MY MANY LIVES

Anna Freud
1946

MY MANY LIVES

BY

LOTTE LEHMANN

TRANSLATED BY
FRANCES HOLDEN

GREENWOOD PRESS, PUBLISHERS
WESTPORT, CONNECTICUT

Library of Congress Cataloging in Publication Data

Lehmann, Lotte.
  My many lives.

    Reprint of the ed. published by Boosey & Hawkes,
New York.
    1. Lehmann, Lotte. I. Holden, Frances, tr.
II. Title.
ML420.L33A37 1974   782.1'092'4 [B]   74-3689
ISBN 0-8371-7361-2

Originally published in 1948 by Boosey & Hawkes, Inc.,
New York

Reprinted with the permission of Lotte Lehmann

Reprinted in 1974 by Greenwood Press,
a division of Williamhouse-Regency Inc.

Library of Congress Catalog Card Number 74-3689

ISBN 0-8371-7361-2

Printed in the United States of America

Looking back at the time when opera was the very breath of life to me, I dedicate this book to the memory of my husband, whose kindness and understanding were my quiet harbor amidst the storms and tempests of those years.

Looking forward into the present and future I dedicate it to Frances, who shares my life in close companionship—a life whose horizons are ever broadening with new inspirations and enchantments.

CONTENTS

ILLUSTRATIONS

INTRODUCTION

THE LONG YEARS which I devoted to opera now seem almost like another life to me. To-day I sing hardly any opera rôles. Recitals demand all my time—the world of Lieder has become my world and opera has become little more than a memory for me. Once I *lived* in the world of opera and could not imagine that a time must come when the great curtain would slowly fall and that fascinating odor of make-up, paint and stage dust, which was then the very breath of life to me, would no longer be a part of my experience.

My life has remained full—yes, has become even richer through a deeper penetration into the boundless realm of the Lied. This source is inexhaustible and eternally new—its overflowing wealth is so limitless that in trying to choose between its riches one always makes new discoveries. That is sufficient substitute for the joy I once knew in portraying living personalities.

I am glad of this opportunity to tell of my experience in opera. It made me very happy to be asked after the appearance of my book on the interpretation of Lieder, *More Than Singing,* to write of my ideas, experiences and conceptions of opera rôles which I have sung.

But doesn't it seem rather paradoxical to write a book about opera—to go in detail into some rôles and yet to leave out of consideration the very soul of the work—the music? Yet that is just what I intend to do.

There are many books on opera. There are those which analyse the music, discuss the different styles, the composers themselves, the stories of the operas, and the history of opera with its early lack of success and final triumphant victory. All this has been told and is of great value. I want only to speak of opera rôles as I have seen and felt and lived them—as an actress —and shouldn't every opera singer be an actress? I want to talk of my rôles, explaining them, illuminating them and making them human. We live in a time when we are no longer satisfied to enjoy an opera solely as music—no, we want to find joy and inspiration in the drama as well.

But it is far from my intention to try to indicate a way of acting by describing gestures or postural attitudes or any of the superficial details of acting. No: I want only to look into the souls of these rôles as I feel them. If one understands the essence of the being whom one is portraying, all that is superficial develops quite naturally from one's own thought and feeling. It is quite immaterial which gesture conveys the right impression—the important thing is to penetrate the rôle to its last detail and become completely one with it. Then for the singing actress with any natural talent, all else is child's play.

Now I'm sure the layman will say: "But surely we can take it for granted that any one who sings a rôle has a complete understanding of it. It seems rather disparaging to suggest that any explanation is necessary. . . ." But experience has taught me that this is not so—that it is just this type of explanation for which young singers are most eager and that the kind of "stage direction" which I am attempting in this book is far more important than a knowledge of gestures and positions. . . .

At the beginning of my own stage career when my desire to be a good actress far exceeded any indication that I ever could become one, opera gave me the impression that so far as acting was concerned, singers were but stepchildren of the drama. . . . There was so much to keep in mind—the music, one's partner, the conductor. . . . How could one ever really feel free? But as I developed as an actress, I soon realized that the situation was quite the reverse: music is the guide, it opens the way to one's gestures, to the details of the representation. It is upon the wings of music that one's spirit is borne, inspired and manifests itself in a thousand facets. . . . The actor stands upon firm ground. He cannot err if he knows the music and fully understands the drama.

The portrayal of an opera rôle will develop from one's psychological insight into its character but the music will be the soil from which it springs. So music is both the wings upon which one soars and the ground upon which one stands, it transports and supports. . . .

But it is understanding which first infuses the body with a soul, and it is this understanding which I shall try to capture and penetrate.

In any case this was the way to my own characterizations.

How often one hears: "Opera cannot survive much longer. The farther we advance, the nearer the films come to achieving artistic perfection, the more realistic our stage becomes, the surer it is that opera will disappear. The people of to-day can no longer endure this cross between reality and make-believe."

This seems to me very short-sighted! I feel that just the opposite is true. To-day more than ever before one needs the opportunity to lose oneself in the world of imagination, in the world of make-believe, a world which may offer an escape from the reality of the present. Reality is to-day so barren, so un-gratifying, that it is incomprehensible to me that anyone who has ever known the world of imagination could ever thrust it aside. . . . Just as people, who through the present crisis have been bereft and torn asunder, have found the courage to go on living through a deep religious faith, so does one find comfort through art, through music.

The word which stands as reality in a play becomes harmony through being sung. Is there not concealed within all of us a longing for harmony? We strive for happiness. Is not happiness harmony? Harmony of the soul, harmony of the senses, of experience, of expanding knowledge, broadening tolerance. And we long for harmony of the imagination which may lead us away from the conflicts of reality.

Isn't the opera one of the harmonious phantasies which gladdens, moves and uplifts us? How could this wonderful world ever be silenced? I do not believe it possible.

As long as man in his inmost being continues to seek an escape through his imagination (however cynical he may seem outwardly) so long, I believe, opera will survive.

To take part in the creation of this imaginary world, to set aside the reality of one's own personality and be transformed into the exalted being whom one represents, who is born of the imagination and carried by the music, makes the performing singer creative: he breathes his own soul into the melodious figure of the opera rôle, awakening it to life.

To portray a rôle means to transform oneself into the being whom one represents, to become completely the personality of this rôle, but to imbue it with one's own soul, the stamp of one's own personality. "When two do the same thing, it is not the same thing", is an old saying. The stronger the personality of the actor the more individual and interesting will be his interpre-tation of his rôle, and the more impossible will it be for another to "duplicate" his performance. Everything else can be only imitation and no longer the expression of one's own individuality. Imitation is basically inartistic and a sad confession of one's own inadequacy. I, myself, have always feared the danger of unconscious imitation so much that I rarely listened to an opera with the intention of "learning". For years, in Vienna, I lived in the opera house—high up in our artists' box in the third gallery, but I went to almost every performance there because I felt that I couldn't breathe without absorbing the atmosphere of the opera. . . . I wanted to hear every one, and see everything and decide for myself what I liked and what I didn't like—and wanted then to close my eyes and ears and with complete independence do what my feeling drove me to do. Without any model, without wanting to copy—perhaps even without being *able* to copy: for imitation is a talent in itself—a dangerous talent which I fear almost more than a lack of talent. One can perhaps awaken a slumbering talent—but it is difficult to transform a clever imitation into the expression of a real personality.

The imitator (I mean one who copies without projecting through his own soul the inspiration which he receives) will soon be consumed by the activities of the opera—he will become a part of a machine and will become mechanized through the ever unchanging routine of the repertory. He becomes a utility singer. He will be a useful member of the opera, never spoiling anything, always ready to do what the conductor and stage director tell him to do. He will never be inspiring and will never do anything badly. He will always be just "average". . . .

I must say I prefer soaring between heaven and hell, between great exaltations and deep disappointments. That alone can make life vital. Not the deadly uniformity of mediocrity. Not the comfortable satisfaction of feeling that one has given a good performance. . . . It is far better to suffer under self-reproaches, to face one's own inadequacies clearly, and then (perhaps once in a year, if one has good luck) to feel: it really happened to-day—that was absolutely as I wanted to say and convey it! These climaxes of satisfaction with oneself are so rare and so dearly paid for through a thousand curses of one's own judgment. . . . Yet I would ten times prefer such a life to the contentment of the unambitious.

I was always as if upon a swing—soaring between emotions. . . . To-day these ups and downs of yesterday seem to me like a crazy dance. . . . Looking back into the period of my opera career the confusion of those passionately glowing years strikes me anew—and my life in the forms of many lives passes before me like a surging melody. . . .

To be sure I do not belong to those people who love to live in the past. I belong to the present: no—to the future. Yesterday is buried in to-day—to-day hurries on to to-morrow. . . . I really drive my life to death. But the ridiculousness of this breathless rush means happiness for me: for the approaching day lies before me filled with new promises and anticipations. . . .

It is said that it is a sure sign of growing old, if one begins to live in the past. Now in that sense, at least—even if I can look back over many years—I am far from being old. . . .

The opera was my past—the Lied is my present—and the future? How can I know that? Who can say how many worlds of creation lie before me in the future? There are so many ways —all of them lie open there. The choice is really difficult. . . .

So, in writing this book, I swing between different periods of life. I will enjoy looking back, for I know it is only a short pause on the long road before me—and I will enjoy considering the foolish, sweet past with the wiser eyes of the present—feeling the fire which I once experienced in the quieter glow of the present.

Chapter I

ELSA—"LOHENGRIN"

THE HAMBURG CIVIC THEATRE[1] opened its doors to the young beginner. It was in the year 1910.

Gustav Brecher was the musical director, the young Otto Klemperer the new great sensation as a conductor. Bachur, the general manager of the Civic Theatre, presided over the whole with his good business sense and his desire to produce the very best in art. Good, very good music was performed—even I vaguely realized that: I, who in my innocent ignorance was getting my first glimpse of a world which seemed excitingly strange and mysterious and which until now had seemed filled with threatening dangers. . . . Every one was kind to me. I was pleasantly surprised: for stage life had been pictured to me as a "sink of corruption", and all my relatives, with great distrust, had offered to watch over me from the distance. My good parents moved with me to Hamburg, my father resigning his official position, for how could they let their child go out alone and unprotected into this "sinful" world?

Neither the manager, nor the conductors, nor the stage directors seemed to have any interest in me. I was given insignificant little rôles to sing—one of the boys in *The Magic Flute*, an apprentice in *Meistersinger*, a page in *Lohengrin* and *Tannhäuser*. . . . These rôles, of course, were only a feeble beginning which one should take by storm with a running leap, to emerge glamorously as Elsa, Elisabeth, Sieglinde. Nothing seemed to be lacking but the opportunity to show what I could do. . . . I made the life of every one who had anything to say in the opera house quite miserable, for I pursued them with everlasting demands and requests.

But the very slowness of this climb was *good* for me. On the whole I was still a rather immature child and by no means capable as yet of giving a really artistic performance.

I couldn't believe that I wouldn't be able to sing Elsa as she should be sung. Standing in the wings with clenched teeth, I

[1]Hamburger Stadttheater

6

listened to the Elsa on the stage. O, I could do that too! And wasn't I young? Wasn't the Elsa out there much too old? Perhaps already "over thirty"—much, much too old to play a youthful part. . . . How cruel is youth!

How much I had to learn, how far I was from any really deep understanding.

But I was soon to have the opportunity to show what I could do: a colleague became ill, the *Lohengrin* performance was endangered since no really adequate substitute was to be found. Then Klemperer proposed that they try me out. With his help, supported by his belief in my capability, I dared it and—won.

This was my first decisive success.

But *was* I Elsa? Did I really know more than how to sing prettily and—judged with kindness—act passably?

Generally Elsa is represented as so lost in her dream that she seems to lose any personality which she might have, in a sickly sweetness. To know why Elsa is in this trancelike state at her first entrance is very important, is decisive for the whole characterization. . . .

Elsa, the daughter of a duke, is accused of the murder of her brother. Overcome by her grief at the mysterious disappearance of this brother whom she loves so deeply, she is completely broken by the enormity of this accusation. The thought that she has enemies capable of conjuring up anything so incomprehensible is almost unbearable for her. It was Telramund who brought this monstrous accusation against her, the same Telramund to whom as their guardian their dying father had entrusted her and her brother's fate—never suspecting that his confidence might be so bitterly and incomprehensibly betrayed.

Friedrich von Telramund had wooed Elsa as she grew into a beautiful and desirable woman. But Elsa, seeing in him only the fatherly guardian, had rejected his suit. Ortrud, who then became Telramund's wife, hated Elsa from the depths of her savage and evil heart. She longs to destroy Elsa and so to free for herself the throne of Brabant by robbing Elsa's brother Gottfried, the rightful heir to the throne, of his rights. Ortrud is a woman who pursues her desires with a savage determination. She has made her husband Telramund a willing tool through the hypnotic power of her sombre and forceful will. It was she who told him that with her own eyes she saw Elsa drown her brother in the pond in order to free the throne for a lover of whom no one has as yet heard. (Actually it was Ortrud who through sorcery had changed this boy, Gottfried, into a swan. She has, of course, invented the lover of Elsa.) Telramund was only too happy to believe these malicious insinuations: Elsa's rejection had wounded his vanity—and although he himself would never have been capable of fabricating anything so horrible, he welcomed his wife's shocking tales and accused Elsa without any further consideration or investigation.

Elsa was imprisoned. In consideration of her position she was permitted to retain her ladies-in-waiting, but they must share her imprisonment. Although she has been surrounded by love and respect, the burden of this experience has been intolerable. Not only has she been tortured by worry over her brother who vanished so mysteriously, but her own fate, in spite of her innocence, has become a dark and terrible tragedy.

The blissfulness of hope has returned to her in a dream: from out of the clouds a knight has appeared to her who will save and avenge her and conquer for her. This is more than a dream, it is a premonition which fills her thoughts day and night. Reality seems a frightful entanglement in an inextricable network of lies. The dream is a peaceful awakening to the feeling of being again free and to an intimation of a future happiness which may comfort her for the loss of her beloved brother.

Elsa is summoned before the court of justice—she is rudely awakened from the rapture of her dream. Still half under its spell she goes forward to meet her judgment.

This is the first time that any one has dared to command this royal child to appear instead of paying her homage. Curiosity seems to creep around her and waves of sympathy envelop her. She makes her way through the people to the throne, undisturbed. As she walks she must hold herself erectly. She is accustomed to appearing in public—though certainly in a very different rôle. But experience in appearing before people has given her her bearing: she moves forward with her head raised. Her eyes are lowered as she is still dreaming. They are not lowered through guilt or shame: there is no reason for her to be ashamed— her conscience is pure—but the strangely vivid dream which has penetrated the darkness of her prison like a ray of sunlight has weakened her and taken from her her last strength.

Unconsciously her steps falter as she nears the mass of people, but with a sigh she continues and stands before the throne.

King Henry bows to her graciously. This accusation has affected him deeply. He has known the child of the Duke of Brabant and has been charmed by her innocence. But he must give a hearing to one who has been accused, and so it was necessary for him to summon Elsa before the court. In his own mind he cannot accept Elsa's guilt. Seeing her as she stands before him in all her loveliness he feels a deep sympathy for her, and his voice is soft and kind as he puts to her the questions which the trial introduces.

"Are you Elsa von Brabant?"

Elsa nods her head in assent. This gesture should not be exaggerated, as it often is. Why should it be? There should only be a slight bending of the head, no abject bowing down. Elsa is the daughter of a great duke, she will show deference to the king but she will not be overawed by his presence.

"Do you recognize me as your judge?"

With the music she slowly turns her head towards him and with a gesture of assent looks with confidence into his eyes.

"Then I shall continue. Is the accusation known to you, which is here raised against you?"

This question strikes to the core of her heart. Turning away, trembling, she looks up into the morose eyes of Telramund which are levelled upon her. She shudders before the power of evil which seems to shroud Telramund and Ortrud, and sadly turns back to the king with a gesture of assent.

"What is your reply to this charge?"

What answer can she give? How can there be any answer to such horror? With a sad smile she shakes her head, as if to say: I have no answer. . . . This movement of her head should not be hasty. It would not be according to the style of Wagner to introduce any commonplace gesture here. It should be just a slow turning, in denial.

In earlier days these Wagnerian movements were so exaggerated that they almost reached the point of becoming ridiculous. I recall the time when I was a beginner, when we learned to make "Wagnerian steps" and were assured that this was the way it had to be done in Bayreuth. Never having been in Bayreuth I can't judge from my own experience, but I really can't believe

that this senseless exaggeration and distortion was actually taught
there. Of course taste as to what is artistic changes with the
course of time. If one looks at photographs of those who were
once great, it is impossible to imagine how they could ever have
been touching or thrilling in such outfits. . . . Accustomed to a
different conception of beauty, our eyes demand that the figures
upon the stage fulfill an illusion. We demand youth and beauty,
and these attributes must be simulated even if they are not
actually present. We are no longer satisfied (as apparently our
forbears were) with singers who sing well and are good actors—
no, they must also look like the figures whom they portray.
To-day a singer must not only fulfill his task as an artist—he
must also be as satisfying as possible from the visual standpoint.
I belong to another generation: when I was young there was not
the emphasis that there is to-day upon strict diets which
keep one slim. . . . But I regret this very much and cannot
advise young singers too strongly to consider their figures and
regard the cultivation of beauty as one of the commands of
which there are so many in preparing for this very exacting
profession.

I want to say another word as to so-called "Wagnerian style":
there is not sufficient space within the limits of this book to go in
detail into the conception of how one can conform to the demands
of "Wagnerian style" and still not appear old-fashioned and unnatural. One must learn to make natural gestures soar with the
musical phrases. When one allows one's feeling to be carried by
the swing of the music, one learns to understand this. It is the
beauty of gesture, originated in the Greek drama, which finds
new life, borne by music—in Wagnerian figures. Nevertheless
one should never become "rigid" in any pose. One must make
the dramatic Wagnerian bearing *living,* approaching naturalness
as far as possible.

But let us come back to Elsa.

King Henry is startled by Elsa's failure to make any reply to
the accusation. His question: "So you confess your guilt?" is
expressed with fear and increasing vehemence.

But Elsa does not even hear him. . . . She is again shocked and
overwhelmed by this charge of murder, by the mysterious disappearance of her brother which can only mean that he has been
murdered. At this moment she is indifferent to her own fate, for

with renewed desperation the realization has swept over her that
her brother must be dead. She can only whisper with a sigh of
pain: "My poor brother." Astonishment grips the mass of people.
The king, deeply moved, speaks to her not as a judge but as a
fatherly friend: "Tell me, Elsa, what have you to confide to
me?"

Elsa must now begin as if completely lost in her dream. It is
as if she does not realize that she is speaking before all these
people. It is, so to speak, not "a speech before the court", but
a return to her dream which has taken her so completely away
from reality. Again she experiences that strange realization
which has changed her sighs of grief and despair into a floating
song which soars into the distance like a flying bird. Again she
experiences the sinking into slumber as if touched by a magic
wand. . . . Now, as though sleeping, Elsa's head sinks slowly
upon her breast—she remains motionless, her eyes are closed, she
neither hears the murmuring of the people nor heeds the warning
of the king. It is her dream to which she listens, and with the
mounting tones of the music which lead into the theme of
Lohengrin she slowly raises herself, opens her eyes and gazes into
the distance with an expression of ecstasy as she sees before her
a radiant vision. In her imagination the knight stands there as
she saw him in her dream, glorious and triumphant in his shining
armor. It is he whom she chooses as her knight—he shall be her
defender! In rapture she spreads out her arms and remains in
this position, only slowly, very slowly, coming back to reality
when she hears the voice of the king warning Telramund to consider once more what support he can offer for his shocking
accusation.

Telramund's answer is a violent repetition of his charge—he
says, now distinctly and with great anger, that the knight of
whom she tells is in all probability her secret lover.

Generally Elsa just stands there completely indifferent. I
never did that although it can be made to seem absolutely convincing that Elsa, wrapt in her dream, is completely oblivious of
all that is going on around her. But I always tried to vitalize the
much too passive Elsa, even in this first scene. Later on she
proves that she can be passionate and wilful—after all, it is
her passionate questioning which robs her of her happiness. So
Elsa is not quite so vapid and colorless as she is usually
represented.

Elsa should react when Telramund makes this senseless accusation. It is enough to show by a glance, by an increasing tenseness, that she reacts, but one should not get the impression that this charge has struck her like a blow—and the natural reaction of innocence would be a proud and challenging attitude. Telramund swears by his sword to the truth of his statement. To this Elsa must react very vigorously. For a knight, his sword is the holiest of possessions—that he should resort to anything so holy to him is injurious to her case—but even more painful is the fact that Elsa now realizes how deeply he must be convinced of the monstrous ideas which he has advanced.

The king, embarrassed by Telramund's reminding him of the service which he has rendered his country and his king, hastens to assure him of his goodwill. Elsa's head is now bowed in almost hopeless dejection. But King Henry wants to be a just judge—and feeling that this decision requires more than his own strength and wisdom, he seeks the judgment of God. In a fight between Telramund and a knight who will defend Elsa, God shall decide who is guilty, Elsa or her accuser. It is all placed in the hands of God—so that it can be and will be just and fair.

From this moment Elsa is completely changed. . . .

She knows that whoever fights for her must win, for she is innocent. Knowing that her fate now rests in the hands of God she knows that she is saved, and so she stands very erect and takes an active interest in what is happening around her.

She awaits Telramund's answer with vivid anticipation when the king asks him for the last time if he will defend his accusation even before the judgment of God.

When he assents, Elsa must react perceptibly. She simply cannot understand how Telramund can persist in this absurd charge which can only end in his defeat.

When the king asks Elsa if she agrees that a knight shall fight for her she replies softly but decisively: "Yes". Wagner's direction here is: "without looking up". In my opinion this should not be confused with her dreamlike trance which is so often exaggerated. Aware of her innocence, and proud of it, Elsa should agree softly and with a restrained eagerness. This whispered "yes" is already the message which she sends to the distant knight of her dream. With this "yes" she summons him and begins to sense his approach.

When the king asks whom she chooses as her defendant every

one listens in tense expectation, spurred on by Telramund's malicious whisper: "Hear now the name of her paramour", but Elsa does not notice it. Her whole thought is centred upon the saviour who will come, who must come. With decision she repeats: "I await the knight, he shall be my defender." She offers him her crown, she offers him all her property. In humility she bows before her future husband, with proud modesty she surrenders herself in love for him.

She stands erect and confident, not noticing the whispers which pass among the people. They are all saying that it is a beautiful prize which awaits the champion—but who knows how it will turn out?

The first time that the herald calls in all directions she follows his summons with radiant anticipation. She listens towards the distance, her face lit up with expectation. But no one comes. . . . There is only silence. Oblivious of the murmuring of the crowd, of Telramund's triumphant cry, she reaches out her hands to the king in a mounting plea: "My king, let me plead for one more call to my knight—he may well be far away and not have heard it." When the king assents, she makes a sign of gratitude and stands waiting in trembling expectation and sudden fear. It seems inexplicable that the knight should not appear—he must come, for she is innocent. But the uncanny stillness all about her increases her anxiety, she seems surrounded by a darkness through which no ray of light may penetrate.

Leaving the row of her ladies-in-waiting and moving forward agitatedly, she falls upon her knees in passionate prayer. This prayer is a great dramatic outburst and proves that the dream-like Elsa knows how to fight, even if it be only a fight in prayer. But she does not surrender to her fate, she demands of heaven the fulfillment of her dream. And into her last ecstatic outburst: "let me see him as I saw him, as I saw him, let him be near me . . ." the chorus breaks in an outburst of astonishment. Still upon her knees Elsa listens, her arms outstretched. She must follow the call of the chorus as if she herself sees the knight approaching, although she is in the foreground with her back to the scene. Her desire, her joy, her confidence are so great that it is not necessary for her to see with earthly eyes what the power of imagination paints so vividly before her: she sees the knight, sees him coming slowly down the river, leaning upon his sword, drawn by a white swan. . . . Slowly, very slowly, she rises and stretching upward with outspread arms turns very slowly as if compelled to do so. It is as if she would delay the lovely moment in which for the first time in reality she will see him of whom she has dreamed—as if she lacks the strength to withstand this overwhelming fulfillment which the sight of the noble knight will bring her. But with the great *crescendo* of mounting grandeur in the music she turns and sees the knight. She utters a cry but remains standing in a blissful trance, her back turned to the audience. Slowly her arms are lowered as if unconsciously.

Now as the loveliest of realities unfolds before her, Elsa is more than ever in a dream. . . . She gazes uninterruptedly at Lohengrin without hearing his words, feeling only his nearness, only the joy of his presence. Elsa should now be standing amongst her ladies-in-waiting—in no circumstances should she be separated from them. When Lohengrin, recognizing her, calls her from their midst, it must be a miracle to which everyone reacts. If, as usually happens, Elsa is separated from them and is also distinguished by her costume, it is quite understandable that Lohengrin should recognize the accused, who is the Princess of Branbant. When he addresses her, she only makes a slight movement in answer. She is not astonished in the way all the others are. She knows that he will recognize her. The miracle which has brought him to her is so stupendous that nothing can any longer seem miraculous to Elsa. She humbly accepts the fact that Lohengrin is superhuman. She falls at his feet, her voice is ecstatic but she is not yet really awake. When he forbids her to ask his name or to question from where he comes, she looks up at him not really to hear what he is saying but because the long speech to which she has at first listened with bowed head draws her upward. She looks at him, gazing into the blinding radiance of his eyes, without understanding what he is saying. She only half hears him— and her answer is almost unconscious. But Lohengrin tries to awaken her. He wants her to understand exactly what she must promise.

Monsalvat, from which he comes, is inaccessible to ordinary mortals. He is a knight of the Holy Grail who has come to defend virtue. But he must remain unrecognized, for his world is so exalted and so beyond that of everyday life that no one may speak of it. No human curiosity must ever touch him. Lohengrin returns to Elsa all that she has lost—he gives her happiness

in choosing her as his wife, but she must trust him completely
and unquestioningly.

All listen with reverence to the speech of the noble knight,
seeking to understand this wonder and eager to fulfill his
command—all but one: Ortrud, the sinister enemy. She listens to
his strange tale with great eagerness—dark plans already foment
within her as she prepares for her husband's revenge if he should
suffer defeat at the hands of this strange and glamorous knight.

Elsa knows nothing of the world around her. She has now
heard his command which he has repeated with even greater
intensity; she has understood it, and from the depths of her
heart promises faith and never-ending confidence.

Lohengrin bows to her and calls: "Elsa, I love you."
Generally every Lohengrin sings this like a real declaration of
love. I feel that it is a cry of *warning*. Overwhelmed by Elsa's
purity, beauty and devotion, Lohengrin fears that she may be too
weak to keep to her oath. Her weakness would then force him
to leave her. This is the law of his knights' order. But to leave
her would mean the loss of a great happiness. For this reason
he warns her: "Elsa, I love you, but trust me or all will come to
an end. If you do not trust me I must leave you, and that would
break my heart, because I love you . . ."

Elsa is now upon the royal throne. She stands there quietly
and with dignity, taking no part in the preparation for the
combat. She must await the combat with tranquillity and complete confidence, for she knows that it is out of the question for
Lohengrin to be anything but victorious. Since she is innocent
it could not, according to law, turn out in any other way. Her
prayer is sincere and fervent but filled with confidence—even
when the struggle actually begins she remains standing in quiet
anticipation, her hands folded in prayer. I have often seen the
Elsa follow the fighting with great excitement. Why? She only
awaits the right ending which is certain to come.

To the general outcry which greets Lohengrin's victory, she
reacts with a gesture of jubilation. When Lohengrin says:
"Through God's victory your life is now mine," she turns away,
she does not want to see Lohengrin deliver the death blow
to Telramund even though it is his right. But Lohengrin is
magnanimous: "I spare your life that you may devote it to
repentance." Turning rapturously she crosses the stage to him
with quick, eager steps.

The song of jubilation which Elsa sings and in which Lohengrin and the chorus join, is a single hymn of ecstasy to the end of this act. Elsa and Lohengrin are raised upon shields and borne through the exulting crowd. Her voice soars over the chorus and orchestra in her radiant: "O if I might have ways of rejoicing, equal to your glory!"

Elsa's song at the beginning of the second act should be sung as simply as possible and with the least superfluous acting. She should not wave her arms in the air but should stand leaning gracefully against the railing of the balcony in a quiet and joyful surrender to the beauty of the moonlit night.

Her destiny now seems to be fulfilled—life spreads before her in a rosy hue. When Ortrud's cry breaks in upon her, she shudders. It is a strangely sinister discord which penetrates the stillness of the lovely night, disturbing and frightening her. She leans forward, shading her eyes from the blinding moonlight, trying to see who it is that calls her name in such weird complaint. When she recognizes Ortrud she is surprised and frightened, for Ortrud has no longer any right to be here, since she and her husband have been banished. Elsa pities this enemy who caused her such indescribable suffering through the slanderous accusation to which she influenced Telramund. But in the depths of her soul Elsa is now so happy that she has no place for thoughts of past misery or contempt for the dastardliness of those who caused her suffering. So in her outcry: "What are you doing here, unhappy woman?" there is only pity and sympathy. Ortrud's unjust accusation: "What have I done to you?" grips her painfully. Conscious of her own innocence she can scarcely understand what her enemy may mean, when, clever and sly as a snake, she distorts the facts and tries to put Elsa in the wrong. Confused, Elsa asks how it is possible that Ortrud now accuses her—but instead of going away and leaving Ortrud to her dark fate, she remains standing on the balcony listening to the senseless charges which Ortrud hurls against her. She must react to the absurdity in Ortrud's suggestion that she acted through envy because Telramund had married Ortrud when Elsa rejected him.

At this moment Elsa realizes the complete worthlessness of her enemy and turns with dignity towards the door. She has no intention of listening to any further accusations and wants to enter the house. With a quick change of tactics Ortrud now tries to arouse Elsa's sympathy for Telramund. She has estimated Elsa rightly, for she now returns and listens with distress to the increasing complaints of Ortrud. It has been very sly of Ortrud to appeal to Elsa's generosity, for in her overflowing happiness Elsa cannot bear to see any one made miserable because of her, even if it is not her fault. She will forgive and forget and save them from their deserved misery. In the fullness of her own happiness she promises Ortrud to invite her to her home.

This is just what Ortrud wants. Her plan seems to be working out. And as Elsa disappears into the house she does not hear the cry of revenge nor the triumphant and malicious prayer of the evil woman who is determined to destroy her.

Shifting from her fierce cry of revenge to an attitude of deceptive humility, Ortrud, playing her rôle skillfully, sinks upon her knees before Elsa, who has now appeared in the courtyard. She knows how to touch the heart of this guileless one. With deep pity Elsa bends over Ortrud. It moves her to see this woman who has been known for her extravagant splendour, her unflinching pride and harsh arrogance, so humble and dejected. She is full of kindness, forgiveness and friendship, and is only too ready to take the evil-doer to her heart. The more Ortrud abases herself the readier is Elsa to raise her to her old glory. Yes, she even overrides the king's command and invites Ortrud to attend her wedding on the following day. Away with the rags of penitence! Ortrud as before shall appear as the most glamorous of all the guests. And with the guileless pride of a child, she tells Ortrud of the bliss with which she awaits the coming day when she will become Lohengrin's wife before God. She spreads out her arms radiantly in anticipation of this solemn moment. Only with difficulty does she pause in her exultation and turn to Ortrud, who seems to be finding a morbid satisfaction in her own self-abasement. When Ortrud describes herself as a beggar, Elsa makes a kindly gesture of denial. Slowly Ortrud approaches her unsuspecting victim, ensnaring her with words drenched with poison. When she says: "That no evil may overtake you let me look into your future for you," Elsa shudders with suddenly mounting fear. She would like to tear herself away from Ortrud, but she stands behind her, encircling her with her black cloak (without really touching her) as in a satanic spider's web. Elsa is petrified with breathless fear. Horror seizes her as Ortrud

dares to question Lohengrin's purity, implying that some day he
will leave her as mysteriously as he has come to her. Elsa seeks
to escape from this strange spell which Ortrud weaves about
her. One must feel that Elsa is held against her will through the
demonic power of her sinister enemy. Finally, with an almost
superhuman effort, she tears herself away. I repeat: Ortrud has
never really touched her physically. It is only her words which
have trickled down like poison upon Elsa, only her hypnotic
power which has made Elsa helpless.

Through her great love and confidence in Lohengrin she tries
to find the strength to escape, seeking her way into the house
with faltering steps. But her pity again proves greater than her
distrust: she turns to Ortrud with a serene and noble dignity.
Ortrud stands in humble obeisance before Elsa—with clenched
teeth she must admit to herself that this first attempt seems to
have been a failure. Elsa steps towards Ortrud and speaks to her
with great kindness. She again pardons her, for she can only feel
regret when she sees a soul so harrowed by misery. Here, too,
Elsa should make as few movements as possible. The more
quietly and nobly these wonderful phrases are sung the more
convincing they will be. Of this whole opera I love most this
duet, and I have always found great joy in singing it.

Elsa again invites Ortrud to follow her into the house. Ortrud
refuses with deceptive humility. Elsa quietly turns to her, and
raising her from her prostrate position leads her towards the
house. On the threshold Ortrud refuses to enter before Elsa.
Bowing in friendly acknowledgment Elsa precedes her into the
house and does not notice that Ortrud has straightened up with
a defiant gesture before following her.

In the following scene Elsa enters in her bridal costume. She
descends the broad steps slowly and with a charming dignity.
(The singer should never give the impression of having to keep
her eyes on the steps!) As she descends, her gaze should be
directed before her. She is deeply moved and scarcely aware of
the people who pay her homage—the nobles and knights who
have gathered for the wedding. (On many stages Elsa first
appears on the balcony from which she has sung in the preceding
scene and greets the assemblage with a sweeping gesture. This
is a matter of stage direction, and the singer who plays Elsa must
do as the stage director decrees. I have always found it very
effective to greet the people in this way. It is a lovely climax

if Elsa appears on the balcony with the jubilant *forte* of the music.)

Elsa walks to the cathedral radiant with joy. Ortrud follows her with much pomp. Just as Elsa is about to ascend the steps of the cathedral Ortrud throws herself before her. This scene between the two women can very easily degenerate into an un-dignified squabbling, if Elsa is not played with great discretion. Perhaps if she still felt as "Elsa von Brabant" she would have found no answer, considering an argument unworthy of her. . . . But she has the feeling of being already the wife of the exalted knight who has saved and chosen her, of the knight whose name she does not know but whom she trusts with her whole being. *As his wife* she cannot permit this woman whom she has saved from destruction to insult her before all these people. At first she does not understand the sudden change in Ortrud's behaviour —the art of pretence is so foreign to her that she has accepted her humility as genuine. But then a deep exasperation sweeps over her and she repulses Ortrud's attack. However, Ortrud knows how to get the better of the hated Elsa: with a subtle craftiness she has prepared the ground for making Elsa doubt Lohengrin, and she is sure the poisonous seed which she has sowed will ripen. She speaks to Elsa of the good name of her own husband—a false judgment, an unfortunate occurrence, has robbed him of this. But what does Elsa know of *her* husband? Nothing—not even his name. . . . Here she pierces Elsa's heart. For even if she has no doubt of him, credulous and trusting as she is, there is still an unhappy feeling of deprivation in never being able to know the name of her husband, in never being able to call him by the name his mother gave him. Everything about him is strange and foreign—and must remain so. This is secretly a great grief to Elsa, and it is this grief which Ortrud stirs with such malicious cleverness. Yes, more than that: she injects into Elsa's heart the fear that he may some time leave her just as he has come to her, that he must keep his name secret because disgrace clings to it. Elsa is very much taken aback. She had never thought of the possibility that Lohengrin could be associated with anything but splendour and virtue and beauty. Overcoming her perplexity she finds glowing words of vindica-tion. His purity seems unassailable—she asks all the nobles, all the people to agree with her. There is not one amongst them who does not share her confidence. But Ortrud hurls a word like a poisoned arrow at Elsa's heart: was it magic which brought him here? What kind of magic was it? He came drawn by a white swan. From where did he come? From what country? What is his fate? Won't Elsa ask him? Or is she afraid to ask him because in her heart she knows that this miracle was brought about through sorcery? . . . Elsa thrusts her hands before her face, trembling. She will hear no more, she will escape from this evil voice which so strangely takes possession of her, which says things that she will not—cannot—believe if she is to keep her oath of silence to her beloved.

At this moment she hears the trumpets announcing the approach of the king and her betrothed. With these sounds she straightens up—it is faith which breaks through the clouds like a ray of sunlight . . . he is near, he who has once rescued her from sombre tragedy and who will rescue her again to-day from the enshrouding web which her sinister enemy has spun about her. . . .

Rushing to Lohengrin she tells him with trembling voice of the frightful state to which her kindness has brought her, of how Ortrud, pretending humility, has turned against her and un-veiled her evil soul. Her last words: "She reproaches me for trusting you too much," should be sung *ritardando*: the first shadow of the doubt which has been so deeply concealed within her begins to emerge. She looks up into his face with an expression of anxious questioning.

With quiet dignity Lohengrin thrusts Ortrud away, assuring her that she will never be victorious over this pure heart which is now his. Elsa bows down—she cannot recover herself so quickly. The deep confidence which radiates from Lohengrin's words puts her to shame—weeping, her head sinks against his breast when he asks tenderly: "Tell me, Elsa, was it possible for her to poison your heart?" Elsa cannot answer this question, but Lohengrin trusts her. He raises her lovingly and with the the words: "Come let these tears flow yonder in joy," leads her to the church. Again Elsa goes forward radiantly happy. Ortrud is forgotten, through Lohengrin's kindly confidence the power of evil seems to have been dispelled.

There—just as she is about to ascend the steps of the cathe-dral, Telramund steps before her with renewed and violent accusations.

From this moment Elsa is completely changed.

The horror which makes her fly across the whole length of the stage is the horror of a human being who has been awakened from a beautiful dream and has been plunged into hideous reality. Doubts besiege her . . . Ortrud's careful preparations now find completion. That these two outcasts, who have been outlawed and condemned should dare a second time to interrupt the wedding in such a scandalous way, that they should dare to attack Lohengrin's inviolability, almost proves to her that Lohengrin has come through sorcery, that he really has reason to conceal his name, a reason which makes silence advantageous to him. Of course, all this is not clear to Elsa. She only feels a deep and menacing disquietude, she doesn't know what to believe, what to think. With deep excitement she listens to Telramund, each time reacting violently to his "Who is he?" (There is great danger here that Elsa may overact. She should not forget that at this point she is not the central figure—neither the center of the stage, nor the center of interest. Her interest in the proceedings should come from a full heart but should not force her into the foreground.)

Her faith and confidence seem to return when Lohengrin repulses Telramund and explains that it is beneath him to converse with one who has been condemned by God. Yes, it is true he is too great, too exalted to argue with Telramund—Elsa realizes this anew and so feels freed. But Telramund is prepared for this. He calls upon the king—won't he be worthy perhaps of learning his name? Elsa stands petrified. The king. Yes, to him he must give an answer. But even before the king Lohengrin maintains his silence. With this blow Elsa again falls victim to her doubts. The king! There is no higher authority in the country! If Lohengrin refuses to answer him what can be the reason for his silence?

With dignity Lohengrin replies that his virtuous deed is his only evidence—one must believe him. There is only one whom he must answer, if contrary to his command, she should ask: Elsa! Shuddering and with a gesture of denial Elsa buries her face in her hands. And there opens before Lohengrin the abyss into which they will be plunged if Elsa should be driven to ask the question: the abyss of their misery, the grave of their love. . . .

The next ensemble, usually known as the "ensemble of the secret", is frequently cut out, which I have always regretted.

Musically it is very beautiful, and it is important for the action. All are absorbed in their thoughts—and the expressions of faith and doubt, of love and hate, of evil and innocent confusion are finally silenced through the magnanimous words of the king: in his opinion Lohengrin is above all doubt. He assures Lohengrin of his confidence, and all the knights agree with him and again pledge their faith.

During this time Ortrud and Telramund, observing intently Elsa's rising doubt, have been at her side and concealing her from the eyes of the crowd have whispered their sombre incantation with urgent vehemence. She tries to turn away from them, tries to escape them, but half fainting still hears Telramund's dark promise that he will be close to her in the night and if she calls to him can quickly get it over without any danger. It is murder which they are planning, murder of which they whisper to her. Lohengrin's sharp warning: "Elsa, with whom are you talking there?" tears her away from their criminal slander. His voice gives her strength to free herself from their hypnotic spell. As if annihilated she throws herself at his feet, and after he has in a violent rage driven away and banished them, he turns lovingly to her. She rises very slowly, and through his words, in which trembles his fear for their mutual happiness, the power of the evil spell falls from her. She looks up at him with quiet determination and for the second time swears that she will trust and obey him. The oath sounds sincere and deeply felt. It is forged in the fire of suffering which Ortrud and Telramund have kindled in her heart. A suffering which has almost seared her, a suffering from which she rises to new joy.

Lohengrin and Elsa now undisturbed approach the altar of God, feeling that they have become one, with only the single thought that they now belong to each other for ever. . . .

Upon the top step leading into the cathedral Elsa turns to greet the jubilant people. As her glance falls upon Ortrud standing very erect in the distance with a threatening gesture Elsa shudders—but Lohengrin's cloak is thrown about her shoulders protecting her from all evil. Leaning upon Lohengrin's arm she enters the church.

In the third act Elsa appears with her ladies-in-waiting. Lohengrin enters with the king through the opposite door. Elsa and Lohengrin walk to the center of the stage and remain standing there during the ceremony while the ladies-in-waiting and pages walk about them taking from them their heavy cloaks and crowns. Both stand with their backs to the audience. This may sound exaggerated but they should also "act with their backs". One underestimates the audience if one thinks that it will not see and feel whether Elsa and Lohengrin are pleasantly amusing themselves with the king (as is so often the case) or are inwardly experiencing the emotions which belong to the opera. Just a slight leaning toward one another, in a quiet, dignified and motionless attitude will make their figures expressive here—that is all, but it will convey everything which it should convey.

When the king and after him the chorus have left the stage, Lohengrin's eyes follow them for a moment; then he lovingly turns to Elsa, who goes to him as if on wings of joy and is enfolded in his arms.

The love duet which follows should be sung with exquisite exaltation. At its close Lohengrin tenderly leads Elsa to the resting place. When Lohengrin says that he feels as if they had always known each other, Elsa again appears to be lost in her dream. The dream is now a vivid and living reality to her, and she tells Lohengrin with deep conviction that since finding him in reality she realizes that it is God alone who has sent him to her. Without any question—God. Perhaps it may seem strange that she emphasizes this. A maiden as pious as Elsa couldn't very well think anything else. But she feels the doubt buried deeply within her, boring like an evil worm. . . . And she is trying to resist this *subconsciously* active doubt by emphatically assuring herself and her beloved that it could only have been God —no one else. "Be still, my heart," her disturbed subconscious mind is saying. "Be still, it was God who sent him, not sorcery, nor evil magic which has deceived me and threatened my happiness." Her passionate question: "Is this only love?" trembles from an inner constriction. And without meaning to or realizing that she is doing so she already asks his name, asks it timidly—in an inverted question. "This word so inexpressibly wonderful, like your name . . ." It is not yet an actual breaking of the command, it is still only like a tender caress—and Lohengrin, folding her in his arms, takes it as such. His cry—"Elsa"—at this moment is not a reproach, it is an answer charged with emotion, a loving reaction to her expression of love. And Elsa's passion increases through this delicate understanding. Oh, only when they are alone, only then, does she long to be able to say the name which signifies all of life for her. . . . Why can't she? She is his wife—why shouldn't she, like other women, be able to say she loves him, whispering his name. Why? Why? . . .

Lohengrin tenderly disengages himself from her embrace, from the intoxicating spell of her words. He is an ardent lover, but above all else he is a knight of the Holy Grail and as such he must fulfill its command. In Elsa's nearness lies danger. He tries to avoid it by releasing himself from her arms. He turns to the window, drawing her attention to the beautiful moonlit night. But his words, which suggest a subtle and gentle reproach: "without any question I yield to your enchantment" scarcely penetrate Elsa's consciousness. She is upset, she feels rejected. She half turns away from him with an expression of sorrowful resignation. Here she must not under any circumstance give the impression that she is "hurt" in any petty sense. She cannot be sulky and so let the figure of Elsa degenerate into something commonplace. Elsa is a woman, a passionately loving woman, who longs for perfect and complete communion with her beloved husband. When Lohengrin says: "I felt no need to ask who you were, my eyes saw you, my heart knew you," she realizes how much more exalted is his unshatterable confidence. Lohengrin had found her when she stood under a harsh and dreadful accusation. But he had believed and trusted. She has seen him in splendor and victory and glory—and she dares to doubt? This makes her feel so small and unworthy that in despair she seeks a way of being worthy of him. She abandons herself to dreams of self-sacrifice. O, if only he were in danger and distress as she has been! If only she might save him, as he has her! Leaning towards him she whispers in his ear the fear which is secretly gnawing at her heart: "If the secret is such that you must keep it from the world, perhaps tragedy awaits you if it should be discovered?" She does not realize that with this doubt she questions his virtue, his inviolability. She knows but one thing: it would be a joy to sacrifice herself. And from her oppressed heart breaks the primitive but ever new longing for death of one who loves: "For you I would gladly die."

Lohengrin feels the passion in Elsa's love; his cry "Beloved" is filled with tenderness, he almost forgets that danger is imminent, that doubt lurks like an evil beast behind this overflowing passion. He would like to seal her lips with kisses to put a stop to her stormy questioning.

But again Elsa tears herself from his embrace, and then as she clasps him to her, her questions—her challenge, become more and more urgent. "Let me look into your secret, that I may know who you are." In a sudden spasm of fear Lohengrin tries to silence her. His cry: "Be silent, Elsa" falls upon deaf ears, however. She is frantic. She must know, she must be able to feel completely one with him, to be completely and without any reticence his own, knowing all, asking nothing more. She puts the question, the momentous question of his fate in an indirect form. It is still veiled in passionate and torturing doubt, in eagerness to sacrifice herself in a firm determination to share his fate. Lohengrin can still disregard the question, can still brush it aside with a sharp warning which should awaken her to the fact that she is approaching dangerously near the edge of the precipice when she doubts and questions.

He must now be firm with her. He must try to preserve their happiness by *commanding* and no longer just *requesting*.

He rises with great determination and stands very erect in the middle of the stage. Elsa, who had sprung up during her last unbridled outburst, turning her back to him, struggles for composure. She is deeply shocked by Lohengrin's harshness. She is like a child—a child who has done wrong and is being scolded. She accepts his severity as her due punishment. It is as if she awaits his judgment in order that she may accept it, even if it be death and destruction. In speaking to her at this moment, Lohengrin is no longer the tender, loving husband: he is the knight of the Grail who is above all earthly doubt. His grandeur overwhelms Elsa. But when he says: "If you should never waver before the command, you would seem to me more worthy than all other women," she straightens up in sudden delight. For the moment everything is forgotten—all doubts, all passionate demands are silenced before the one supreme fact that she, she alone, seems more worthy to him than all others. She throws herself passionately upon his breast when he calls her to him: "To my breast O sweet and pure one," blissfully drinking in his words of love.

Lohengrin now makes a psychological mistake: he should have forgotten everything which has happened before and should not again refer to the questions which are consuming Elsa. But he wants to comfort her, wants to give her security for the future and show her that her doubts are senseless. It is not disgrace or danger which forces him to be silent, it is the most exalted distinction which places him *above*, not *below* other people. He says all this to comfort her but the result is terrible: she listens in mounting horror. If the mystery had been one of his suffering she could have shared it with him, she who is experienced in misery. But that it is splendor and magnificence which surrounds him, a splendor which he has renounced and upon which he might look back with longing—O how can she ever make up to him for all that he has renounced for her? Her doubt of his integrity was bad enough, but she would have been capable of facing suffering and death with him, of atoning with him, of dying with him. But how can she ever be worthy of his splendor? How can she, who is so inadequate, ever be worthy as a substitute for all this glory? In what way? Clearly and with great tenderness he tells her: "The one thing which will reward me for my sacrifice I must find in your love." Her love! Is she strong enough and great enough to be everything to him? She feels so small and worthless in comparison to him—and his last words: "for I do not come from darkness and suffering, I come from radiance and glory," plunge her into abysmal despair.

What Elsa now says and does is something over which she no longer has any control. Her emotions have been overstrained: she has been saved from the slanderous accusation of which she was innocent, but the doubt which Ortrud has planted in her heart begins to mature. Her wedding day has been brutally disturbed and her wedding night is a fluctuation between ecstasy and gnawing doubt, between surrender to her loving confidence and self-defence against her better convictions. Through all this Elsa has completely lost her balance, and instead of expressing what she really feels—her fear of his very exaltedness—she lets the evil doubt which has been smouldering within her win the upper hand, the doubt which Ortrud had so cleverly awakened and which Telramund had nourished through his vicious challenge.

There is only confusion in Elsa—her faith in the truth of Lohengrin's words, her doubt, her deathly fear that he may leave her, to return to the splendor from which—perhaps—he has come. Into his despairing cry: "Cease to torment me" she hurls the whole weight of her own despair: "But how you torment me." She is wild, unjust, uncontrolled, unmanageable in this moment. Lohengrin tries a last request: "Your charm will never be lost if you remain free of doubt." But with these words he strikes too deeply into her frightened heart: she knows nothing of the charm which she holds for him. Who is she? Of what worth is she? And who is he that came to her so miraculously? What was this miracle? Was it sorcery? Yes, it is through sorcery that he has come to her—O how could she ever be equal to one who has sorcery at his command? Suddenly a horrible vision possesses her: she sees before her the swan which had drawn the skiff in which Lohengrin had stood leaning upon his sword, beautiful and godlike. In vain Lohengrin tries to bring her to reason, in vain he tries almost by force to tear her from her evil dream. Violently rejecting his embrace she throws herself across the stage. She stands very erect, committing herself to her fate. All restraint has left her. With great dramatic power she asks the fatal question: "Your name, from where did you come, who are you?" Telramund breaks in upon her last cry. True to his sinister promise he has waited behind the door. Seeing him and knowing that he has come to kill Lohengrin, Elsa cries out: "Save yourself, your sword, your sword." And while Telramund sinks to the ground fatally wounded, Elsa falls as if lifeless at Lohengrin's feet.

Deep silence.

Lohengrin's sword slips slowly to the ground. He stands erect beside Elsa, his eyes looking sorrowfully into the distance: "Woe, all our bliss is now ended." He raises Elsa tenderly and leads her to the couch, upon which she sinks half fainting, sighing: "Eternal one, have mercy upon me."

She remains there motionless, fainting, until the ladies-in-waiting whom Lohengrin has summoned, help her to rise. Then swaying, supported by two of her ladies, she moves past Lohengrin to the door. With the musical motive: "never shall you ask me" she raises her faltering glance to him, while he stands looking past her into the distance into which he will soon vanish, never more to return. . . .

In the last scene Elsa should appear changed. Life seems to have left her. It is as if she is extinguished—completely passive. When she enters supported by her ladies-in-waiting she must give the impression of someone who is ill. The king goes towards her, she greets him with a weary and abstracted gesture. When he asks her kindly: "Why do I see you so sad? Does the separation affect you so deeply?" she does not meet his eyes. He thinks that she might be sad because her husband is going to a war which will bring victory and glory to her country, for he, the noble knight, will lead it to victory. No one knows that she has lost him, no one knows that he will never return. Exhausted, she sinks down upon the couch which has been prepared for her. But she immediately rises as she hears Lohengrin approaching. He is greeted by the people with great enthusiasm, she alone is sorrowful and stands bowed in humility. When Lohengrin announces that he cannot lead the army to battle as he had hoped to do, Elsa withdraws into herself more than ever (she does not sit down), for she now realizes that she has destroyed not only her own and her husband's happiness but that she has also wronged her country. Her guilt increases, her repentance is devastating. When Lohengrin speaks of Telramund's guilt Elsa does not react, she stands withdrawn into herself. But when he accuses her before all the people of having broken her sacred oath she turns to him with a sorrowful and pleading gesture. When he announces that he will now reveal his name, his origin and his mission, she slowly straightens up and follows his words through the narrative of the Grail with increasing tension. As he says: "If known to you, he must leave you" she is seized with a terrible fear and tries to interrupt him. She does not want to know anything, she does not want to hear anything. It is very difficult to find the right balance in acting this: Elsa should not even for a moment push herself into the foreground. All the attention is centered solely on Lohengrin and must not be diverted from him. On the other hand it is very wrong for Elsa not to react at all. She knows that in the instant when he tells his name he is lost to her for ever, so at the last moment she tries to stop him. If she doesn't step out too far from the row of her ladies-in-waiting a restrained gesture is possible and right. I have always played it in this way, and I don't think that I was in any way too assertive.

When Elsa sees that her pleading is in vain she devotes herself completely to his revelation: with wide-open eyes she drinks in his account of his nobility. At his name: "Lohengrin" she falls to the ground as if struck by lightning. Her ladies try to raise and comfort her. She rises slowly and dizzily, and groans in barely more than a whisper—"The earth sways beneath me, O what darkness!? O air, air for me, miserable one."

"*Upon the top step leading into the cathedral Elsa turns to greet the jubilant people.*" LOHENGRIN (page 22)

"*The cry of the people: 'The swan, the swan!' awakens Elsa from her lethargy . . . and turning . . . with horror she sees the swan slowly approaching drawing the boat.*"

LOHENGRIN (page 29)

The following speech of Lohengrin and a further outburst of Elsa's are generally cut, as is the ensemble and Lohengrin's prophetic prediction of future victory. And I think quite rightly. We sang it all uncut for a long time in Vienna—I think from the time it was revived by Richard Strauss. But I have always found it much too long-winded and the action too dragging. The objection that Elsa would not let her husband go away without a word, that she would pluck up her courage in a last attempt to hold him, does not seem to me convincing. Elsa is now absolutely broken. She knows that everything has come to an end. She has resigned herself to her cruel fate. This holding him back I have always found almost painful. It is only a matter of postponing the end, which can easily become "too much". Generally it is cut from Elsa's sigh to the appearance of the swan. The cry of the people: "The swan, the swan", awakens Elsa from her lethargy. She straightens up, and turning, looks with horror into the distance, from which she sees the swan slowly approaching drawing the boat.

Lohengrin sees the summons of the Holy Grail bidding the lingerer to return—and he says with agitation: "The Grail now summons him who had delayed too long." Elsa stands as if paralysed, her back to the audience. With trembling anxiety she follows Lohengrin's words as he greets the swan. In an outburst of anguish he turns to her. Since he must part from her he may now explain everything. Now he may tell her that she would only have had to hold to her oath for one year—only one year. Then her brother would have returned to her. Elsa is deeply shocked. With a gesture of despair she covers her face with her hands and remains in this position, broken, devastated.

When Lohengrin gives her his horn, his sword and his ring, she takes the gifts almost unconsciously. She holds them tightly to her and passionately kisses the ring upon her finger. But she must give the impression of swaying, of half fainting, and when Lohengrin, drawing her to him, kisses her good-bye she drops the horn and sword. (She must be careful that they don't clatter as they fall to the ground, she must let them drop slowly and cleverly in the folds of her dress so that they will fall as noiselessly as possible. One of her ladies gathers them up.)

Lohengrin draws away from Elsa who has scarcely the strength to cling to him any longer. She sinks into the arms of her ladies who try to help her, while Lohengrin strides towards the rear of the stage.

Ortrud who, concealed among the people, has followed all this with a sinister joy, now breaks out of her concealment, unable any longer to bear her triumph in silence. She wears the grey dress of a penitent but her attitude is that of a triumphant victor. However, in spite of her snakelike cleverness she is led through her malicious jubilation to commit an act of great stupidity: she discloses to every one, and above all to Elsa, that her brother still lives in the form of the swan. She has bewitched the boy, and the very swan which has brought Lohengrin here and will bear him away is he who is believed to be dead. Elsa, who has straightened up and listened to Ortrud with mounting horror, again collapses. But Lohengrin with great solemnity falls upon his knees, raising his hands before him in prayer. Amidst the breathless tension of the assemblage he prays for the release of the young prince. Great excitement sways the crowd as a fluttering dove, appearing from above, slowly and gracefully circles down to the boat. Suddenly the swan dives into the water, the dove appears upon the prow of the boat as its leader—and Lohengrin helps a youth out of the water: it is Gottfried, Elsa's brother, whom Lohengrin's prayer has freed of his enchantment. Lohengrin names him as the leader of Brabant, and steps into the boat. In the general uproar he rides away quickly without being noticed.

Ortrud with horror has seen the dove of the Holy Grail as it descended, and with a last cry of terror at Gottfried's appearance has fallen to the ground—dead.

With radiant joy Elsa stretches out her arms to her brother. With delight they fall into each other's arms. Then Elsa, embracing him tenderly, leads him to the king before whom he bows and who blesses him with the touch of his sword. In her overwhelming joy Elsa has taken no notice of Lohengrin. But now in sudden fear she looks about for him. With the cry: "My husband, my husband!" she hurries toward the rear of the stage. At this moment she catches sight of Lohengrin disappearing into the distance and falls to the ground lifeless.

It is actually rather difficult to make the ending of the opera really convincing. In my opinion Elsa shouldn't fall to the ground too quickly. I always remained standing upright for a moment looking backward. Then I fell very slowly to my knees; Gottfried took me in his arms, and while he seemed to lay me carefully on the ground it was just time for the curtain to fall.

Chapter II

ELISABETH—"TANNHÄUSER"

AFTER THE SUCCESS of my first Elsa—a success which was due more to my youth and childlike innocence than to the performance itself—I was given one rôle after another. In this way I was, so to speak, lifted out of the group which for some years had been formed by the four pages from *Lohengrin* and *Tannhäuser* and the apprentices from *Meistersinger*. We were intimate friends, and our friendship was not at all disturbed by a success in which the others did not share and which even in later years they were not quite able to share. This is evidence of the real spirit of comradeship which existed in the theatre.

One often hears reports of wild intrigues, of envy and ill-will between the singers, of egotistical quarrels and inconsiderate attempts to push one another out of the way. It is really too bad that these ridiculous stories seem to circulate over the whole world. Good heavens, in any profession where there is competition there is also conflict! Every one who must struggle to get ahead thinks of himself, of his own success—this goes without saying! But I don't believe that this quite natural and human struggle for existence is any greater on the stage than it is in any other profession. On the contrary: I have always found that artists of the stage stick very closely together. All are in a certain sense victims of the moment. An artistic performance can be ruined through nervousness, a sudden hoarseness, an accidental stumbling, a thousand details over which one has no control. Every singer is at the mercy of the moment and knows that this is equally true of his colleagues. This creates a bond between them. Knowing that the same thing might happen to oneself any moment makes each helpful to the other. I have only known of rare instances on the stage in which a colleague was not as helpful as possible. The few who are entirely self-seeking, whom thank God one seldom encounters, always remain outsiders, considered as "uncooperative"—a much-dreaded reputation in the life of the stage.

Memories of my life in opera are little darkened by such

unhappy experiences—if there were any, they have faded away as something not at all typical and quite unimportant.

When I became Elsa and the others of our group were my pages it in no way affected our friendship—and though our ways have parted we still remain bound by the same ties, and when we come together we share again those memories of far-off days with all their sweet nonsense and glowing intensity. We forget the long years which have intervened and feel as closely bound to one another as in those days of our youth.

How well I remember the little apartment which I shared with my friend and colleague Annemarie. It was of course just opposite the theatre, for we practically lived there! How we loved to drive around the Alster, that lovely lake in the centre of Hamburg. This was a great luxury which we only permitted ourselves on the first day of each month, for the carriage—a venerable one-horse affair—meant real extravagance for us. Annemarie always had some money left at the end of the month while I was always in a state of embarrassment, even though my salary was already higher than hers. I remember a time when we both bought tickets in a lottery and, of course, expected to win a prize. For weeks the chief topic of conversation was what we would do with all the money which would pour into our laps in such rich profusion. Of course we took it for granted that whoever won it would share it with the other just as it was also taken for granted that one of us would win it. I promised Annemarie the exact half. But she said if she won it she would not just give me the half outright, she would put it in a bank for me where it would be safe and where I wouldn't be able to draw it out without her permission. . . .

I boiled with fury. . . .

"And may I ask why?" I asked with icy disdain.

"Of course," she answered quietly, "if I give you the money, you will give it away immediately and will have nothing from it."

I didn't at all appreciate her concern for me. I remember I threw my pocket-book at her head and she was showered with loose change (it must have been the first of the month!). Our mutual anger and disdain were quieted through our eager search for the money: we had to laugh, and peace was restored. Of course I don't need to add that neither of us won the lottery. But I was too busy learning new rôles to bother very much about this disappointment.

My repertory grew in a short time—to-day I cannot understand how it was possible to absorb so many rôles with an almost ravenous hunger without having a breakdown. In a colorful array I sang the most varied parts and quickly learned to battle my fear of a new rôle.

Nevertheless, I must confess that this fear continues to torment me in a certain sense even to-day: I seldom approach the study of a new song, of an unaccustomed style of singing without the fear that I am not equal to it. However, my attitude towards this faintheartedness has altered with the course of years: in earlier times I would set the rôle aside despondently, whereas later on it became a challenge to me to conquer my pessimistic weakness. I reached this attitude through an almost humorous experience. My kind director in Vienna, Franz Schalk, was familiar with my dreadful habit of always sending back a new rôle, the first time it was sent to me, with a letter of regret. It was "an old custom" that he would then send me the rôle for the second time with a few encouraging words—and then I sang it. So one day I received the rôle of the wife of the dyer for the *première* of Richard Strauss's *Frau ohne Schatten*, but Schalk wrote in this case that we must save time; and so I should imagine that I had already received the rôle once and had already refused it and sent it back to him and that this is now the second part of the accustomed procedure—and I should say yes just as I had always said "yes" the second time. I said "yes".

Later, when Clemens Kraus became director of the Vienna Opera and I received a rôle for the first time under his direction, I returned it as I had been accustomed to do. But he was not Schalk. He took it back with delight and gave it to another singer, whose success was nearer to his heart than either the opera or I. Very much disconcerted I had to admit to myself that I really wanted to sing this rôle very much! This time the only impulse I ever had to play the *prima donna* (pfui!) was punished severely. A good lesson, I must say. . . .

But to come back to the time of my first successes: a change of management had brought an unwelcome standstill. Dr. Löwenfeld, the new director of the Hamburg Opera, arrived with a large following of singers whom he wanted to use in preference to those already established there. Quite ridiculously, although only a young beginner, I suddenly belonged to the ranks of "the old ones" whom Löwenfeld wanted to replace with members of his ensemble. The conductors Brecher and Klemperer left the Hamburg Opera, and with them I lost two good friends and champions. Weingartner, the new power on the throne, concentrated his interest for the most part upon his adored wife, the soprano Lucille Marcel. I did not sing very much under his direction. But the ever restless Weingartner soon left this position, and many of the new singers whom Löwenfeld had brought with him disappeared. Selmar Meyrowitz became the first conductor and gave me the rôle of Iphigenie in Gluck's *Iphigenie in Aulis*. With this rôle I emerged from my undesired inactivity and was again plunged into the confusion of *premières*.

I now made my own a rôle for which I had longed for some time: Elisabeth in *Tannhäuser*.

To-day I cannot judge whether at that time I really *was* Elisabeth. I had not yet experienced any deep suffering. My life, to be sure, had been rich in heights and depths—I had experienced disappointments and known joys. But to be able to portray Elisabeth, suffering, the greatest teacher, must have sung its painful and sombre melody. . . . In my opinion, one cannot represent great emotions if one has not experienced them deeply oneself. The contention that the singer, the actor, must have enough power of imagination to be able to create from imagination alone, is incorrect and unconvincing. Naturally every portrayal of an emotion is created through the power of one's imagination because it is the experience of *others*, of those whom we represent, with whom we identify ourselves, to whom we must give expression. The feeling of the other, the imaginary figure is so to speak sublimated through the power of our imagination. But this must be approached through one's own depth of feeling. . . . One's own experience, one's own griefs, one's own joys must arise in the representation of another's fate. The richer our own life has been and is, the fuller is the scale which is at our command. This necessity for living life fully and ardently through suffering and joy, lifts the artist beyond the moral standard of everyday experience. He cannot live amidst restrictions, he cannot let his senses be tyrannized by the conventions of a narrow average way of living. He exists to give to the average being an emotional exaltation which may lift him above his everyday experience. And he can only do this fully if he himself has gone through fire and water.

I would almost like to say that this applies especially to the experience of great spiritual suffering. Suffering such as one must represent in "Elisabeth".

I remember with what deep emotion I, many years ago, visited the Wartburg in Thüringen. I had just sung Elisabeth and the fading images of this experience were still before me when my vacation brought me to the neighbourhood of Thüringen. I felt I had to visit the Wartburg, to enter the dwelling in which the mythical—perhaps the actual—Elisabeth, lived and loved and suffered.

The dimensions of the hall in which the singing contest took place were rather disappointing, but my imagination was vivid and deeply stirred. Looking down upon the green valley which stretched before me, I imagined the lovely Elisabeth—what does it matter whether she was a real or purely imaginary figure? For me, she lived, for me this dwelling had reality as hers, and the saga of Tannhäuser lived again just as Wagner evolved it and gave it immortality.

The hall of singing was before me. Elisabeth stood upon the threshold, I myself was standing there—I *was* Elisabeth. . . .

Elisabeth had been through a deep emotional experience. The hero of her dreams had gone away. Without him, without his wonderful songs, this hall had seemed desolate to her and she had shunned the singing competitions to which she had loved to listen before Tannhäuser went away. At that time he had been the centre of the singing contest. Elisabeth does not realize that she loves Tannhäuser. She cannot explain her restlessness even to herself, she cannot understand the grief which she has suffered, nor describe the joy which she feels now that he is returning. She is aware of but one thing: to-day she must be here, to-day life begins anew for her, life which had seemed distant like a far-off song.

She enters the hall filled with joy, with deep emotion, the emotion of a heart overwhelmed by happiness. For this reason the first phrases: "Beloved hall again I greet you, joyfully I greet you again, beloved hall," must be sung in the same flowing, swinging *tempo* as the prelude. Not more slowly, nor with dramatic breadth. A surging joy pours from these words. They must give the impression of an outburst, in order to be convincing. Generally those who sing the rôle of Elisabeth grow sad when they look back over the suffering which Tannhäuser's departure has caused them. ("Since he left how empty you have seemed.") No: it is suffering which is past, which has been eclipsed by the radiant present. Elisabeth looks back over this suffering as she would over a bad dream with the confused astonishment of the fortunate who can no longer believe that the poor heart once suffered so deeply. . . . It is a remembering with a half smile, a contemplative wondering remembering. And now the realization of great joy breaks radiantly through the half light of recollection: from: "Now that my heart is lifted by joy, you seem to me proud and lofty" to the end of the aria the singer and the orchestra become one surging pæan of joy. And much as I hate *fermate*, generally speaking, I would have fought with every conductor if he had not permitted me to sing with a little more breadth (*allargando*) in the finale of the aria.

I remember the time when the young Jeritza sang this aria incomparably. The golden radiance of her voice was as if made for this surging music. And at the end of the aria she did something which only she could permit herself: she sang the last phrase with her back to the audience, really greeting the hall with an all-embracing gesture. Naturally I would never advise any singer to try this who doesn't have a very large dramatic voice or who couldn't make this dangerous nuance convincing from their own inner conviction. La Jeritza, with her flair for theatrical effect, was breathtakingly convincing. Her voice, scorning the handicap of her position, soared over the orchestra like a flame of gold.

During the postlude Elisabeth walks eagerly through the hall, until seeing Tannhäuser upon the threshold she stops abruptly. She vainly seeks to conceal her overwhelming emotion, and turning away from him tries to control herself. Tannhäuser throws himself at her feet—she does not know what to do. With great timidity she starts to leave the hall. Elisabeth must now actually convey the impression that she means to leave. As he kneels she must quickly hurry past him to the little door through which the Landgraf enters later. This door leads to an inner room—she will try to escape that way. At the moment when Tannhäuser cries: "O stay and let me remain at your feet," she pauses. She accedes to this welcome request only too gladly. Having succeeded in composing herself she turns to him with quiet dignity. She is now very much the "great lady" graciously welcoming her guest. In her words: "Where have you been so long?" trembles the aftermath of her grief, of the longing for him which she has suffered. The change from her gracious welcome to this trembling recollection must be very subtle. Just as the in-between tones of a painting make the real picture, so life itself is not just black or white, but shines and glistens in a thousand shadings—joy and pain often flowing imperceptibly into one another. To find the fine, infinitely subtle expression for all these delicate shadings—that is the task of the true artist. That I call acting. That is what makes the portrayal of an otherwise lifeless opera figure convincing. . . .

With astonishment, Elisabeth listens to his strange explanation. She cannot understand him. She feels only the deep homage which he pays her when he says: "That I no longer hoped to meet you, nor ever again to lift my eyes to you." The delicate upward sweep of the music like a soft whisper is the reflection of her gesture as she turns her head slightly towards him in her confusion—and there is quivering anticipation in her question: "What was it, which brought you back?" At the moment she hears the word "miracle" a flash of enlightenment sweeps over her. Yes, it is a miracle! A miracle that he has come, a miracle which brings me fulfillment, a miracle which I will try to understand and which when I do understand it will make me incredibly happy. Soundlessly her lips form the word "miracle" even before she frees herself of her inhibition and cries exultantly: "I praise this miracle from the depths of my heart." Tannhäuser, surprised and overwhelmed by the lack of restraint with which she offers him her love, makes a sudden movement as if he would draw her to him. Elisabeth immediately controls her feeling. She realizes with confusion that she has quite forgotten herself—and her startled expression restrains Tannhäuser. She feels that she must explain to herself as well as to him why she has lost so completely all her natural reserve. She needs his help, for she can no longer understand herself. Her touching cry: "O help me to solve this mystery of my heart," moves Tannhäuser deeply. Having lived for a whole year in the Venusberg, lost in a sensual ecstasy of which this royal child hasn't the remotest conception, he has almost forgotten that such purity and lovely innocence could ever exist. Tannhäuser should react here with great subtlety—every violent gesture, every expression of love would have silenced Elisabeth. That he looks at her as a man would

look at a child who has asked a question makes it possible for
Elisabeth to speak with the fullest of confidence.

A singer once asked me: "What do you actually do in the
short interlude which follows this question? It really isn't right
to do anything, is it? I make a gesture with my cloak, to fill out
the pause . . ." In my opinion that is just the antithesis of art.
"Filling pauses" is something which makes my blood boil. . . .
One must have the courage to do nothing, just to stand still. In
real life one does not run around and gesticulate incessantly!
Elisabeth must just feel *inwardly*—then she will be convincing.
To try to bridge a pause with an empty gesture is senseless, inartistic, insincere. And in the end the audience always detects
insincerity.

This applies also to all the great "sensational successes" of
which I have seen so many come and go like the wind. The
public, with a certain eagerness for the sensational, may be
deceived for a time. But after a while it comes to appreciate
what is genuine and right. It is my deepest and innermost conviction that only that which springs from a sincere heart will
have lasting value. Real gold lasts for ever, false gold fades and
wears away.

This brings me to a question which I received in a letter from
a young singer. I would like to quote a part of this letter, for it
seems to me typical of the bewilderment of many young singers:
"One of the things which seem to bother most of us when we
talk of stage singing is how to shove our own personalities into
the background. Does this come with confidence in ourselves?
We hear of losing oneself in a part—is this possible without
running the danger of forgetting lines or cues? We hear of artists
who are nervous until they step on the stage—and from then on
I am Carmen or Elisabeth or Walter or whatever he is singing!
None of us has ever had that feeling. Does it mean that we are
not meant for the stage, that our self-consciousness is a form of
conceit, or is it just a lack of experience?"

I can only say that one steps into the background quite of oneself if one is really a part of what is going on. This is the great
and wonderful blessing of the stage, that one learns to forget
one's own small personality and becomes identified with the rôle,
so that one lives, suffers, rejoices and dies with it. Of course,
one loses oneself in a rôle—but one does not do it without control.

Every emotion in life is controlled by our reason to some extent. The more cultivated one is, the more this self-discipline controls the natural reactions of our senses. The primitive being, for example, goes at his food like an animal, if he is hungry. The man who is trained to bring the beauty of culture to the sensual enjoyment of eating will master his hunger and be moderate, even if he would like to let himself go and forget all that he has learned. Hunger and love are the two most powerful emotions in life, are they not? Now will not love be something really beautiful if it is raised to the sphere of imagination? If this were not so there would be no difference between human beings and animals. We are human beings, with a God-given power of realization. So the singer must learn to bring this realization to the experience of a performance. Then he will truly master it. Feeling the experience, he must learn to raise himself above this feeling. Only then will he learn to master and to hold in check that which can only be really beautiful when it is restrained. No emotion can ever be realized to its fullest unless it is controlled.

When I sang a rôle I was never Lotte Lehmann. Not for a moment. Perhaps I was—when I was in bad voice or had to struggle against some indisposition. At such times it is difficult to surmount these material limitations. But I do not speak of these exceptional instances.

Stage fright is a part of the life of an artist. It is the usual prelude to one's entrance upon the stage, a painful prelude, I must say. . . . One lives through a thousand hells, one swears a thousand oaths that in the next life one will be anything but a singer, will never again endure this frightful experience of appearing before an audience. And then comes the self-discipline which one can only acquire through an iron will. Then the soaring flow of music raises one above the fear and trembling of the moment before, the everyday self is thrust into the background and one is released and transformed into the personality of the rôle one is playing. No beginner can really have this experience to start with. At least I can't imagine that this could be possible. I don't like to use that detestable word "routine"—for routine is the antithesis of art—I might better say one must learn to be at home on the stage. That is absolutely necessary. The road is a long one—there is so much to learn. One must have patience. But with this feeling of being at home will come the realization of losing oneself while at the same time controlling

oneself. Oh no, this is no contradiction! Above the deep
feeling of identification with the rôle, one's brain guides the
purely technical production—it keeps one from forgetting what
one has to sing, it makes one sing in harmony with the conductor,
with the orchestra, the ensemble—and makes one able to attend
to the action of one's partner.

But now let us come back to Elisabeth. How did I get started
on this long detour? Oh yes, it was the gesture with which
Elisabeth "filled out" the musical phrase. (For Heaven's sake
never "fill out" anything!) She should stand quietly as if
searching within herself—seeking to explain what is not at all
clear even to herself. Then she begins very simply: "To the
minstrels' songs I often loved to listen." She sings this phrase
with a friendly contemplation as if she were placing a frame
about the picture in her heart. But as soon as she feels her own
experience becoming vivid again, she changes. With an inner
trembling she tries to explain, both to Tannhäuser and herself,
the strange restlessness which his singing has awakened in her.
"O what a strange new life your song has awakened in my heart"
is a stormy confession of her love. Elisabeth is filled with passion
for the first and only time, for the first and only time there is
a sensual glow in her words and in her impetuous bearing. "I
felt a sudden desire within me." This passionate outburst makes
a deep impression upon Tannhäuser, who had almost gone to
pieces as the slave of his senses. He receives this naïve love
which is offered him as a surprising and fabulous gift which
quite overwhelms him. But he must not react impetuously—
never that! That would immediately bring Elisabeth back to
herself, would immediately dispel the intoxication of her confession. Tannhäuser trembles—he ceases to breathe, he is almost
overwhelmed by his emotion. But he remains motionless with
wide open eyes, drinking in this confession. With a sudden break
Elisabeth resumes her story. It is as if she finds her way back
from the intoxication of her thoughts to that painful time when
Tannhäuser was away from her. Her voice is soft—it almost
breaks as she tells him how forlorn and forsaken she had felt.
She is again astonished to realize how flat and dull the songs of
the other minstrels had seemed to her, how far from her had been
all joy and desire. The dreams which oppressed her seem to
disquiet her even in recalling them. Her hand clutches her

throat in fear as she sings: "In dreams I felt dull pains"; and the
pathetic outbreak "Joy left my heart" is the climax of all that
she had suffered—the summation of all she has experienced, of
all she has undergone. Turning directly to him she reaches out
her hands beseechingly, saying with tears: "Heinrich, Heinrich,
what have you done to me?" This is not a reproof. It is a
plea: free me, release me from this strange and oppressive
feeling, tell me that what I feel is not wrong. All this should
be conveyed in this trembling "Heinrich, Heinrich . . ."

Overwhelmed, Elisabeth buries her face in her hands and
Tannhäuser's joyous outbreak in the prelude to the following
duet soars over her without affecting her. For a moment she is
completely lost within herself, awaiting his words with averted
face. When he sings: "You should praise the God of Love"—
she slowly lowers her hand. With a sudden shock she has
realized that Tannhäuser has found the right word. Yes, it is
love which has wrought this change in her, her lips form the
words even before she sings "love, love", and she throws herself
blissfully into the radiant duet: "Praised be the hour". Here
neither Elisabeth nor Tannhäuser should indulge in gesticula-
tion. This duet is pure song. It should be sung with scarcely
any acting which would disturb the hymnlike unison of the two
voices which must dominate the stage.

When in parting from her Tannhäuser kisses the edge of her
cloak, she seems to want to bend over him—but he tears himself
away and she remains standing in the centre of the stage for a
moment, deeply moved. Then with quick steps (without being
too hasty!) she moves towards the background, her eyes following Tannhäuser. He seems to greet her from afar and she makes
a gesture of response. I have seen an Elisabeth who resorted to
too much play of facial expression as Tannhäuser presumably
greeted her, while disappearing into the distance. When she
imagined him out of sight her face became very sad so that she
could suddenly be radiant again as if Tannhäuser had once more
turned back to her. That is of course very bad and very false
theatre. There is no reason for Elisabeth to be sad: she knows
that her beloved will return. So I see no reason for her to
plunge from joy to despair when she sees him going away for a
few minutes. (Poor Tannhäuser, what a dreadful punishment to
be so loved! That would seem to me very annoying!)

Elisabeth hears the Landgraf approaching. I want to mention

here a detail which can easily be disturbing: every reaction must
be subtle. It would be illogical for Elisabeth to react too strongly
to the Landgraf's entrance. She certainly knows that he is
coming. The festivities are soon to begin and she awaits him,
so why should she act as if she is astonished to see him? With
amazement I have often seen her give this impression. She
should greet him with a welcoming smile and then quickly
move towards him. He, who is like a father to her, should be
the first to learn of her happiness. His eyes tell her that he
reads her heart. So she hesitates a moment as if overcome
with feeling, and then going to him buries her head upon his
shoulder.

The Landgraf gently disengages himself from her embrace,
and as he speaks to her is himself quite overcome with emotion.
He covers his feeling by jesting tenderly with her: "Do I actually
see you in this hall, which you have avoided for so long? Does
this festival of song, which we are preparing, really lure you at
last?" He knows very well what it is which draws Elisabeth
here to-day! It is not the festival, but Tannhäuser's presence.
Sensing the delicate reproach, the tender kindliness of her
fatherly friend, Elisabeth breaks into tears of gratitude. "My
uncle, O my kind father . . ."

Her voice is soft: she trembles, deeply moved. Her head sinks
again upon her uncle's breast. And he who has never urged her
to confide in him, knows that to-day it would perhaps do her
good, that it would help this confused child to open her heart
to him. He says tenderly: "Don't you want to open your heart
to me at last?"

Here I can't help thinking of the man who seemed to pour out
his whole soul with these words: the unforgettable Richard Mayr
of the Viennese opera and of the Salzburg festivals. Tears come
to my eyes as I think of him, of the infinitely tender and kindly
gesture with which he took my head in his hands and looked into
my eyes as if he would fathom the depths of my soul. . . . Elisabeth's plea—"Look into my eyes—I cannot speak"—came from
the depths of my heart and my last words were almost choked
with tears which often enough rolled down my cheeks. Certainly
one should always be above the experience—I know that my tears
were out of place. But I wouldn't have missed this thrilling
moment for anything in the world. Even if under the spell of
the moment my feeling did overpower me, this vivid almost un-

controllable flood of emotion was something beautiful and never to be forgotten.

The Landgraf now speaks to Elisabeth as if he were her own father. He has come to the decision that since song has awakened something so wonderful in Elisabeth, it should be the means through which she will find her happiness. Elisabeth not entirely understanding his words makes a questioning movement, but is interrupted by the pages who announce the arrival of the guests. She bows graciously with a gesture of modest protest, when the Landgraf assures her that the guests will come in greater numbers to-day than ever before, because they have heard that Elisabeth, the princess, will attend this festival after being absent for so long.

During the procession of the guests Elisabeth must never forget that without being in any way conspicuous she must nevertheless always be a part of the action. *It is very inartistic ever to step out of the rôle.* So long as one is on the stage, one belongs to the action, is a part of the whole. Elisabeth cannot stand there as if she were bored and imagine that no one notices what she is doing because her back is turned to the audience. It knows very well when a singer is just faking and when she is a part of the action.

I have seen a singer, a very well-known singer, who always made use of a moment when she thought she wasn't observed to pull a lozenge quickly from the depths of her gown, unwrap it and thrust it into her mouth—always with the blissful conviction that the audience would never notice it. But I saw it and many others must have seen it. How can one be convincing as an actress if one only "plays" when one is actually involved in the action onself? One is always a part of the action—silent and motionless—but always the personality whom one represents. Only then can it be called a complete performance, not just empty theatre.

When the Landgraf and Elisabeth have seated themselves upon the throne the procession of minstrels begins. Elisabeth must follow this scene with great interest. She is only waiting for the appearance of the one: Tannhäuser. But she must realize that she sits before the eyes of the whole assemblage: all the nobles of the land are gathered before her, a great part of the attention is centered upon her. So Elisabeth must not react too violently when Tannhäuser enters. All exaggeration is very much out of

place here. By reason of her high position Elisabeth is accustomed
to controlling her emotions when in the presence of others. She
certainly will not show before the whole assemblage the exaggerated reactions which so many Elisabeths bring to this scene:
tense expectation at every entry, disappointment when it is not
Tannhäuser but another who enters. Of course Elisabeth knows
that he will come! In spite of her youth she is a "great lady",
she has the dignity of her position, the dignity of her maiden-
hood. So she greets him as he enters impetuously, with charming
friendliness, without betraying through more than a smile of
delight the deep feeling with which she has awaited him.

During the address of the Landgraf she listens with quiet
attention and does not return Tannhäuser's glances, which are
directed towards her with increasing intensity. On the contrary
she looks away from him, for she wants to listen undisturbed to
her uncle's speech. Only once when the Landgraf refers to the
minstrel who has returned home does she, forgetting herself for
the moment, turn with emotion towards Tannhäuser who is
bowing before her. When the Landgraf says: "It seems to me
a wonderful secret which has brought him back to us," her face
is transfigured with a rapturous smile: she knows what it is
which has brought him back—his love for her. Wherever he
may have been he longed to return to her, to the truest, most
loving heart, which is his alone.

The Landgraf, knowing well that there is no singer who can
compete with Tannhäuser, offers as the prize the hand of Elisabeth, assuming—and what a certain assumption it seems—that
Elisabeth would find in the winner the fulfillment of her secret
dream. She bows graciously and willingly agrees. In blissful
expectation her eyes turn to Tannhäuser.

Elisabeth should not betray any deep disappointment when
the first to sing in the competition is not Tannhäuser but
Wolfram. It seems rather superfluous to mention details which
should be taken for granted, but in attempts to "act" I have seen
such incredible absurdities committed that I want to warn
against them, even if they do seem self-evident.

Elisabeth listens to Wolfram with great interest. His song
pleases her immensely. When his words "I lift my eyes to only
one of the stars" are clearly directed to her, when his eyes, filled
with tenderness, are raised to her declaring his deep and reverent
love, her glance is lowered. She has realized for a long time that

Wolfram loves her. She respects him, she has the friendliest feeling for him—but her whole heart belongs to Tannhäuser. She is unhappy that she must hurt Wolfram, her wonderful noble-hearted friend. But she cannot help it. One must feel that Elisabeth is kind, that it hurts her to cause him unhappiness. Elisabeth pays no attention to Tannhäuser while Wolfram is singing. Had she done so, his reaction to Wolfram's words would have disquieted her: through this song extolling love, Tannhäuser, who has barely escaped from the sensual charms of a Venus, is again transported to the ecstasies which he had freely and gladly forsaken. While he is deeply touched by Elisabeth's innocence he has lost the ability to love without desire. His whole being is pervaded by the fascination of Venus—her spell has not lost its hold over him, her wiles have for ever destroyed his purity. Looking up at Elisabeth, so lovely as she sits upon her throne with such dignity and radiant purity, he begins to feel a violent desire for her, a desire such as he had for Venus, such as she had taught him to feel. Venus and Elisabeth become one in his thoughts and desires.

Wolfram extols love as the source of pure joy; he extols renunciation—not even by a thought or desire does he want to touch her who seems unattainable to him, the true lover. But Tannhäuser finds this passion for renunciation quite ridiculous. He covets what he loves.

Elisabeth listens with increased agitation as he begins to sing. Her bearing and her radiant smile express the deepest concentration. She listens to his words without really taking in their meaning. His cynicism is so completely foreign to her being that she really has no idea what he is saying. She hears the sound of the words, she hears the enchanting quality of his voice and is enraptured.

When Tannhäuser finishes there is an embarrassing silence. Elisabeth who would like to applaud vigorously is restrained by a slight gesture from the Landgraf—and looking around she notices with surprise that the nobles seem wrapped in a gloomy silence, a silence indicative of a harsh judgment.

Walter's song is a sharp reproof to Tannhäuser. Elisabeth, listening to him with horror, sees with increasing amazement that all the others seem in accord with him. Questioningly she turns towards Tannhäuser. From now on he is completely under the spell of his passion. An expression of scorn flashes from his eyes and plays about his mouth—he waits impatiently for Walter to finish so that he may start a new song which is frivolous and cynical. Elisabeth begins to understand but is again reassured by his words—words which she misinterprets: "To praise God in unattainable sublimity, look up to Heaven, look up to His stars." That is the language with which she is familiar! To speak of God, of the sublimity of the heavens, it is of that which she is accustomed to hear! So with a deep breath she straightens up— joy in his song again seems to fill her with rapture. But suddenly it dawns upon her that these words which had seemed so noble and good were only the introduction to the song which now pours in a flood of passion from her beloved's disturbed mind. Certainly she does not entirely understand his words, but she feels their inherent impurity, she senses the strange world from which Tannhäuser speaks to her—a world which she cannot and will not enter.

Bitterolf challenges Tannhäuser to a duel; quarrelling and disputes rage through the hall where before has been only beauty. Elisabeth, withdrawn into herself, is as if petrified, her anguished gaze fixed upon Tannhäuser, who, forgetting all around him, seems to have fallen completely under the spell of his impure desire. Wolfram's sincere and beseeching prayer, instead of awakening him, excited him still more. So has he also sung in the Venusberg, so has he extolled love, even so did a hymn pour forth from him in his excitement, a hymn of sensual lust, a hymn of desire. Within him Wolfram's words are altered into an unbridled stammering of passion—and scarcely waiting for Wolfram to end this song which he has sung like a prayer, he plunges forward embracing his lute as if it were his beloved. There resounds through the lofty hall a song such as has never before been heard there: a song extolling sin, a wild confession of lascivious pleasure. The nobles file out of the hall horrified to know that he, who was once so honoured as a minstrel, has sojourned in the evil Venusberg and is capable of taunting them with this fact. As he says "enters the mountain of Venus" Elisabeth collapses upon the throne.

But this collapse should not be an indication of any inner weakness: a world falls in ruins before her, the world of her happiness, the world of her faith in him whom she loves and whom she has supposed to be pure and noble. In this moment she must seem to age years: she has learned the meaning of sin.

Sin, which until now had been nothing more than a word, now stares at her from the eyes of her beloved. At the same time a torturing fear rises within her: she knows the harsh laws of her country, she knows that Tannhäuser, as an unworthy sinner, will now be the prey of the knights whom he has sullied through his worthlessness. He was one of them—he has stained them all through his sin—for this he must pay with his life. With this realization Elisabeth awakens: with an effort she rises, fighting her weakness with superhuman strength. She must save him.... She cannot let him be destroyed.... Consumed by anxiety she watches the action of the knights: she foresees the end to which their shouts of indignation are leading. She plunges between their drawn swords and Tannhäuser, protecting him at the risk of her own life.

One must consider what it meant in this period for a woman, a virgin, to take the part of a sinful man so fearlessly. She, the child of a duke, defends an outcast.... The knights, unable to understand her, yield in horror.

It now must be another Elisabeth, an altered Elisabeth, who struggles to save Tannhäuser. She has lost all her shyness, her reticence is transformed into glowing action, her dreaminess into passionate challenge. Filled with the realization that it is not God's will to punish in the way in which the world punishes, knowing that God has chosen her to speak for him, to plead for him, she bares her heart before these men, confessing her love. A love which is magnanimous enough to forgive, a love which rises above earthly grief, a love which has become an intercessor, a love which will not cease to hope and to believe.... Until the end of her plea Elisabeth seems apart from reality: she is love transfigured as prayer, she is sacrifice and passionate renunciation. But at the moment when Tannhäuser collapses, annihilated, stirred to the depths of his being by so much love and purity and goodness, of which he is now unworthy, she also breaks down. Tannhäuser's words—"Woe! Woe to me, miserable one"— reveal to her his deep, inhuman, unbearable suffering; and in this misery, not her own but his, she falls upon her knees.

From a purely visual standpoint it isn't advisable for them both to fall to their knees at the same moment. It is always only a short step from the sublime to the ridiculous. One must find a way of avoiding this without doing anything which is contrary to one's conviction. One must always hold in mind the *complete picture*, not just the effect which one creates oneself. Theatre is essentially an art of the ensemble, the coordination of the one with the whole. There is nothing for Tannhäuser to do but suddenly fall to the ground—he is felled, as a tree is felled, by the grandeur of Elisabeth. Elisabeth can, of course, remain standing and yet convincingly give the impression of a breakdown. It is the expression, the trembling, the gesture of selfless exhaustion which conveys this effect. I myself have always sunk upon my knees very slowly—as if I did not want to fall but could no longer hold myself up. Elisabeth at this point must be like a flower which is broken, a withering flower. She remains upon her knees until Tannhäuser begins to sing. Then she slowly raises her head, and begins to find her way back to reality. With increasing pain she hears the words with which he accuses himself. It grieves her unbearably to see him who was once so radiant, so shattered, so broken down. At his words "Have mercy upon me" she raises herself and covers her face with her hands, trembling like a leaf in the wind—her whole being a figure of despairing entreaty. Slowly she begins to realize that her intercession has perhaps not been in vain: the knights seem deeply touched—and she stands amidst them with renewed pleading, her hands raised in entreaty—the angel of his liberation.

In my opinion Elisabeth in her pleading should not turn to any one individual, as is often done. I feel that she should, with outstretched arms, address her plea to the whole assemblage, not just to this one or that one. Much of the grandeur of this situation is lost if she turns to any one in particular. Standing in the centre of the stage her entreaty soars over them all. At the end of the wonderful (and very difficult!) ensemble she remains withdrawn, and she makes a lovely and convincing picture if she stands with outstretched arms, so that her figure conveys the suggestion of a cross.

When the music again indicates action she turns away hesitantly, listening to the Landgraf with a deep inner anxiety. Here Elisabeth should step further towards the background—not in her participation but physically: she has now said and done everything which it was possible for her to do. Now the decision rests in the hands of the Landgraf.

He is now the center of the stage, the center of interest. Elisabeth, though turned away from him, listens to his words. She listens but makes no movement of any kind. It is always a mistake to draw attention to oneself through some unnecessary movement when one should be a part of the background. Without ever neglecting the most important thing: being a vital part of the complete situation, one should never try to be conspicuous in a way which is not essential to the ensemble and so simply stands out for itself.

When the Landgraf thrusts Tannhäuser away, damning him as a sinner, Elisabeth is gripped by the terrible fear that her entreaty has been in vain. She cannot agree to the words of the Landgraf when he says: "and Heaven itself looks threateningly on this roof which has sheltered you too long." With a questioning plea Elisabeth looks up towards the heavens. She does not believe that Heaven would refuse forgiveness to a sinner. She feels that it is hypocritical and devoid of understanding to say that Heaven will never forgive. No, God could not want that. The Redeemer who died for our sins knows that they are committed through weakness, not through evil intention. He will forgive this weakness. With the music of the transfiguration which emerges from the emphatic rhythm, she turns with an imploring gesture to the Landgraf. It is a last entreaty—a last attempt to save Tannhäuser. And she feels that her plea will be granted: she sees it in the eyes of the Landgraf, which rest upon her filled with kindness.

Listening, she moves slowly towards the throne. (Tannhäuser lies outstretched at the front of the stage.) She does not see him, she pays no attention to him. It is as if his body—he, the man Tannhäuser whom she has loved—no longer exists for her: he has become an empty shell, even as the dead body is the shell, the insignificant shell of the immortal eternally living entity—the soul. He himself, his life, is not as important for her as his immortal soul which must not escape from his body without atonement and forgiveness. Saving him, saving his life, she saves his soul—for from now on his life shall be dedicated to one purpose: expiation, the plea for absolution.

Once again the minstrels seem about to raise their swords, once again they seem overcome with rage, doubtful that he can ever attain forgiveness. Once again a gesture of Elisabeth's restrains them. But this is more a gesture of rebuke than of entreaty, for she knows that the knights must obey the command of the Landgraf, and since he has ordered Tannhäuser to go to

Rome to seek the forgiveness of the church he cannot permit them to injure him.

The great final ensemble is very often cut—and I must honestly say quite rightly.

As the singing of the pilgrims sounds from behind scenes, Elisabeth listens, deeply moved. To Rome! The Pope himself will forgive him—he, who is the voice of heaven, will understand and absolve him!

Taking his leave Tannhäuser throws himself at Elisabeth's feet and kisses the edge of her robe. Elisabeth scarcely realizes his presence. . . . Her face is raised towards heaven—and the only thing which it is possible for her to do is to lower her hand almost unnoticeably, as if she were laying it in a gesture of benediction upon his head—but of course she must not touch him.

She is withdrawn from earth. She has become prayer: prayer which will accompany him until he finds absolution in Rome.

At the beginning of the third act Elisabeth lies stretched out before the cross. The figure of the praying Elisabeth should, of course, be a picture of great beauty, but I want to warn against a too-conscious draping of her dress. The robe should not have too long a train, for although a long flowing train will look lovely and will be theatrically effective, it isn't quite credible that one, dedicated to heaven, should have so much earthly vanity. Certainly all this is in the nature of a fairy tale and so perhaps unrealities which would make it more beautiful might be permitted. But they should never be lacking in taste, never so out of character that the illusion is destroyed. For me, the illusion of the nun resigned to heaven would be decidedly shattered if she wears a train long enough to make a sensation in any concert hall.

The best effect is achieved with apparent sincerity, if Elisabeth just before the curtain rises lets herself fall with the inner feeling of sinking down before the cross. The train will then drape itself without much need for arranging it in the right lines, as the slow and deliberate sinking down draws the robe into the right folds.

When the first tone of the pilgrims' chorus sounds in the distance Elisabeth raises her head very slowly. (She has, of course, taken no notice of Wolfram.) With a few clever lines her make-up must be altered during the intermission: death has now laid its hand upon Elisabeth. The grief which she has suffered has broken her heart, so naturally she cannot look blooming and healthy. She is pale, emaciated (the arrangement of the veil about her face helps to create this illusion), her eyes have deep shadows. Her voice is faint, her movements lifeless. When she straightens up after she has finished singing, she supports herself in her weakness by clinging to the cross: her movements are dragging, weary unto death.

The arrival of the pilgrims moves her to the depths of her being. But she must never forget that a too vividly displayed interest would be false here. Elisabeth is no longer capable of making vivid gestures. It is best for her to remain half leaning against the cross (this is also visually very effective), and only when the procession of pilgrims is drawing to an end should she very slowly and with dragging steps pass among them (without going more than a few steps from the cross) searching with desperate anxiety for that face which she longs to see more than any other. But Tannhäuser is not among the pilgrims—God, through the person of the Pope—has not pardoned him.

With a gesture of pain, Elisabeth clutches her heart. She stands motionless. Her gaze is directed into the distance. Left alone, she says softly, almost inaudibly and without any expression: "He does not return" . . . It must seem as if her lips form the words without being conscious of it. Since her task of saving him has failed it is as if she were extinguished, dying.

Swaying, she wants to climb upward to the castle, but her eyes fall once again upon the cross at whose base she has prayed such countless times for the salvation of his soul. Slowly her arms are lifted towards the cross. Once again she wants to surrender her whole heart, once again offer herself upon the altar of Her the all understanding. . . .

The more transfigured, the more unearthly, the more ethereal is the prayer: "Almighty Virgin, hear my pleading", the better. It is the prayer of one who is transfigured. It should have no earthly quality.

She, the pure one, feels that she is too sinful to plead for the salvation of that lost soul for whom she fears. She searches within herself for the weakness which has made God heedless of her prayer. She now lays her whole heart in the hands of the Holy Virgin, through whose intercession God may yet, in the last hour, bestow forgiveness, where even the emissary of God, the

Pope, has found no pardon. During the postlude she rises very, very slowly, crosses herself, tries to go on—as Wolfram, with a gesture of tenderness, approaches her. At the moment when she sees him and feels that he wants to speak with her, she tries through a gesture to restrain him: she no longer belongs to this earth, she no longer is a part of human life, she had dedicated herself to God and knows that silence is the law of the order which she will obey until death. But Wolfram tries again to approach her. He who loves her so truly and deeply hopes that he may have the blessing of leading her to her goal, up to the heights of the cloister which will shelter her lovely form, as a grave closing over her for eternity. He sees her weakness—he longs to help her.

The pantomime through which Elisabeth expresses her gratitude and asks him to honour her silence, shows him that she now belongs to heaven and no longer to an earthly existence. To work this out so that it may seem credible is a great and wonderful task.

She begins slowly and arduously to climb the hill towards the cloister. As if borne by the music she moves upward with swaying steps almost in an undulating dance—though this may be a dangerous suggestion, for it could be easily misunderstood, and it would be better if I could find another description. But her steps should have no earthly quality—it is as if she is uplifted, driven on, as if she is soaring.

One must feel: this is the end. The end of all that is human, the beginning of *life*. . . .

Wagner was the first to expect living characterizations from his singers. The demands which he made upon them in regard to dramatic action were revolutionary—and he often met with a complete lack of understanding. He gave the rôle of Elisabeth to his niece Johanna Wagner, a very lovely young girl with a beautiful voice, but when she first undertook it she was quite lacking in any real understanding of the character of Elisabeth. In his autobiography *My Life* he tells how Madame Schröder Devrient asked him if he really believed that Johanna, a young girl of only nineteen, was capable of representing Elisabeth. As she put it: "A young and pretty voice without any soul or without any real experience of life which alone could give the true feeling to this interpretation." Wagner sighed and said that in

Lotte Lehmann and Lauritz Melchior in TANNHAUSER

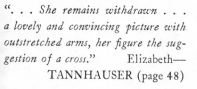

"... She remains withdrawn ... a lovely and convincing picture with outstretched arms, her figure the suggestion of a cross."   Elizabeth—
TANNHAUSER (page 48)

"... Question and answer now become a subtle duel of words. It is a game which they play with one another, a kind of verbal hide and seek ..."
Eva—MEISTERSINGER (page 75)

"... And now as she remembers h eyes are lowered as if she sees befor her the running brook whose wate had mirrored her face: and it was h face! ..."
Sieglinde—WALKÜRE (page 108

this case her youth must suffice and he must resign himself to a singer who was certainly not his ideal. He himself and his Brother Albert (the father of the young Johanna) painstakingly worked over the rôle with her and she became a great success. Yes, she became a renowned Elisabeth although, as Wagner says, her talent was more theatrical than dramatic.

I myself feel a kind of personal connection with this first Elisabeth. My charming friend Lili Petschnikoff gave me a beautiful and treasured gift. It is a gold pendant with two very delicately cut cameos, an ornament which had belonged to Johanna Wagner and which she bequeathed to my friend Lili. Johanna had been so delighted by the young, beautiful and talented violinist that she set aside this lovely ornament for her. Lili who, now retired, lives in her old ivy-covered house in Hollywood, wanted to give this gift from the first Elisabeth to another Elisabeth—and I hope that Richard Wagner, looking down from heaven, may not be displeased. . . .

Chapter III

ALONG THE ROAD TO AN
OPERA CAREER

TO-DAY IT SEEMS rather strange that it took me so long to come to a real understanding of the *art of acting*. I think it must have been due to the fact that a stage director generally has neither the time nor the patience to work intensively with a young and inexperienced beginner. It is so important that someone should explain the real meaning of the rôle and not be content with showing how one should act so far as outward gestures are concerned. It is far more essential to explain the "why" of a rôle than the "how". For from the "why" the "how" will develop of itself.

In an opera house where the repertory is changing constantly and there are always new *premières*, new rehearsals, as was the case in my youth, it is easy to understand that the stage directors are much too overburdened to "waste" time on a beginner. But such a serious neglect should be corrected by the assistant stage directors. They should teach—not only with slavish detail all that the "lord and master" says—but they should also instruct the young singers in the underlying meaning of their rôles. It is essential that both the time and the persons qualified for such a task be found. Then opera will also have something to offer from the standpoint of acting and people will no longer go to the opera just to hear music but to enjoy real drama. To-day good actors on the operatic stage are the exception. I am sure this would no longer be true if young singers were trained in the right way.

Very often I find in my mail letters which are difficult to answer: letters from young singing students asking for my advice. They say that they feel they have finished their period of study, that their ambition is the stage—do I think they are ready for an operatic career, and if so how can they go about it? Do I think they have the right qualifications for such a career, and by the way what are the right qualifications? They write that they feel an inner urge towards the stage. Is that sufficient?

I sit quite helpless before these letters. I hate giving an unsatisfactory answer to questions which come from a confused heart—and yet how can one offer advice about something which is so purely individual when one knows nothing of the surrounding circumstances? Let us speak first of the instrument, the voice. In my opinion no young girl should start to sing with the determination: opera or nothing. Only through years of study will the voice be developed to the point where a decision can be made as to which type of career it is best suited. The experience of my own early years may serve as an example. In my own case no one, least of all myself, thought of a stage career as a possibility for me. From the beginning my voice was soft and of a pleasing quality, but it was very small and lacked dramatic power. I began to study with the idea that I might perhaps become a good teacher, and my father, who was very much in favor of anything which would offer "security", preferred that I work towards a school position where a pension would be "assured". The idea that I might develop into a concert singer, one in which I only indulged in secret dreams, seemed absurd in moments of clear thinking.

I was very shy, but gradually as I went on studying I began to develop the ambition to sing at concerts, and then slowly the thought of opera became more than just a dream. . . . It became a goal. . . . I remember very distinctly that an elocution teacher to whom I owe much gratitude once said to me with horror: "For heaven's sake, Fräulein Lotte, you don't really have the idea that you could go into opera? Your voice is much too small!" I tell this to show how absolutely wrong a premature judgment may prove to be. My small voice under wise direction developed astonishingly and I had a long operatic career—not without success.

For this reason I myself am very hesitant about giving advice to young singers even when I have had the opportunity to judge them, for in view of my experience how could I say: give it up. Only when I have had a chance to work with a singer over a period of time, so that I may hear how the voice develops, am I willing to give advice which might be taken as the determining factor in a career. But I always add that where there is a vital compulsion to drive on towards one's goal, my advice should be disregarded. Had I followed the advice of one teacher I would have given up singing entirely, had I followed another I would have sung, but never in opera. . . .

The first and most important task is the *training of the voice*. You must study indefatigably and pray that you fall into the right hands—for finding the right teacher is often a matter of good luck, and sometimes becomes a very serious and difficult problem.

It is a great mistake, and often an irreparable one, for a child to be permitted to study singing too early. It goes without saying that a boy must be past the dangerous period when his voice breaks, but a girl also should not begin to take lessons before she is around sixteen. There may be exceptions who are precocious and are ready to study earlier, but they are the proverbial exceptions. One must begin slowly and with great care. The untrained voice often takes strange courses, and to develop it in the right way demands great understanding and infinite caution.

But what is the "right way"? Is there a correct method? At the risk of having many singing teachers at my throat I must say that I doubt it from the depths of my heart. Every larynx is constructed somewhat differently, every voice has its own individuality. In my opinion one is only a good teacher if one can recognize and develop this individuality. This does not apply only to interpretation; no, it applies just as much to the training of the voice. Through some lessons the teacher should just study the voice—just listen, so to speak, and should not be afraid to experiment a little to find what may be the right thing for this particular voice which he is to train. You must have confidence in your teacher—that is absolutely essential. But how can you be certain that your confidence is justified? That question is a very difficult one to answer. Only really advanced singers will know whether this or that "method" (I hate the word) is right for them. There is nothing more individual than the training of a voice. What is right for one may be wrong for another. Etelka Gerster was a wonderful teacher for many, but her method of singing was almost fatal for me. It was my good fortune that she threw me out of her school because of what she considered "a complete lack of talent"—it saved my voice.

The problem of finding the right teacher is a very difficult one. I know of no advice which I can give which will help you to recognize whether your voice is developing in the right or the wrong way under your teacher's guidance. Of course one cannot give up any teacher after just a short period of study. That would be very wrong. You can't simply run from one teacher to another. You must give any teacher a fair chance—that goes without saying. A new "method"—or better, a new way—of singing only develops slowly. You must first learn to understand your teacher and this takes time. You can't run away after a few lessons, saying this isn't the right teacher for me.

Even under the best of conditions learning to sing correctly requires long years of study, and for this reason I feel that one should begin to concentrate on it as early as possible, although certainly not before the age of sixteen, and should not attempt a general college education before beginning to study singing intensively. This work is much too serious and demanding to be treated as a side issue and I do not believe that it can be given sufficient concentration in a general college curriculum. Certainly one's life becomes rich in proportion to the breadth of one's knowledge, but if you intend to devote yourself to music you must devote all your time to it and not scatter your energies during these important years.

Let us suppose that you have found the right teacher, that the foundations have been well established and that your voice has developed as you had hoped it would. There now lies before you the decision as to which type of career you will select. Of course if you are in doubt as to this question some experience in each field is of great importance, but knowing when to give up one type of career is often very difficult. As I have said before, I was engaged by the Hamburg Civic Opera for some years, and until my first success as Elsa was only entrusted with very small parts. But even in these unimportant rôles my clumsiness made me the terror of the director. I flatter myself that I have become quite a good actress—but it was by a long and arduous road, and often enough I heard: "Why, for heaven's sake, don't you give up the stage? You will never learn how to move gracefully, you will never learn to play a rôle even in a mediocre way...." *That is a fact.* So what right have I to advise a young singer: if you feel you cannot act give it up? No: *only* give it up if you do not feel within you the glowing determination to master what is difficult for you. . . . Then, and then only, give up.

But do not forget that your art, in whatever way you may serve it, is an all-demanding goddess who makes no concessions.

Never forget this! So long as you serve her there can be but one thought for you: complete devotion to her and to her alone. Once you have dedicated your life to your art it is no longer your own. I do not mean that you should seek to withdraw from life. On the contrary, live it in all its facets, for only through your own experience can you nourish your art with your heart's blood. I only mean never let your art be overshadowed by the circumstances of your private life. I had to sing a *première* when my mother, whom I loved above everything, had just died. It seemed impossible, but the great blessing was granted me of becoming for a few hours a different person, of being able to forget for a few hours what had been taken from me. It would have been so easy to say I wasn't able to sing. Everyone would have understood. But it was a great *première*—Richard Strauss's *Arabella*—and there was no one to take my place. The house was sold out. The director implored me not to leave them in the lurch. I had to sing, it was my duty to my profession. It must come first, before any personal considerations.

The best of health is of the utmost importance in this profession, for the life of a singer is certainly not an easy one, and when you are singing in repertory there is scarcely any opportunity for relaxing and resting. Rehearsals require as much strength as performances—in fact they are even more taxing because of the everlasting interruptions which tear you out of the mood and then demand that you immediately recapture the full intensity which has been lost through being interrupted. There is no such excuse as: "I am not in the mood." The layman easily imagines that singing is chiefly a matter of mood. Oh, no! It is a matter of will-power, of being able to disregard all limitations and with an inner elasticity rise from out the prosaic world of reality into the far nobler world of art. You must have good nerves to endure such a life and you can never allow yourself to be the victim of any personal indisposition. Even if performances could be arranged so as to spare you for a few days there are always rehearsals which you cannot afford to miss. You soon cease to make excuses for yourself. In comparison to men, women are handicapped in any profession. Every profession is exacting, but the singer must do more than the mere fulfillment of her duty: she must give all the beauty of which she is capable, she must be radiant, she must show temperament. Like a well-trained acrobat or dancer she must have complete control over her body and must never betray through a weary gesture that she is not feeling well. In such a profession as this it is impossible to pamper oneself in any way and anyone who does so will never make a career. There is the strain of endless travelling which is of especial importance in the life of a concert singer. Even the best trains are tiring in spite of modern comforts. And how often after a taxing concert one must either rush for a train or sit waiting in the cold or badly overheated waiting-rooms of miserable stations only to go eventually through ice and snow to the train. Yes, one would appreciate a nice warm bath and a comfortable rest after the strain of an exhausting concert, but a singer is not "a lady of leisure" and must have the strength to endure every kind of strain.

Even if you do not feel well you must give your utmost vocally. The orchestra remains the same. It will not be dampened because you are in poor voice. In concert-singing concessions can be made much more easily. The more submissive piano can follow you, can be played more softly or can be made to cover you if it should be necessary. This is not possible when you are singing with an orchestra. In rôles which demand dramatic force you must give dramatic force—and give it without restraint. I remember a performance of *Fidelio* in Salzburg years ago, when I wearily dragged myself to the theatre after a severe attack of influenza—and sang. . . . The orchestra seemed like a raging sea against which I must struggle—I had the feeling of being drowned beneath its waves even though my kind director Schalk was conducting and did everything possible to make it easy for me. Only an iron will kept me erect. How healthy you must be in every fibre of your being to endure such experiences, to sing and be an artist in spite of physical weakness and suffering, in spite of emotional shocks.

You must have this strength, this capacity for self-effacement, if you are to be a really great artist. And I would add: art is born of grief and pain, joy and passion. Life itself is the eternal source from which one draws strength and illumination for one's singing.

When I was young, one did not make one's way so rapidly as to-day. It took years before I had a real success—years which at that time I considered lost but which I realize now were an excellent education. To-day in my opinion one does an injustice to youth in making it possible for inexperienced children to become "stars" overnight. In principle such an opportunity as is offered by the auditions over the air is something very wonderful: it affords an opportunity to young students chosen by the public to win a contract with a great institution. The longed-for opportunity has come to them—in the most glamorous way. But that is just the danger: it is too glamorous to ensure any further progress. It is a spectacular success, but all too often a success which is deceptive, and it is something at which to wonder, if such sudden adulation doesn't turn the head of the young and inexperienced beginner. Publicity stretches out its tentacles and seizes its young victim. . . . Immature girls appear on the greatest stages of the country, in the most renowned concert halls and the great outdoor bowls. Glamor surrounds the young victims, applause engulfs them, their careers seem assured. . . . And then suddenly they become only one of many, awaiting a new opportunity—and most often waiting in vain. They may get rôles and, appearing before an audience which is no longer intoxicated by the glamor of a sensational début, be judged for just what they are: young beginners who have yet very much to learn. . . . Or they may get rôle after rôle if they happen to have a popular success, with the result that they are overstrained and their voices lose their youthful brilliance.

In Europe this was all so much easier: each little city had its own theatre in which plays and operas alternated. When a young singer was ready for an engagement she had, so to speak, a "choice" of possibilities, for there was never a lack of opportunity—and when the voice seemed promising she could be certain of getting an engagement. Developing slowly into her (or his) work, the beginner learned self-confidence on the stage and how to maintain contact with the conductor and the other singers. A period of apprenticeship on a smaller stage was of infinite value to the inexperienced young singer, for when this promising talent was later engaged by a larger theatre the first period of confusion and awkwardness had already been overcome and it was possible for the career to develop on a more secure basis.

Unfortunately, America cannot offer this opportunity for slowly growing into the profession as it does not have sufficient opera houses to provide opportunities for young singers. It is easy to understand that the half-ready beginners standing upon the threshold of a career here feel lost and insecure. The Metropolitan cannot be a refuge for all of them. Other opera houses have only short seasons·and naturally use experienced singers in order to fill these weeks successfully. So where can a young beginner find an opportunity for experience? There is always the radio and there are the films—both distinguished arts in themselves but not adequate substitutes as a preparation for an opera career. Of course for those who have beauty and who want to make a glamorous career quickly, the films certainly have an unequalled attraction. I don't want to be misunderstood: the films offer great possibilities, they have a great future artistically speaking, but there is one drawback. From what I have seen so far a film career seems to have a cheapening effect which it is almost impossible to escape. The great masses which make the darlings of the films so quickly popular demand of a star a very different attitude towards music than do the opera or concert audiences. Whenever I listen over the radio to the young singers who are so successful and so talented, who could be certain of success as first-class singers—I hear them, for the most part, singing the greatest "trash" which one can imagine. . . . It makes me very sad. . . . If only the great firms which engage these young singers as their stars and pay them very high fees would not insist upon lowering music to a sphere which is unworthy of these fine young talents. . . . Radio has a tremendous educational influence throughout this country. One hears marvellous concerts, one hears the great artists of the day; but with the exception of a very few none of them is permitted to sing an artistically worthwhile program. The less experienced the singer, the more he is forced to sing purely "popular" songs. Soloists should be allowed to select their own programs. One should be proud of having an educational influence, proud of opening the way to musical understanding. Sponsors of radio programs should work hand in hand with those who are seeking to give the people an appreciation of the world of music which is infinitely more enriching than mere sentimentality.

A young talent is easily spoiled. . . . Since it has great success with cheap music it sings to a cheap public, singing *down* to its listeners instead of *uplifting* them. . . . And how can one criticize the young singers if they make their lives easier in this way, when

the opportunity is offered them on a platter? I understand it
very well. But it is sad that radio cannot find a way to utilize
these talents in a manner worthy of them instead of squandering
them through cheap successes. Who can say where these young
talents, which seem so promising, will end? It is not a momentary
success which makes for a long career, it is the kindly understanding and helpful hand of a careful guide who helps to train
that which is worthy of training, combined with the opportunity
to develop gradually through experience. Young beginners should
be given a chance to develop on a normal and healthy basis.
They should approach success slowly, maturing under wise
direction.

I know it is hard to believe but I am often asked whether it is
necessary for a singer to know what happens in all the scenes of
an opera in which one has a rôle. That one must know just what
the opera is about. . . . Good Heavens! ! ! When this strange
question revealing such an abysmal lack of understanding was
first put to me I really couldn't understand what was meant by
it. How can one portray a rôle in an opera if one does not have
a complete conception of the whole story with every detail which
relates to the rôle and all the action which has preceded it?
Otherwise it would be nothing but empty and incredibly stupid
theatre. If one doesn't know the story from which the opera was
created, the libretto itself, every gesture will be superficial and
all the action lifeless and false.

If you are not aware of the deep inner meaning how can you,
for example, react to your partner, especially if the partner is a
stranger to you? Let us say that in a certain place you are
accustomed to having your partner make a slight movement to
which you react, and then one day you play this rôle with a guest
artist, or you yourself sing in a strange theatre and there is no
time for a stage rehearsal. This happens very often. I have had
the experience of meeting a guest artist for the first time on the
stage during a performance where the artist had no opportunity
to introduce himself until after the curtain had fallen, although
we had already played a glowing love scene together. In such
cases you must be prepared to have your partner play his rôle in
a way totally different from that to which you have been accustomed. If you really understand the essence of the rôle your
partner is playing it doesn't matter at all what he does—I mean
what gestures or movements he makes or how he expresses his

emotions. You just react *logically*—that is all. I have sung with many different partners. I have sung guest performances throughout Europe, and we always had many guests at the Vienna State Opera. I always enjoyed the challenge of singing with a different partner—the more his conception differed from that to which I was accustomed the happier I was. It brought new color into an old story. I remember, for example, Leo Slezak's wonderful Otello at the Vienna Opera. He played this rôle superdimensionally. He stood upon the stage like a dark rock from which there glowed something deep and uncanny. In the scene where Otello insults Desdemona and her tears flow in vain, her innocent pleading misunderstood, there was something inescapable in his sombre, menacing personality. He was like a great beast which, conscious of its overpowering strength, can destroy anything which it wishes to destroy with one blow of its frightful paws.

Then Richard Schubert (of the Hamburg Civic Theatre) sang Otello with us as a guest. Entirely different from Slezak, and just as convincing in his own way, he was like a panther, a supple cat—and I remember that in the scene which I have just mentioned he sprang across the stage upon me in such a terrifying leap that my cry of horror was absolutely genuine and spontaneous. All his movements were different and I had to react in an absolutely different way from that to which I had been accustomed with Slezak. That delighted me tremendously, for I believe that acting must always be vitally alive. Please don't misunderstand me: of course, one must conform to the instructions of the stage director. What I say here refers only to the presence of mind which is required through being forced to adjust oneself to such changes. Disorderly confusion would reign upon the stage if one simply altered one's pattern at random and felt one's colleagues uncertain of what to expect. But even within the established pattern of stage action one can always introduce slight variations, according to the feeling of the moment, which make the action more vital.

At the Vienna Opera we had a very excellent singing actress— Marie Gutheil-Schoder. She was a model for me when I was a young singer. Yet to-day I see that our ways were worlds apart. She was fanatical about exactness. Her rôles were always worked out to the last detail to the point of perfection. She never altered anything, not even the slightest detail. She was deeply disturbed by any deviation from what had been found good and definitely established, to which she had become accustomed. Any variation seemed to her inartistic and indicative of a lack of discipline. Yet at the same time she was an actress of great temperament and if, as was so often said, she had only head and no heart (which I don't believe) one must take off one's hat to such a head, for in that case her apparently genuine temperament was incredibly well acted. But such exactness is far from my nature. I could never be tied down to a definitely prescribed gesture or movement, no matter how convincing it might be. I would inwardly perish if I had always to do the same thing. In the same way as it is impossible for me to understand how a concert singer can sing the same program throughout the country for months—yes, for years—just because it is certain of success, it is impossible for me to understand actors who say: that is right now, I will do it that way as long as I sing the rôle.

Many singers have a bad habit which has always made me terribly nervous: they never look directly into your eyes as they sing, but always at your forehead. The theory is that this is supposed to make one's eyes appear clearer and brighter. Ye Gods! How is it possible to sing with any warmth if one considers such superficialities. I have often implored my partner to look into my eyes as otherwise the mood was completely destroyed.

I am often asked if it matters whether one likes one's partner or is indifferent to him. My experience except in the rare cases where I felt a definite physical antipathy for my partner, has been that while I was acting with him I felt for him that same passion which I should experience in the rôle. It was for me another indication of his real artistry when I was told what Lauritz Melchior had said following the celebration of his twentieth anniversary as a member of the Metropolitan. We had sung together that evening the first act of the *Walküre*, an opera which we had sung together over the whole world. He told the friends who had gathered about him that, although he had never been in love with me as a woman, he was always in love with me when we sang together, and felt that I was with him in the same way. The completely impersonal passion which one feels for the personality one's partner represents (however one may feel towards the real man in ordinary life) arises from the vital feeling with which one lives the rôle. But this is controlled by the ever alert brain which never allows the *person* to be confused with the *rôle*. In this way the real personality is eliminated from the glowing embrace of the operatic rôle—it is Sieglinde who embraces Siegmund with fire and passion, not Lotte Lehmann who embraces Lauritz Melchior, for their brains control the surge of feeling which flows between them in their portrayal of the characters which they personify.

One can, of course, only be really free when one has mastered a rôle completely. It seems quite superfluous to say this! Yet there are singers who depend upon the conductor with a desperate helplessness. There is nothing which can spoil the illusion so much as this and I hope all the conductors won't be furious with me if I say that it is much better to make mistakes, to be slightly inexact, than to stare fixedly at the conductor's pit. When one watches acrobats on a trapeze one hasn't the faintest notion of the difficulty of their act. The greater artists they are the more one has the impression that what they are doing is as easy as child's play. It should be the same with opera singing: the audience should never realize how difficult it is. One must give the impression of great freedom, as if singing requires no effort at all. The layman never imagines that the life of a singer is one of hard work. He thinks the voice is there, so the singer just opens his mouth and sings—that is all there is to it. Let him keep this idea! Let us never reveal to him the difficulties of our profession. He should never be allowed to suspect the precipices we skirt and the abysses we cross. . . . So let there be no faces contorted with fear, no petrified glances at the conductor. One can keep contact with him out of the corner of one's eye. One must be clever and in this case know how to bluff.

An inescapable hazard of a stage career is stage fright. Never let this fear become so uncontrollable that it masters you! This is, of course, very easy to say! I have gone through such hell because of stage fright and yet have learned to control it up to a certain point, that I feel I must speak of it.

In the office of the Stage Club in Berlin there hung a marvellous cartoon of stage fright. The picture is divided in half: one side shows the stage with the curtain lowered. An actor in the costume of a knight (the bold knight is side-splitting) looks through a hole in the curtain at the audience. His knees tremble. His shadow, frightfully menacing, falls across the whole stage on which he will soon stand to act his part as the dauntless knight. The other side shows the audience as a loathsome vampire. It lies stretched out lazily, its malicious eyes looking up at the stage expectantly. Only evil radiates from those eyes, those ears, those horrible limbs which seem to reach out in eagerness to destroy their piteous victim. I managed to get a copy of this picture and it hung on the wall of my dressing-room in the Vienna Opera House.

There is a great difference between the repertory of European and American opera houses. In America there are not many *premières*. For many years in Vienna I went from one *première* to another, stage rehearsals scarcely ever ceased and one no sooner learned one rôle than one had to begin another. I would seem that with ever-increasing stage experience, stage fright would decrease. But the more one sings, the further one advances in experience and in artistry, the more one appreciates what it means to stand before an audience, what it means to live up to a growing reputation. . . . One reaches a point where so much is expected of one and realizes how difficult it is to satisfy this expectation.

I was never a great technician. If I still sing "quite decently" to-day in spite of being well along in years, it is because of a technique which I have developed through long years of actual experience rather than through concentrated study. When I was young I sang without very much consideration for technique as such. My voice was healthy, well placed and caused me no difficulties worth mentioning. But if my attention was drawn to the difficulty of some phrase, I could be quite sure that although this phrase had seemed until then quite easy for me, a sudden stage fright would make it impossible for me ever to sing it well again. . . . The realization that something was technically difficult and that I really didn't know a great deal about technique made it impossible for me to sing as I otherwise would from my natural feeling, which would lead me over technical hazards as a guardian angel would lead a child across an abyss. For example, as the "composer" in Strauss's *Ariadne auf Naxos* I had to sing a lovely little song—"Thou son of Venus givest sweet reward". I had always sung it with great ease and freedom. It had never caused me the slightest difficulty. One day a former singer, who entertained lavishly in Vienna and whose teas were very fashionable, said to me: "It surprises me again and again to see with what delicious ease you sing that difficult and exposed little song, as if it had no difficulties for you at all. And it is so very tricky. . . ." I was very much astonished. "But it really isn't so difficult," I answered, more amazed at the moment by my technical surety than was my hostess. "But that is just what is so charming, Fräulein Lotte: You don't realize it at all."

I had forgotten this conversation—but my subconscious mind recalled it at just the wrong moment: in the next performance of *Ariadne* I sang this lovely song miserably and was never again able to sing it really well. . . . Our stage was especially arranged for this particularly glamorous performance of *Ariadne*: in singing this song I had to sit on a ramp which led into the audience, directly over the heads of the orchestra. I can still remember how those good members of the orchestra looked up when I began to sing in a trembling voice the same little song which I had always before tossed off as if I were throwing brightly colored balls into the air. . . . This time they were very labored notes which quavered over the heads of the orchestra.

I began to suffer increasingly from these sudden attacks of stage fright. I began to imagine all sorts of things: for example, that I had to swallow in the middle of a phrase—this became such a tormenting compulsion that singing was torture for me. . . . In my despair I went to a doctor who was supposed to be able to help with such a difficulty through hypnosis. I am very suggestible, and was certainly more so in my youth than I am now. So I gave myself up to this mystical magic and for a short time believed in it. However: hypnosis or not—the main thing was that I found a support which restored my faith and self-confidence. But fortunately I soon freed myself from this "Trilby" situation. I am and was also at that time a much too healthy person fundamentally not to find my own way out of this confusion of rebellious nerves. I no longer remember how I found the way—but I never again consulted a nerve specialist and have tried to stand on my own feet in every situation which life has brought me. So far I have been successful. . . .

In connection with the question of stage fright I remember an amusing incident. Richard Strauss had revived Weber's *Der Freischütz* in Vienna. I sang Agathe, a rôle which lay very well for my voice. In the third act I had to sing the lovely, softly sustained *Cavatine*: "And though the clouds may cover it, the sun still remains in the heavens." High exposed *piano* notes

were always a horror for me. . . . This time I had sworn that
I would sing them "blindly", that I just wouldn't recognize any
difficulties and would be oblivious of them in singing. . . . I
was armed, prepared. . . . Then Strauss, psychologically speaking, made the fatal mistake in a rehearsal of saying to me with a
smile: "Now just don't get nervous here! . . . You sing this
very beautifully. Just don't make a drama over it, it sounds
wonderfully." Oh God—I knew I was lost! In the first performance I sang the lovely *Cavatine* simply dreadfully. The long
sustained high note wobbled and trembled, so that I was in a
terrible state of fear. . . . After the performance Strauss came
to me. I expected him to be very angry, but he laughed and
said: "A guest in my wife's box said something very funny. He
doesn't know *Freischütz* and thought the *Cavatine* had a trill on
the high note. He said very flatteringly that he hadn't realized
that you could sing such a lovely trill. . . . That evening I certainly didn't have the humor to be amused by this!

Of course my lack of sureness was due in part to a lack of
technical knowledge. But it was due still more to my consciousness of my own inadequacy. I tried to study further and went
as often as possible to Felicia Kaszowka. She had been a
renowned singer in earlier days and was now an excellent teacher
from whom I learned much. It was very difficult in the midst of
a constantly changing repertory to study vocal production in the
right way. One reaches a point where one's production is
neither one thing nor the other, which is very difficult for the
voice. One should sing and want to sing as one is being taught
—but standing upon the stage one must be able to forget entirely
the technique of production, for one can only be a real artist if
one is able to rise above technique. . . . And when my vacation
came after the season of intensive work, I needed it as one needs
food when one is hungry, so there never seemed a suitable time
for studying. Nevertheless I profited very much from the lessons
and can give the good advice to every one to continue studying,
and to seek always to perfect oneself. For there is never any end
to what one may learn. Especially for a young singer, who,
scarcely out of the singing school, is suddenly confronted with
a repertory full of new demands.

Elsa—LOHENGRIN

Eva—DIE MEISTERSINGER

Sieglinde—WALKÜRE

Chapter IV

EVA—"DIE MEISTERSINGER"

EVA WAS FOR YEARS one of my favourite rôles. To present upon the stage this warmly human and vividly created burgher maiden in all her natural simplicity is a wonderful task.

A burgher girl of the sixteenth century, who had the daring to elope with her lover, must really have been a warm and forceful personality. Eva is not, as she is often represented, a sweet shy child. On the contrary, she is wilful, independent, definitely thinks for herself and is quite capable of standing on her own feet.

In the first scene in the church the exchange of glances should not be coquettish. To be sure Wagner directs and even repeats: "She lowers her eyes shyly," but her bold determination to speak with Walter Stolzing and the artful way in which she arranges the opportunity for a secret word with him doesn't exactly seem to be an indication of shyness. Her eagerness to break the shackles of convention is certainly much greater than the power of the convention itself. So her shy turning away is more a matter of reminding herself how she should behave—but it is overruled by the impetuous warmth of a young heart in love for the first time.

Of course nothing is further from my thought than making of this first scene an open crossfire of amorous glances. That would be absolutely out of style and is certainly not my intention. One must find just the right balance between recklessness and restraint in order to do justice to this very difficult scene. Even in this first scene Eva must appear as she really is: impulsive, passionate, wilful, intelligent, out of the ordinary, and she has also that kernel of conscious coquetry which is latent in every true woman—it is there as a tool, a weapon, as a charming expedient.

While the chorus has been singing, Eva has worked out her plan: with a watchful side-glance at Magdalene, she carefully lays her kerchief and brooch on the back of the pew—"forgetting" them. Even if Magdalene had seen it she wouldn't have taken

69

any notice of it, for she loves Eva and is already aware of Eva's eagerness to meet the young man whom she had seen the day before for the first time and of her schemes to bring about a meeting. Perhaps out of the corner of her eye Magdalene has watched the whole manœuvre and has decided to help her, just as in real life there are always good friends who enjoy helping in such matters and so vicariously experiencing a second life.

She seems to pause in prayer and in this way gives Eva a chance to leave the church alone. From head to foot, Eva is a "good" girl. She walks across the stage with the proper lowered glance. When she sees that Walter is approaching her, she doesn't respond to his whispered call but turns to Magdalene: "My kerchief, look, it must be on the seat." The good Magdalene plays convincing theatre. Her reproachful: "Forgetful child, that means search for it," gives Eva time to exchange a few quick words with Walter. But he is quite overcome with emotion, and in the determination to say as much as possible in this brief moment can't explain himself so quickly. How fortunate and foreseeing it was of Eva to have left not only the kerchief but the brooch in the church! But she is not the only one who is foreseeing. Magdalene, noticing the young knight's excitement and eager to give the youthful couple as much time as possible, "forgets" her Prayer Book and must go back a third time.

Finally Walter gets to the important question: "My Fräulein, tell me, are you already betrothed?" That is all he wants to know, whether or not she is free. To this daring and determined young man the fact that she is free means that she will become his own.

Magdalene feels that it is now time to make clear to this youth that Eva is under good protection. This talking on the street is something really quite unheard of—and she hastens to put the acquaintance on a formal basis with her question: "May I announce to Meister Pogner the visit of the noble knight?"

But Walter is not certain that he would really be welcomed. As a knight he belongs to quite another, higher class which is separated from the burghers almost as if by law. It annoys him that he must fight against class distinction in order to win this lovely girl with whom he has fallen head over heels in love. So he refuses bitterly: "O, I have never entered his house!"

In this guarded remark Magdalene sees something akin to

criticism of Nürnberg's hospitality and appears rather annoyed. But Eva draws her aside and whispers to her that he has just asked her if she is free. At this point Magdalene suddenly recalls everything which is good form in Nürnberg in the sixteenth century. . . . Diverted by the presence of David who, though quite a young boy, has fallen in love with the ageing woman who knows how to soothe his perpetually gnawing appetite with such wonderful tit-bits, Magdalene explains to Walter how he may win Eva's hand. He must become a Meistersinger, one of the guild, only then can he think of winning Eva. For Walter that is just child's play! A Meistersinger! Why not? He is quite accustomed to being successful with song as well as with sword. He will win Eva. Eva shares his confidence in his success. Her farewell is a radiant promise for the day when, singing before the whole world and winning with his song, he will be hers—he, who has won her heart without either sword or song.

In the second act Eva enters the scene with her father. She is very nervous and restless: she knows that Walter was present at the meeting of the masters this morning but she hasn't been able to find out what happened. Her father doesn't like to discuss such things with his daughter. Walter has said that he would meet her in the evening. Now evening has come and her father doesn't seem at all in the mood to go home. Eva wants to be rid of him in order to be free for Walter. Her whole bearing must convey the impression of restlessness, nervousness, distraction. She half hears what her father is saying and half listens to what is going on in the narrow street, longing to hear the sound of those steps for which she waits so eagerly. It must be absolutely clear here that Eva is accustomed to using any means in her power to get what she wants—any means which a woman, a real woman, knows how to employ. She is the obedient child: "An obedient child only speaks when she is spoken to." She is the anxious daughter: "Isn't it too cool? It was quite close to-day." She quite takes the place of her dead mother when she says: "Dear father, come! Go change your clothes!" She wants to make him go into the house and not stand right beside the door where he will interfere with her rendezvous with Walter. Trustingly and good-naturedly he enters the house.

When Magdalene tells her that she has bad news, that Walter, who is so accustomed to being successful, seems to have made a complete failure with the masters, she is desperate and doesn't know what to do. But Magdalene knows how to advise her: Hans Sachs—he will know what to do, he will help her. . . . Yes—Sachs! He loves her, he will know what to do! And Eva decides to make Sachs tell her everything which she is so eager to know.

Between Sachs and Eva there has always been a very tender and romantic friendship. Eva has looked up to him as if he were a second father—but he is more than that. It has been he, the poet, the philosopher, who has awakened her first dreams. . . . He has watched her develop from childhood, he has loved her as if she were his own daughter—and yet there was more. . . . He has watched her passionate willfulness develop so charmingly, he has felt that he was much more to her than a fatherly friend— and in a tender and romantic way he has reciprocated her feeling, but always with a smiling wisdom and resignation. Never really desiring her he is yet charmed by her youth, her beauty, her unusually spontaneous outpouring of feeling.

To this friend Eva now comes in confusion over her first love and all its problems. . . .

I remember, standing in the wings waiting for my entrance, how often I have listened to Sachs's wonderful *monologue of the lilacs,* delighting in the noble music and in the beautiful warm voice of Friedrich Schorr, with whom I have sung Eva countless times over the whole world.

Sachs is a rôle for which every baritone longs, just as Isolde is probably the dream of every soprano. Schorr was warm, human, touching. Dr. Schipper, Vienna's much-loved Sachs, German to the core and powerful like a mighty oak in a northern forest, who might have been outstanding alone through his powerful figure and heroic blond head, but who was also vocally magnificent, was more the kind fatherly friend, the genial, humorous master, while Schorr was more the poet and philosopher. Of the many Sachses with whom I have sung, these two made the greatest impression upon me.

It always seemed as though I had to tear myself away from the spell which Sachs's voice wove about me when as Eva I ran down the steps to him.

Eva has waited until she knew that he was alone. Then she runs quickly down the steps of her father's house and begins to talk with him in her usual half joking, half coquettish way. She knows that she must give herself time to work up to her goal. She knows that she will only find out what she wants to know if she enters half playfully into all he says and acts as if she had only come to chat with him. But she falls under his spell just as she always does when she is near him. He, who knows better than anyone else how to make a lively and exciting game out of question and answer, who seems to look into the depths of her heart yet can conceal it with a joking word, is close to her and completely one with her in a way in which Walter never will be. Walter means for her: passionate desire for self-surrender, giving way to a strong and overpowering compulsion, her first experience, the first awakening of her senses. But Sachs means a deep inner understanding, a strange, romantic bondage and— boundless faith. . . . How often Eva has dreamed that he, the widower, would some day woo her. It seems to her only natural and logical that she should some day be his wife. But Sachs is wise. . . . He takes the love which is offered him half playfully and cherishes it in his heart like a precious jewel, an inviolable treasure.

Of course he sees through Eva to-day. He knows perfectly well that she has come to him to learn about Walter—that strange, wistful singer, who so enraged the masters this morning—but who pleased him in spite of the wildness of his songs. But it amuses Sachs to keep Eva waiting. He will help when he sees that the right time has come for helping. He thinks it well over before he lends his aid.

So he makes use of every possible roundabout course. He tells of Beckmesser, who is presumptuous enough to woo the lovely Eva. Yes, to be sure—he is a bachelor and it must be a bachelor. Now every bit of coquetry in Eva is awakened—but more than that: she wishes again that he himself, the honored and beloved Hans Sachs might woo her. O mysterious heart!

When I sang Eva I was never quite sure (putting myself in Eva's place) what I would have done if Sachs had really wooed me. I felt so strongly attracted to the poetic, wonderful characterization of Sachs; he always seemed to me so much more exciting, so much more worthy of being loved, than Walter, that I myself would never have hesitated: *I* would have chosen *Sachs*. This should not be taken in any way as advice regarding the conception of Eva. Perhaps she only speaks as she does out of coquetry, only flatters him in order to get from him what she wants to know. Perhaps my feeling is entirely false. But in developing my ideas of the different opera rôles I must be honest enough to say what *I* thought and felt in attempting to portray this rôle in all its psychological subtlety. The infinitely tender gesture with which Eva leans towards Sachs, the lovely expression of devotion in her words: "Couldn't it be a widower?" always seems to me like a distortion of Eva's personality if they are not intended to be taken seriously. And if they are intended seriously—how could she want it, if it were not the desire of her own heart? Eva is no calculating coquette. Eva loves Sachs, loves him more than she realizes or will confess. It is the fate of Sachs and Eva that youth with all its impetuosity and reck-lessness has taken by storm what the discreet maturity of age has permitted to bloom only hesitantly and with many ifs and buts—always prepared to resign, and to resign with a smile. . . . Gently, Sachs frees himself from the spell of the soft hand, which has lain upon his arm. His voice is choked and tender: "My child, he would be too old for you."

Unconsciously this makes Eva think again of Walter. Sachs has often spoken of his age to Eva, has often resisted her fascina-tion by taking refuge in the realization that he is much too old to take this child seriously. And I am sure that Eva has always found a quick and convincing answer. But to-day it is as if one door closes and another opens which leads to the radiance of youthful experience. So half jestingly she answers him with a coquettish evasion: "What is this, too old! Here it is a question of art—whoever understands art can win me."

To the core of his being Sachs senses the change in Eva—and with a half-smile he admonishes her—"Dear Evchen, are you teasing me?"

But she is quick to answer. Quick to reproach—a reproach which is without any foundation and which he disclaims with a delicate jest. That he should mention his wife at this moment again arouses in Eva the longing to be more to him than a beloved child. Doesn't he see that I am no longer a child? Doesn't he know that he was and is dearer to me, dearer in a certain sense, than anyone else could ever be? So the words: "But your wife is dead and I am now grown up" are a passionate challenge. And Sachs's answer: "Yes, tall and beautiful" is like a soft and resigned caress. Eva is completely under his spell. With deep devotion she again leans towards him, and as she reaches out her hand to him, her voice trembles in the fervent plea: "I thought you might take me as both your wife and child?"

This is the moment of decision for Sachs.

But he is much too wise to want to hold fast to a deceptive happiness—he is no King Mark who binds Isolde to him only to lose her to Tristan.

So with a light jest he crosses the abyss and goes his way, leaving the flower which is budding at his side to bloom in a spring in which he will know no part. . . .

Eva is hurt. She feels rejected and misunderstood. Her heart which, in these confused days, has known so many changes now turns away from the friend who has disdained it.

Sachs skillfully leads the conversation back to Walter. Putting his own personality in the background he re-awakens Eva's desire to learn, to hear, to know . . . Question and answer now become a subtle duel of words. It is a game which they play with one another, a kind of verbal hide-and-seek which, I am sure, Sachs enjoys more than Eva. . . . The climax is reached with the harshly expressed statement that Walter this morning has been the proverbial duck out of water and a complete failure. Counting on his help Eva in her fear and anxiety reveals her whole heart to him. Sachs's haughty, defensive attitude, the scorn with which he seems to abandon the knight to his fate, his apparent unwillingness to offer any help is of course all in fun! Yet nevertheless there is a kernel of bitterness in it. Sachs is much too great a person to leave Walter, in whom he senses the true artist, in the lurch. But it gives him a kind of grim satisfaction to pretend that he is indifferent, to act as if he were just an ordinary person whose routine has been disturbed by this youth's storming impetuosity.

Eva misunderstands him just as he had intended she should. She thinks him narrow-minded. By her misunderstanding she proves how little she really knows him, how far she is from any real appreciation of him. She can assume that his scorn and bitterness are due to envy, she thinks him small and commonplace like his fellow-singers, like his guild which seems to have degenerated into all that is humdrum. Her words for him are sharp, and weeping with fury she leaves him sitting at his window and crosses the stage. But his eyes follow her with a smile. These bitter accusations do not hurt him for he knows

that they are kindled by the confusion of her heart—and at this
moment their very sharpness almost does him good, at this
moment when, resigning, he has decided his own fate. . . .

His "I thought that, now the time has come to give advice . . ."
reveals him in all his understanding, his wisdom, his great kindliness, his love for Eva.

Magdalene comes and tells Eva that the knight, as they both
had feared, has really been a failure, and so all hope of Eva's
hand seems to be lost.

Eva is nervous, distracted, and only concerned with seeing
Walter. . . . Hearing his steps, she runs towards him, throwing
herself into his arms. . . .

Perhaps she might have acted very differently if Sachs had not
so upset her with his sharp and, as she thought, unjust scorn.
She has been well brought up, but she now throws everything she
has learned to the winds, she forgets her shyness and her usual
ladylike restraint. She is no longer Evchen, the naïve and playful
child, who can be so charmingly coquettish with Sachs. No!
She is an ardent, loving woman, ready to do whatever her lover
may want, whatever he may ask of her. . . .

Walter is bitter and disillusioned. He hates the masters who
have failed to understand him, he despises them for being unable
to appreciate the flight of genius in his verses, for only seeing
that they were unconventional and rejecting them as bad just
because they were unconventional. . . .

It rather amuses Eva to hear him give vent to his hatred for
the narrow-mindedness of the masters. She is to-day imbued
with a revolutionary spirit, she is ready to despise all which until
this moment she has honored. Walter means everything to her.
His outlook is the right one, any other is false and "small-
townish". From now on she is his from head to toe. . . .

When Walter begs her to fly with him, she hesitates only for
a moment, then she flings out her arms with an ecstatic "Yes".
One should again recall what that must have meant in the sixteenth century. A burgher girl eloping with a knight! . . . But
Eva is strong and willful. Eva is filled with passion and ardor.
She will follow him blindly, without any questioning. . . .
Walter works himself into such a rage over the objectionable
masters that the call of the night-watchman finally mixes with his
words like a call to battle—and accustomed to battle he draws
his sword. Eva's next phrase: "Beloved, spare your anger, it

was but the night-watchman's horn," should be sung without any sentimentality. The music may tempt one to be sentimental here—it generally does—but the tender and poetic melody only echoes the fabulous and romantic beauty of Nürnberg in the sixteenth century with its narrow streets flooded by moonlight, with the fragrance of lilacs and the sleepy song of the night-watchman. . . .

Eva sings with humor, very tenderly and very discreetly—but without any sentimentality. Even to Walter's anxious question: "You will fly with me?" she gives an answer which in spite of the love it conveys still has a humorous note: "Don't I have to?" and to his trembling cry: "You will fly?" she answers with great charm: "The judgment of the masters!" Wagner indicates here—"with tender determination". Yes, she will fly, she will fly with him to escape from the masters. She says it with a smile, tenderly, reflectively. Quite the child of Hans Sachs. . . . Grown up and educated in his way. . . . He would have been delighted by this answer. . . .

She enters the house with Magdalene and when she returns is wearing Magdalene's dress. This disguise is a part of the carefully worked out plan which will prepare the way for her flight with Walter and at the same time punish her annoying suitor, Beckmesser.

Eva has not the slightest pangs of conscience—she is imbued with an overflowing joy in adventure and wants only one thing: to escape as quickly as possible. . . . She now feels misunderstood and foreign to all which was once dear to her. Everything which in any way interferes with her plan is seen as hostile—and when Hans Sachs throws open his shutters at just the wrong moment, so that it is impossible for her to escape without being seen in the flood of light coming from his window—he, too, becomes an enemy. She calls out—"Woe to the shoemaker if he should see us." She calls him *shoemaker* to make clear to herself that for her he is now only a member of the guild which is hostile to Walter and has ridiculed him. . . . When Walter, feeling that Sachs is his only friend, would approach him trustingly, Eva robs him of his last illusion saying that he, too, has only said bad things of Walter.

Even if Walter does now want to break open the way to freedom, to which he would carry Eva, to freedom from the shackles of all this detestable convention, he is forced to weigh and consider the matter, for Beckmesser approaches bringing a song for his adored one. Walter cannot dare to get himself involved in a long-drawn-out conflict, for he would not get far in his effort to escape if he should awaken the whole neighborhood with shouting and fighting. . . . So at Eva's suggestion, she and Walter hide themselves beneath the Linden tree. Her sigh: "What trouble I do have with men!" must be *unintentionally* funny. Eva means it very seriously, for she has had trouble enough getting her father out of the way this evening, and then to be sure Sachs had not made her life exactly easy with his obstinacy, and now he even takes his shoemaking outdoors and sits there in the light of the lamp, relaxed and comfortable, just where he has every opportunity to keep them in sight. . . . As the last straw Beckmesser has arrived, introducing new complications, not the least of which is Walter's impetuosity, which it is no easy matter to restrain. Eva really has cause for this deep sigh. She says it with exaggerated weight and impatience—and so it must sound humorous. But one must have the impression that the humor is unintentional. . . .

Walter and Eva seat themselves upon a bench under the Linden tree, resigned to wait until it may be possible to make their escape without being detected. Eva is very much preoccupied with Sachs's song. She listens to his words and says without understanding their meaning: "I hear it now, it doesn't concern me—but there is malice in it. . . ." She is quite certain that there is something malicious about the song, in the facile allusions which Sachs has always made use of to amuse her— but to-day she feels that they are at her expense and she listens with distrust.

Sachs engages Beckmesser in conversation, very much to the distress of the latter, who would like to have the way clear for himself, as he hopes to touch Eva's heart through a beautifully rendered serenade. But in between Beckmesser's songs Sachs sings in a loud voice of Eve, the first woman. . . . Eva is much taken aback and depressed. The friend who has always been so kind and gentle with her, now puts her in the greatest embarrassment and even seems to scoff at her. She seems almost on the point of risking flight by force. But reason finally wins the upper hand: this crazy fracas really must come to an end some time and there will be an opportunity to emerge from their concealment and escape with her beloved into the wide world!

Eva and Walter now disregard the increasing uproar around them. They sit absorbed in one another and only from time to time look out through the overhanging branches on to the moonlit plaza, where a nightmare seems to be developing. Leaning against Walter's breast, Eva sings softly: "Everything seems like a dream, whether it be good or bad, how should I know?"

This is often a little overplayed. In my opinion Walter and Eva should not be too much interested in what is going on. There is confusion enough upon the stage, so from a visual standpoint they should be the point of rest—the one quiet and peaceful spot amidst all the uproar. This is, of course, a debatable idea: certainly they are both tremendously excited and want to be freed from their undesirable prison just as speedily as possible, for at the moment what can this flowering Linden arbor seem but a prison? They will again and again look nervously towards the center of stage, implying to one another through gestures: "Oh, if we could only escape! I have played it in this way and felt that I did not emerge too much from the background. But thinking it over to-day I believe that this is questionable. Certainly they must participate in the action but in a very inconspicuous and unassertive way. Neither should give the impression of being bored. They are in love so they won't find this enforced concealment a very great trial. They have accepted the fact that they must wait for the proper moment to escape. They are happy in being together. Leaning close to one another they are lost in a blissful communion and are quite contented to wait until the nightmare beyond quiets down.

When, taking advantage of the climax of the confusion, they seek to rush away, Sachs places himself across their path. He has not ceased to keep his eye upon them. He will not have his beloved Eva hurling herself into an unworthy adventure which will bring disgrace upon her. He wants her to win her happiness legitimately with the blessing of her father—and he has decided to help her towards this end. But he will not permit the child to rush away in this fashion; he will not let her fly off so impetuously and without protection into an unknown world with this wild young knight, who, though he undoubtedly loves Eva, has nevertheless failed to consider what it would mean for the young girl to throw over all her good traditions. So with a firm hand he grasps the knight, and holding him fast pushes Eva into her father's house, saying scornfully: "Into the house with you,

Magdalene!" Looking about her confusedly, Eva can just see that Sachs has taken Walter with him into his own house. At this point her father closes the door.

During this night Eva has passed the darkest hours of her young life. . . . For the flight has failed—it seems too late for everything. For the festival is to take place to-day on the broad meadow near Nürnberg, and she well knows that at this festival her father is to promise her hand to the winner of the competition. Is it possible that Walter might be the winner? She doubts and despairs. Nowhere is there any help, nowhere any way out. Her dearest friend, Hans Sachs, seems to have deserted her at this crucial moment. Her father, in spite of his great love for his daughter, is much too conscientious a member of the masters' guild to refuse to abide by its laws, and it would be contrary to that law if Eva should marry a man who could not be recognized as a master singer and admitted as a member of the guild. She has pleaded to deaf ears when she has tried to convince her father that her happiness is dependent upon her marriage to Walter.

So she awaits this day with a fear and dread such as she has never in her life experienced before. Quite instinctively she would have found her way to Sachs even if she hadn't seen at the last moment that he had taken Walter with him into his house. Sachs, who knows everything, who is always helpful, may perhaps even at the last moment know of a way out—and so she goes to him.

At the beginning of the third act she is already dressed for the festival. She approaches Sachs hesitantly, looks into the window, opens the door and remains standing there shyly. It is for the first time that she comes to her friend with a feeling of guilt. She knows that he has disapproved of her intention to elope with Walter and she feels ashamed and guilty. But at the same time she is very much upset by Sachs's whole behavior. It is the very first time that he has ever disappointed her as a friend, the very first time that she has come to him in vain for help and advice, the first time that he has let her go away, abandoning her to her helplessness with scornful words.

So she stands in the doorway as if she comes to him almost against her will. She is pale and haggard, her smile is sad and joyless. Sachs is quite delighted by her appearance. Taking her hand he leads her to the foreground. When he says: "You make both old and young covetous when you look so lovely," she half turns to him meeting his glance with a sad smile. It has always been so between them: they have never expressed what they were thinking in everyday commonplace words. . . . They have always found a gracious way of saying what they wished to say. And to-day, even in this hour of desperation, Eva finds her old accustomed way of speaking with her friend. She finds the parable of the shoe which hurts her by which she means the troubles which are tormenting her. Sachs, of course, enters into this, pretending great seriousness. He appears to be very much concerned over the "bad" shoe and doesn't seem to understand at all what she means when she says with bitterness: "I realize that I had too much confidence. I have been mistaken in the master. . . ."

He leads her to his little shoe-bench and she has to place her foot upon it so that he may look at the "badly fitting shoe". With mounting impatience she enters into his playful questioning, at the same time looking anxiously towards the door which leads to the inner room. If Walter is still in the house he must be there. Suddenly she interrupts Sachs and all the misery in her heart rings through her words: "O master, don't you know better than I where the shoe pinches me?" His answer is interrupted by her cry of delight—Walter stands in the doorway leading to the inner room. Wagner's direction—"Eva remains without changing her position, her foot on the stool, gazing at Walter" seems very often to be taken too literally. In my opinion it is very wrong for Eva to remain too long motionless, like a statue, with her arms outstretched. Even holding her foot raised upon the stool the whole time is senseless and unnatural. Eva is not a person to be paralysed at such a moment. She is much too full of temperament and vitality for that. . . . She should follow the wonderful surging phrases of the music which soar several times as if in waves of delight. When Walter sings his prize song, the sudden realization sweeps over her that it has been Sachs's master hand which has led Walter from the unbridled outbursts of passion in his songs to the ways of the old masters—organizing and moulding the output of his natural genius into a work of art which is certain to win the approval of the masters. . . . Eva sees at once how grateful she must be to Sachs. He who had never disappointed her has not disappointed her now: he is helping her to win her happiness. He alone understands her and loves her, helping and guiding her. Her overwhelming delight over Walter's song, her jubilant realization of what Sachs has done, break over her in an avalanche of joy. Hurling herself into Sachs's arms she buries her head on his breast, sobbing, until he, overcome by his emotion, gently but firmly pushes her from him and leads her to Walter's arms.

Here Sachs almost loses control of his feelings. He conceals his inner turmoil by chattering roughly. At first Eva scarcely listens. She is so overwhelmed by this experience, the greatest which she has ever known, that she leans against Walter, almost fainting. But then she straightens up and with one hand holding fast to his, leans towards Sachs. Yes, at this moment Walter scarcely exists for her. He is the future, he is still a shimmering vision. But Sachs is the living present, Sachs is her deepest tie, in him lie her roots, he is "home" for her. When in jest he reminds Eva of how she has scolded him (in the second act) she smiles through her tears, with a deprecating gesture. She must inwardly prepare herself for the great outbreak which is to follow. She must "build up", must become increasingly excited, in passionate self-forgetfulness.

Unable to control his emotion, Sachs wants to leave the room, but Eva holds him back. For the first time in her life she speaks to him with complete and open seriousness. No longer is there concealment behind smooth, gay words. There is no playing, no coquettish duel of words. For once she must tell him what he really means to her, for once she must unveil her heart to him. And so she tells him everything—how much more he has meant to her than just a fatherly friend, that she would have chosen him alone as her husband if Fate had not sent Walter to her. Sachs is moved to the depths of his being. He has suspected this, has really known it. But now hearing it revealed without any reticence makes him tremble. He turns away that he may hide how deeply it has affected him. Eva now turns to Walter— and the love which has taken possession of her so suddenly and so completely pours forth in a passionate confession. There can be no choice, she must be his. It is forced upon her, it is fate, it is the irresistible law of her heart. . . . "And if I am wed to-day, it would be without any choice, because it must be, because it is so ordained" and cradling her head lovingly upon Sachs's breast: "You yourself were afraid."

Sachs is now completely master of the situation. But in the

momentary tumult of feeling he does not find the appropriate joking, veiled words. He also is serious and wants her to know how he feels. So with a half-smile he takes the old saga of Tristan for comparison: "My child, of Tristan and Isolde I know a sad tale." Eva raises her head, and listening, understands what he is saying. . . . I have noticed that those who play Eva generally have here a completely uncomprehending expression as if they had no idea of what he means. That doesn't seem convincing to me. Sachs has often related the old sagas to the child and the maturing girl—and Tristan, that wonderful saga of love, death and fidelity, may have been a favorite story. It is quite improbable that Eva shouldn't be familiar with it. Knowing it she understands very well what he means. Her glance is veiled, her face shows that she understands but does not agree that there could be any similarity to her own experience. Sachs again takes refuge in a jest. But it is a jest with a serious setting: "It was time that I found the right man, or in the end I might have been caught!" And with these words he gives Eva back to Walter.

The tension is relieved. Sachs has known how to lead everything into the right channels, has known how to bridge the excitement. Just at the right moment he sees Magdalene outside the window and calls her in, and with her the festively attired apprentice who enters proudly adorned with gay ribbons.

In a humorous speech Sachs announces to—as he says—"the respectable company", that Walter has composed a master song. A song is a creation. Just as a human child is born and named, so is a master song born and must be named. He will give a name to the song and baptize it. All those present shall be witnesses of the baptism. But no apprentice may witness a baptism, so he promotes the apprentice to a journeyman. The name of the song is "The blissful morning dream's true tale".

Emotion holds them all as if under a spell. All feel that Eva now stands on the threshold of happiness and that her heart's desire will be fulfilled. Eva is deeply moved. Her eyes seek her beloved friend Sachs, her hands are folded half unconsciously as in prayer. Sachs turns to her and taking her hand leads her slowly towards the center of the room, asking her to make the baptismal speech.

The quintet which follows is exceptionally difficult vocally. One needs tremendous breath control for the long sustained notes of the beginning, and the building up to the grandeur of the ending is a task before which every Eva trembles.

And yet it should be quite easy to overcome this nervousness, if one just remains in the rôle and doesn't attack the quintet as a hazard of exposed singing. Bruno Walter who through years was a wonderful guide for me whenever I had the good fortune to sing with him, helped me very much in overcoming this difficulty. I sang Eva with him in London and Berlin. In a rehearsal he noticed my sudden attack of nervousness at the beginning of the quintet, and since his advice took away all my fear and really brought the scene to life for me for the first time, I want to give an idea of what he said: Eva is to be sure among her closest friends, but making a baptismal speech is a kind of "official act" which embarrasses her. She is much too excited and moved to be able to overcome her emotion with a light word. She feels that her fate has been decided—and the baptismal speech which she must make over Walter's song is like a baptism of her own happiness. Moving slowly, on Sachs's arm, to the center of the room, she must think in the *sense* of the *scene*. I mean literally: she who sings Eva should think ahead in the action, so that her mood is in no way interrupted. She should think to herself as if the audience were hearing what she is thinking. Her thoughts run—"O I must make a speech? How can I do that? I am so deeply moved, I will never find the words to express what I feel in this sacred moment. Sachs was so good and so great—I will always love him. But Walter von Stolzing is my fate, I must be his. My life lies before me radiant and joyous—everything is blissful." And there is the beginning of the quintet, leading directly out of her thoughts: "Blissful as the sun which smiles upon my happiness." If the Eva is able to identify herself with the rôle to such an extent that her thoughts obey her and lead her into the heavenly beauty of the quintet, then this will not be just something which is difficult to sing but a devout prayer of happiness. *And so it should be.* At the end of the quintet Eva, in an infinitely subtle way, turns to Walter.... Their eyes melt together as if they want never again to separate. Then Sachs breaks the lovely spell, leading Eva on—the time is already short—they must go to the festival grounds, where everything is prepared for the competition, which will result in the winning of Eva's hand. ...

In the following scene, Eva arrives at the festival on the arm of her father amidst the procession of masters and climbs the steps to the platform. She sits between her father and Magdalene. When the people jubilantly greet Sachs, the great master of song, who is so revered by everyone, she looks about her proudly. This seems to her absolutely right: her beloved friend should be loved and admired by every one—he deserves it as no other does! And she greets him as the others do, with pride and joy. The whole assemblage breaks out into the great chorus—a greeting of homage to Sachs, a surprise for his name day which moves him deeply.

I can't help mentioning here a performance at the Vienna State Opera in which this chorus had a special significance for me: we had that afternoon buried our director, Franz Schalk. Not one of us had been missing, for no one was the distance too great to pay him the last honor at the woodland cemetery in the Vienna mountains where he had wished to be laid to rest.

Franz Schalk had always been a wonderful friend to me. Certainly I don't flatter myself that his affection for me was at all comparable to Sachs's for Eva—certainly not that! But in my memory his image merges with that of Hans Sachs. He was such a good friend to me. He was my guide. I looked up to him as to a father. His death at this time was doubly painful because another had taken his place, one who was unworthy, self-seeking, for whom the beloved Vienna opera was nothing sacred as it had been to Schalk through his whole life. Strangely enough the opera did not close its doors that day. . . . We had *Meistersinger* and I had to sing Eva. Over the opera house the black flag fluttered at half-mast—and over the performance there spread a kind of paralysis. I myself was almost glad that I had finally been persuaded to sing—in spite of the fact that I was so overcome with grief that I hadn't thought it possible. But the performance wrenched me out of my grief—I was Eva and not the saddened Lotte Lehmann. . . . However, when this chorus began, I was gripped by such a violent pain that I almost collapsed. In my imagination I saw below me at the conductor's stand the delicate emaciated figure of Schalk—not the man who was actually conducting that day and who had caused Schalk such bitterness. . . . It seemed as if he were standing there again, surrendering himself to this noble music, with all his characteristic and lavish self-abandonment in the ecstacy of creating beauty. . . .

Perhaps the chorus may have reached up into the world to which he had been raised—and with it the sound of my sobs, which I was unable to suppress. . . . He would have enjoyed the music—and as to my tears, he would have said an abrupt, sharp word, behind which would be hidden his vulnerable soul—just as Sachs would have done. . . .

During Sachs's speech Eva listens intently like everyone else. She nods in bashful acquiescence when it is made known that she will give her hand to the victor of the competition. When, as the first to mount the singer's stand, Beckmesser tries in vain to catch her eye, Eva should not turn up her nose and turn her head away in intentional arrogance (as I have seen done)—it is better for her not to show the slightest interest in the sad figure of her suitor and to carry on a conversation with Magdalene without taking any notice of him. Later, like all the others, she becomes much amused by Beckmesser's confused song.

I remember so vividly the distinguished Beckmesser of the Vienna Opera, Hermann Wiedemann, who by a tragic fate was frustrated in the attainment of his highest goal: to become a member of the Metropolitan Opera Company. He had the contract in his pocket and was ready to come to New York when war broke out in 1939, with the result that he was forced to remain in Vienna—and now it is too late: he died there without seeing his dream fulfilled.

Beckmesser's failure is complete and overwhelming. Since he has no conception whatsoever of Walter's song it is impossible for him to sing it. He distorts it into an unrecognizable caricature. Everyone is speechless when, after Beckmesser has run away in fury, Sachs declares that it never would have been possible for him to have written such a lovely song as Beckmesser has accused him of doing. (When Beckmesser had finished singing he had thrown down the song saying that not he but Sachs had written it.)

Sachs says that if only someone would come who could sing this song as it should be sung, one would know the master who composed it. Eva listens with tremendous excitement: so that was the master's game! He has worked out everything so that it will all come to a good end! Sachs knows his people. Now they have had their fun and will be more eager to listen to the young knight since they have already been won by his good looks and knightly bearing. And the same song which has been a target for scorn will seem even more inspired after such a misrepresentation. Eva now sees through it all, and as her eyes seek Sachs he nods to her with a heartening smile.

Walter appears. He makes a great impression upon the audience—and Eva's eyes rest upon him filled with love and joy. His prize song is a great success. Sachs has awakened all there is in Walter. He had come to Nürnberg as a free singer, and overnight he has become a master under the guidance of the greatest of the masters.

Eva places the laurel wreath upon Walter's head, and her father is about to place the golden chain—the emblem of the master— about his neck, when Walter suddenly and very unexpectedly refuses to be a master. A lover of freedom, he recalls with horror the narrowmindedness of the masters—he remembers the bitter hour in which they had ridiculed him and were incapable of understanding what he had to say. . . . How could he ever become one of them?

With a horrified plea Eva turns to Sachs. He must help— again he must help! For she knows that she may only marry a master, and now in the last moment Walter seems to have ruined everything which Sachs has so painstakingly worked out. . . .

But Sachs rises and speaks to the impetuous youth with great and irresistible authority. He makes it clear to him what being a master really means—how it is the duty of the old German masters to guard Germany's most precious possession: her Art. . . .

In these days it seems doubly thrilling to recall this speech. There will always be masters, who will hold high the greatest gift which mankind can offer, wherev_r it may have been born; there will always be masters to remind the world that one thing is eternal, that one thing stands supreme above all others: Art.

The opera *Meistersinger* ends with a general jubilation among the people. Walter yields—Eva herself places the chain of the masters about his neck—and with a tender gesture she removes the wreath from his curly head and places it upon the brow of her honored friend Sachs. Deeply moved, he draws her to him, reaching out his other hand to Walter. So they stand united amidst the jubilation of the people.

Chapter V

SINGING IN SALZBURG

I HAVE SUNG *Meistersinger* under different conductors. The usual question—"under whom did you most enjoy singing?"—is one which cannot be answered. I don't think that it is possible to compare conductors any more than it is possible to compare singers—or artists in any field for that matter. Even though they may seem equally great they will always be different, and the greater artists they are, the more divergent they will be, for in my opinion being an artist means expressing a personality. One personality may seem more attractive or more lovable than another, but that doesn't mean that one can be considered as right and fine and the other as inadequate. Art is the profoundest expression of personal individuality. For this reason one should give each his due and seek to penetrate all that he has to say and offer. For instance one may at the same time love a Flagstad, a Traubel, a Jeritza and a Lehmann—yet in themselves they are all fundamentally different. It seems to me that it would be deathly boring if one were always to expect the same thing from every artist and if one has a firmly set opinion as to what is right and what is good. . . . I have a vital and versatile appreciation, and can very much enjoy a conception which differs entirely from my own.

This is, of course, also true of conductors. I have gained something from each conductor with whom I have worked and have always tried to absorb the best from each, "his best" being for me what lay nearest to my own personality—so for another singer quite the opposite might seem best.

Schalk gave me my love for the soaring phrase and my joy in it. He could lose himself so completely through music, could find such liberation through tone! He was never very much interested in the action upon the stage. He never concerned himself with questions of stage direction—which I could never understand, for it always seemed to me that the conductor should work hand in hand with the director. But Schalk only existed for the music, penetrating it completely and so re-creating the

vision of the composer—and that was his circumscribed field.
He often concealed his real feeling behind a sarcastic word.
Every bit of sentimentality was repugnant to him. From him
I learned what I have tried to hold fast through years: freedom
from all cheap sentimentality and the expression of music as it
is in its truest sense: the noblest and most forceful language of
the heart.

That wonderful time when I sang Eva under Toscanini is for
me unforgettable. Salzburg—the festivals—those days when
we were lifted above the course of everyday life and repertory
and the confusion of large cities—that period of fanatical work
and endless spending of oneself. . . . I believe there was not one
of us who worked together there who did not love this time and
who did not look upon it as a climax of artistic creation. Perhaps
this Salzburg was not quite the one which Lili Lehmann
pictured when she started the Salzburg festivals. I have heard
that she wanted only works of Mozart performed and sought to
preserve Salzburg as a shrine for worshippers of Mozart.

It is a pity that the Mozart city of Salzburg did not give me
the inspiration to sing Mozart there, in that hallowed place. . . .
And I feel it is evidence of a great lack in me that I find little
joy in telling of a Mozart rôle—how I felt it and portrayed it.
Mozart seems the "nearest to heaven" of all the composers. His
music is the purest, the most clarified, the most ethereal language
of the heart. And yet in my rôles I never quite found my way
to him. Perhaps I have always been too earthbound in my feeling,
perhaps I was incapable of the necessary technical brilliance. . . .
It is well to be clear about one's own weaknesses and failings.
And my great weakness was the lack of a perfect technique. The
music of Mozart demands the most crystal-clear perfection of
which the human voice is capable—each phrase seems finely
chiselled and is very exposed. There are very few singers who
have the ideal combination of a flawless technique and passionate
feeling—I, unfortunately, am not one of these. Yet how can I
find joy in singing if I am unable to forget myself completely—
if I am restrained by imperfections which I am incapable of sur-
mounting? I must be free, delightfully free, in order to be what
it is my goal to be: a singing actress.

I have sung Pamina in Mozart's *Magic Flute* and perhaps
have succeeded in conveying the imaginative charm of this
poetic figure—but each performance was overshadowed by my

nervousness about the great aria: "O I feel it, it has vanished."
How often I have sung this almost unconscious from fear. I
should have enjoyed singing Pamina immensely if it hadn't been
for this aria.

It was the same with the Countess in *Figaro*. The second
great aria almost killed me—I still shudder when I think of the
torture I went through in singing it. . . . In this case there was
good reason for my nervousness: as a young singing student I
learned it in the Etelka Gerster Singing School. I sang it so
badly that my teacher, Eva Reinhold, with the craziest tenacity,
totally devoid of any psychological insight, made me sing it for
weeks until I began to tremble even if I only heard the intro-
ductory music! Because of this aria Mme. Gerster threw me
out of her school and told me that I was totally and hopelessly
lacking in talent. . . . My failure at her school was probably due
to her method of teaching which was almost fatal for me.

The inability to sing this aria really well remained in my subconscious mind like a poisoned arrow. No psychoanalyst could
have helped me, for I knew all too well the cause of my exaggerated fear: the youthful experience associated with this aria. . . .
Unfortunately this clear realization didn't help me at all—and
after a time I gave up my struggle with the rôle of the Countess,
because it was impossible for me to overcome this fear.

The Countess Rosina is a beautiful rôle, vital and interesting.
The lighthearted Rosina of the *Barber of Seville* has, at the side
of her husband, grown into a great lady. But she has not been
entirely happy in her marriage: the Count indulges in his clan-
destine love affairs and does not let his wife interfere in them. . . .
He has remained the adventure-lover that he had been before.
He had won his Rosina through bold manœuvres, but now, sure
of her, he doesn't seem contented with her love, which he once
wooed so passionately. He has even fallen in love with her
chambermaid, and wants again to make use of the old feudal
custom which gives the master the right to any young girl in his
service the night before her wedding. He had magnanimously
renounced this right—as long as none of the young girls in
question pleased him. But now that it is a question of Suzanna,
who is pretty as a picture, he regrets his hastiness and tries in
every possible way to make the girl agreeable to his desire. The
Countess is very much hurt, her love has been insulted. But
through the dignity with which she bears her misery there still

shimmers the old Rosina, who as a girl had such a flair for daring intrigues, for quick and witty inspirations and who has never ceased to take life with a laugh, even when it has seemed blackest. . . . In those days Don Bartolo had threatened her peace, pursuing her with offers of marriage which made her shudder and shut herself away like a criminal. . . . But she was so lighthearted, she loved so much to laugh that she knew everything would turn out all right, for life is good. . . . To-day as the wife who has been deceived she would like to say the same thing. . . . But she has looked through the deceptive face of happiness and has learned to endure pain and to accept humility.

So this rôle has, so to speak, two opposite sides: the melancholy seriousness of the disillusioned wife—and the laughing daring of Rosina who with her mischievous play knows how to trick her husband through intrigue and so bring him back to her arms.

One often hears it said that no passionate expression is permissible with Mozart. A singer once remarked to me that one must, for example, consider how delicately people conducted themselves in the time of Mozart, how carefully they clothed themselves and with what formal politeness they addressed each other. This conception led her to a narrow limitation of expression. She felt that one should glide lightly over the surface of feeling—that nothing should disturb the pure harmony of tone. . . . That is true: the undisturbed beauty of tone must be preserved, it must never be clouded through realism—the realism, for example, which is possible in modern opera—no ugly sound may distort the heavenly quality of this music! But is heaven itself so pale and colorless? Just as dark, dramatic clouds mass together, just as thunder roars and torrents of rain descend upon us—so is there thunder and lightning in Mozart's music. . . . And the people, who at the time of Figaro spoke more daintily than we to-day, were nevertheless human beings just as we are, with all the same passions which do not change with time. . . . The dress, the manner, can't make warm, living flesh cold just because it clothes it more chastely.

And so I feel that in singing Mozart, emotion should be expressed just as warmly and glowingly as in other operas. It only wears a more supple cloak—that is all.

During the Salzburg festivals the lovely Salzkammergut became a fashionable resort for people from all over the world and

Salzburg was flooded with gaiety and splendor, becoming a symphony of varied color and a fascinating Babylon of many tongues. I loved it just as it was: the center of the international world where all discord was dispelled through a common enjoyment of art. During the day the visitors in their gay peasant costumes seemed like a part of the lovely landscape. Then in the evening they emerged from elegant limousines in luxurious evening clothes, furs and brocades, to be marvelled at by the native people of Salzburg who stood in deep rows before the brightly lighted Festspielhaus. . . . Oh that those times might again return, those times when Austria was happy in its art, when everyday problems didn't seem as important as whether the opera favorite was in good voice for the performance. There seemed to be no cares in those blessed days!

I sang Fidelio and Eva in Salzburg under Toscanini, and will never forget the nerve-shattering rehearsals which brought us all to a point of desperation, for the much-feared maestro was never really satisfied with anything. . . . Instead of venting his displeasure through one of his well-known tempests, before which every one trembled and which we awaited with a horrible inner tenseness, he wrapped himself in an icy silence and just looked at us sadly and scornfully. If we hadn't been good this certainly didn't make us any better. . . . We began to stumble over the simplest phrases, exchanged glances of despair and would have welcomed any display of temper. . . . Finally I mustered up my courage and approached the fuming lion. "Maestro," I said, "won't you please tell us what crime we have committed? We want to do everything you want, but won't you please tell us *what* you want?"

He looked up at me with the eyes of a dying fawn and said: "There is no fire . . ."

Deep breath. . . . Fire. . . . All right . . . let us forget that it is the much-feared maestro before whom we are singing. Let us forget that we must be exact to the finest detail. . . . Let us forget that any and every mistake is a deadly sin. Let us just be normal human beings, who are not without faults, like this genius— then the fire will blaze which had been dampened through our fear. . . . Then Toscanini showed us his wonderful smile. . . . And whoever in that ensemble had no real fire was actually kindled through his glowing flame. . . . I remember the dress rehearsal of *Meistersinger*—that very special rehearsal, for I don't believe that there was in the actual performance the frenzied intoxication of this unique rehearsal. The Sachs of the Salzburg performance, Hermann Nissen, was one of those blessed natures who are never tormented by nervous crises, who seem endowed with a wonderful equanimity and seem to be unaware of any conflicts. Perhaps this is entirely wrong, but it is the impression which he always gave me, and I always envied him glowingly for his marvellous disposition. Incidentally he was an excellent Sachs with a warm flowing voice, a real Hans Sachs voice. In spite of his rather phlegmatic disposition, even this man was stirred to his very depths by the great maestro. I can still see him, his eyes overflowing with tears, as he turned around after the "Wachauf Chor" in the general rehearsal, saying: "My God, how shall I be able to sing now. This damned demon down there has absolutely devastated me with his fire."

I myself was quite delirious after this rehearsal. I rushed into the maestro's room without knocking and found him scantily dressed—or rather undressed—and wasn't the least disturbed, much to the horror of Emilio, his chauffer and general factotum. . . . I embraced him in tears and could only stammer: "Thank you, Maestro. . . ." Then I was out of his room. . . .

But I must say one thing: the great fear which every singer feels before him—and I don't know one who would say that he had no fear of him—often keeps one from being really free. . . . The fact that every one trembles before him makes Toscanini terribly unhappy. He is impatient and furious when someone says: "I am so afraid. . . ." He has absolutely no realization of the power of his own personality. He can be so kind and simple, and fundamentally so naïve, so absolutely unbiased and so unquestionably just. But his glowing fanaticism, made doubly expressive through his tempestuous Latin temperament, demands the utmost of every one to such an extent that, expecting thunder every moment, you are confused and consequently often unable to give what you are really capable of giving. . . . You feel how he suffers under any imperfection, so that you tremble for fear of making some mistake, tremble from the fear of upsetting him by doing so. . . . Once in a performance of *Fidelio* in Salzburg I made a bad musical mistake in the last act and I remember well my deep despair—not because the audience might have noticed it and thought less well of me for it, but because I knew how the poor maestro had suffered through my carelessness. After the performance I stole to his room, but didn't have the courage to go in to him until his very kind wife, Signora Carla, led me to him. I wanted to offer apologies before those dark, sombre eyes, but he turned away impatiently—it was forgiven, though I am sure not forgotten. . . .

When I first began to lose my fear of him, realizing that he is always just and kind and that he does forgive, I became really free in singing with him. And then it was as if genius itself carried me with it in its flight, as singing under Toscanini I felt completely one with him, as it is only possible to feel in such an ideal way in moments of boundless artistic sublimation.

Bruno Walter was a wonderful leader for me whenever I had the good fortune to sing with him. He is both conductor and stage director at one and the same time. I learned to understand him so completely that I really wouldn't have needed a stage rehearsal for a new rôle: a talk with him about a rôle made everything so clear to the last detail that the actual "acting" just took its natural course. It enabled me to realize what otherwise might only have developed through long stage rehearsals. To study a rôle with Walter was a very unusual experience. More than any one else he explores the background, the story, which precedes every aspect of the opera. With him nothing is ever "accidental" yet everything is always filled with life and feeling. There was never anything torpid, never a difference of opinion which could not be worked out. Walter loves to discuss possibilities of dramatic conception. His ideas are so convincing that, even if you have a different conception, you generally yield to his. It goes without saying that he demands a complete self-surrender to the work at hand. I remember with shame a rehearsal of *Meistersinger* in London in which I had the misfortune to annoy him deeply. How good it is that with these lines I have another opportunity to offer my apologies! We had given *Meistersinger* at Covent Garden a number of times; it was towards the end of the season and we were all tired. A terrific heat-wave certainly didn't exactly add to our enthusiasm for rehearsals. But Walter felt that the performance had lost its vitality and spontaneity through its many repetitions and decided that these deadly sins must be removed through another orchestra rehearsal. . . . I cannot say that we were delighted. But of course there was no question of any opposition to a Bruno Walter. But when the last scene—the festival meadow—began, I was absolutely dead and not in the least concerned with what was going on around me. At twelve o'clock in the middle of a terribly hot day I just couldn't be enthusiastic about Walter Stolzing. Entertaining myself with Magdalene I let things go on around me without really taking part in them. Oh, the thunder that was loosed upon my head! I have seldom seen Walter so angry—actually I never have, for he is always friendly and has the patience of an angel. But he hates above all else neglect of duty, lack of serious concentration, disrespect for what should be considered holy—always, with no exceptions and under all conditions. . . .

Once he attended a *Lohengrin* performance—I believe it was in London. At the end of the performance I heard that he had been in the audience in order to hear a new singer. On the following day I met him and waited for a kind word about my Elsa. But he was silent. Finally I asked him if it had been so bad that he couldn't say anything. He looked at me very seriously and said: "Yes! Yesterday I saw something which I don't ever want to see in you, which doesn't go with you at all: routine. . . ." I shuddered. . . . Routine is something which I despise to the very roots of my being. . . . Routine means death to personality. To have routine means: to be an official, not an artist. . . . He explained why my entrance as Elsa seemed lacking in interest, and with a few brief words he sketched the whole scene before my eyes. . . . Never again did I sing Elsa with "routine".

Whatever we do or however often we do it, it must be each time reborn, each time—a new creation. It is only when we are able to do this that we deserve the title Artist. . . .

Chapter VI

SIEGLINDE—"DIE WALKÜRE"

I HAD NOT intended to write of Sieglinde, for she is so much a part of the whole *Ring* cycle that it doesn't seem right to consider her as a single rôle. But how can I turn away from the Wagner rôles without including her? It was just Sieglinde who was of the greatest importance to me in America: my début in Chicago in 1930 with the Civic Opera was as Sieglinde, as was also my début with the Metropolitan in 1934. I have been Sieglinde over the whole world—in Europe, in South America, as well as the United States. It is one of my favorite rôles. My Seigmund was almost always Lauritz Melchior, the ideal portrayer of this part. Not soon will there be another with the warm, outpouring brilliance of his voice, the dark timbre which is so necessary for Siegmund, the radiant heights which must with unbroken power pour forth their "Wälse, Wälse" in the first act, in a veritable orgy of richness and radiance.

I am bound by many lovely memories to my colleague and friend, Lauritz—Covent Garden in London, the Paris Opera, the Metropolitan. Siegmund, Siegfried, to which I often listened from the audience, Tannhäuser and Lohengrin, Fidelio, all these are priceless memories of wonderful performances, of artistic bondage.

The limits of this book do not permit me to go into the actual story of the *Ring*, but there are many excellent books which explain and clarify this very intricate and involved saga, so I will restrict myself to the presentation of this single rôle and hope that I may be forgiven for neglecting much that is important.

The characters of the *Ring* are drawn superdimensionally. The humanly simplest, the nearest to our feeling seems to me Sieglinde. Although the daughter of Wotan and so having blood half human, half divine, she is close to the earth and humanly convincing. That should be the cue for the actress who portrays Sieglinde. She should, as much as possible, free this character of "Wagnerian movements". . . . Her gestures should always be borne by the music, they should never be realistic in the sense of a modern drama. But they should never be rigid, they should never cease to be the expression of inner agitation. Only when they originate from true feeling and are borne by the music will they be effective and give the impression of being the vital expression of feeling revealed in a lovely form, rather than that of an outmoded "Wagnerian style".

Sieglinde enters the room quietly. She carries in her hand a flaming torch which she fastens on the door, giving the room a dim light. As she turns her glance falls upon a stranger stretched out upon the hearth. She says quietly: "A stranger? I must ask him." Guests rarely come to this house. She lives amidst a lonely wilderness with her husband whom she does not love and has married against her will. It is seldom that strangers penetrate the deep, somber forest. She is only accustomed to hearing the brusque steps of her husband, Hunding, pushing through the dense brush. No friendly messenger comes to her no being who might ever be close to her.

She approaches the stranger with interest. Receiving no answer from him she goes to him and kneels beside him, putting her ear to his heart: but it beats loudly and forcefully—he has only lost consciousness. Rising, she looks down upon him with quiet contemplation: "He looks fearless, though now, exhausted."

Siegmund, awakening, calls—"A draught, a draught." Sieglinde, taking the drinking-horn from the wall, goes outside to draw water from the well. When she returns she moves slowly towards Siegmund. There is a great deal of music to be filled out between her entrance and her first words. The actress must give the impression that she goes quickly towards this stranger who is dying of thirst. Nevertheless the *music must be filled out*. So her steps should be quick, but she should remain standing hesitantly as if lost in observing him: she doesn't know whether he is unconscious, whether he is dying or whether he is ready for the water which she has brought him. Kneeling down she offers him the refreshment which he craves, supporting his head while he drinks. His consciousness returning, Siegmund looks up at the unknown woman before him. Wagner directs: "His glance is fixed upon her face with increasing interest." Sieglinde is lost in his glance which seems to hold her strangely under its spell. She has taken the drinking-horn from him, has risen and moves slowly backward to the table. That is to say she goes without looking around, without taking her eyes from Siegmund. As if absorbed in her thoughts she lays the drinking-horn upon the table without looking at it. She stands there erect in an attitude of attention and listens to Siegmund's words. He says something lovely and unusual: "My eyes feast upon what is before them." Sieglinde has never before heard such tender words of admiration. She has lived amidst coarse men who have no time to waste on talking to her, a woman. . . . Trembling, with bated breath, she looks before her in confusion. When Siegmund asks who it is who revives him with such friendliness, she takes several steps in his direction but then pauses. Perhaps she has wanted to say: Who am I? A lonely miserable woman who longs for freedom. . . . But she cannot say it—she knows that her fate is irrevocable: she is the wife of Hunding, bound to him, her fate is worse than that of the wild bears of the forest whom her husband often brings home tied with bands woven from the strong fibers of trees. . . . She feels caught and helpless like a wild beast. . . .

Her face is rigid, her voice somber and without warmth when she answers him: "This house and this woman are Hunding's. . . ." Turning away she wants to leave the room quickly, leaving the stranger upon the hearth, but Siegmund's words: "I am un-armed, your husband will not turn away a wounded guest . . ." hold her back.

Sieglinde turns immediately. He is wounded and without weapons—she knows Hunding well enough to be concerned for the stranger. So she approaches Siegmund anxiously, ready to bind his wounds, to soothe his pain. But he springs up refreshed and revived.

Sieglinde listens with eagerness to the story of his misfortune: his weapons were struck from him in battle, he was pursued and harrassed by superior enemies, until in the uproar of the storm and the deluge of the rain they gave up his pursuit and he found refuge—refuge in this house, whose protection he implores. . . . His eyes melting into Sieglinde's, Siegmund says: "My weari-ness departs from me faster than I from my pursuers. . . . Night fell upon my lids but now the sun laughs at me again. . . ."

Sieglinde listens with eagerness to the story of his misfortune: confusion she seeks something which will help her to escape from their hold. She goes quickly to the chest, built roughly into the side of the wall beside the hearth, and takes from it one of the drinking-horns, filling it slowly and gracefully with wine. She moves with a quiet dignity to Siegmund and offers him the drink of welcome with which one seeks to honor a guest: "You will not refuse this sweet drink of foaming mead. . . ." But Siegmund knows that a woman honors a guest most highly when she herself takes the first sip before offering it. It is with a significant gesture that Sieglinde raises the horn to her lips—it is as if she were expressing a sincere desire for his well-being, a solemn confirmation of their belonging together, of their finding each other. . . . And Sieglinde's hands which hold out the horn to him, slowly draw away and remain in a gesture of devoted self-surrender while he drinks. With surprise she sees that Siegmund's manner is strangely altered: his eyes, which fixed upon hers revealed an awareness of destined bondage, are now lowered, his brow is contracted as if in pain, he sighs deeply and letting the horn glide to the ground says in a trembling voice: "you revive a miserable being. . . ." Rising, he seeks to leave the house because always pursued by misfortune he wants to avoid bringing misery into her life through his presence.

With an impetuous gesture Sieglinde holds him back. . . . And when he confesses to her that his fate is one of calamity and misfortune which pursues him wherever he may go, she turns away trembling violently. She struggles with herself, she does not know whether she should open her heart to him. . . . But of one thing she is sure: this stranger whose gaze has touched her so strangely, whom she feels that she has always known and who is in the deepest sense her own—must not leave her in her tragic loneliness, must not again abandon her to the sombre, joyless life which she endures with her detested husband. So, forgetful of herself, she cries: "Remain here! You cannot bring misery to the house where misery dwells."

Siegmund remains. . . .

Their eyes meet in a solemn promise, a self-surrender so complete that there can be only one possible ending for them: a challenge of fate—death or life together. . . .

Sieglinde hears Hunding approaching. Sudden fear seizes her—with a gesture of entreaty to be quiet she makes Siegmund understand that danger approaches in the person of Hunding. . . . With flying steps she hastens to the entrance and opens the heavy door. Hunding stands in the doorway, a terrible and horrifying figure. Seeing the stranger, he turns with a sinister question to

his wife—but she meets his glance calmly and says that she has
found him wearied upon the hearth.

Sieglinde's behaviour must now be *totally changed*: in the first
scene, although she seemed serious and bowed down with sadness, she nevertheless moved with an easy grace and womanly
dignity. But now she is inhibited, her bearing is rigid and
awkward, her elbows are pressed against her body as if she seeks
to hide the trembling which sweeps through her from head to
foot. . . . When Hunding says: "Holy is my hearth, may my
house be holy for you," she shudders visibly: she knows of
nothing holy in this house where she has experienced only
humiliation, where she has poured out tears of despair. . . . She
hates and abhors this man, to whom she has been sold as a
motherless, forsaken child, taken from a quiet peaceful life in
the forest with her mother and twin brother, and suddenly left
alone in the world without protection, not knowing which way
to turn. . . . Her home had been burned by enemies, her mother
murdered, her brother gone without a trace. . . . She was taken
by savage men and sold to Hunding. That has been her life in
the house which he calls "holy". She lives here as his servant,
the servant of his sombre moods, of his abhorred desires. With
a gloomy look she takes his heavy weapons from him and sets
them beside the tree-trunk around which the house is built. She
then goes to the chest to get food for the homecomer, and
arranges the heavy wooden dishes and drinking-horns on the
table.

(I must confess that in Vienna when the two men had seated
themselves at the table, they showed a quite undue interest in my
talent for cooking. . . . We rarely had a performance in which
Hunding didn't ask me in a soft but threatening tone: "What
have you cooked to-day? I don't want always pork and beans.
. . ." and I with modestly downcast eyes generally named a quite
impossible combination of foods much to the suppressed amusement of my guests. . . . In London, Otto Helgers of the Berlin
Opera sang Hunding. He implored me before every performance
not to have any nonsense over the food because it was so easy to
make him laugh until he was absolutely lost and couldn't control
himself. . . . Even his wife begged me to remain strictly within
the picture of Sieglinde and not make her good Otto laugh. . . .
It was certainly very hard to be generous and not bring the poor
man to the torture of a suppressed fit of laughter. . . . Blushingly

I confess: I was *not* generous—Otto was really frightened about this scene. But once he got the better of me: he took a knife and knocked audibly on the wooden ham—with the result that I completely lost my composure and stood beside the table absolutely helpless until my glance fell on Bruno Walter, the conductor, whose complete surrender to the music put me to shame and brought me back to what I was at the moment: Sieglinde. . . . Walter knew nothing of our nonsense, we were very clever in concealing it. . . . Woe to us if he had discovered it! I can only hope he will never read this book—I believe even to-day judgment would still be passed on me—and quite rightly. . . .)

From the household activities which Sieglinde goes through mechanically, she lifts her eyes again to Siegmund—and Hunding, watching them, notices with astonishment that they resemble each other—it is as if one face looks towards him from the features of Siegmund and Sieglinde. Hunding says to himself: "How he resembles the woman, the deceitful worm also gleams from his eye. . . ."

Offering Siegmund his place at the table he asks his name and how he has come here. But Siegmund would like to know the name of his host, the name under which this woman must live, to whom he feels a deep bondage. Hunding is proud of his name, of his clan. All the people who are connected with him are hostile and contemptuous to Sieglinde. With averted face she hears how Hunding speaks of them, and her expression is one of hatred for them.

But Hunding again asks his name and Sieglinde turns towards him as she slides slowly to her seat, raising her eyes to Siegmund's face with a burning look of anticipation.

Hunding sits between them like a great gloomy beast of the wilderness. His eyes, hidden under heavy hanging bushy brows, wander with distrustful attentiveness from Siegmund to Sieglinde. . . . He notices the passionate anxiety with which the woman raises her eyes to the stranger—he sees the mournful absorption of Siegmund in her gaze. . . . A sombre threat sounds from his voice when he says slowly and with an accent of scorn and distrust: "If you have troubles to confide, tell my wife of them—see how eagerly she asks you. . . ."

Sieglinde does not notice the concealed threat in his tone. With undisguised sympathy she turns to Siegmund and says with quiet dignity: "Guest, who are you, I would gladly know. . . ."

Siegmund's eyes rest on hers and he begins to relate the story of his life—for the ears of this woman alone. Both have forgotten ` Hunding's presence. . . .

It is not a gay story which she hears. It is a life overshadowed by tragedy which the young Siegmund has known—pursued by an evil fate, never resting, never happy, never lighthearted. As a child he grew up in the forest with a twin sister. He has a vivid memory only of his father, called Wolfe. From him he learned the use of weapons, from him he learned to be fearless, to fight and vanquish his enemies. . . . But returning home one day from hunting they found the house burned to ashes, the mother murdered, the sister probably burned to death, for no trace of her was ever found.

Enemies pursued them, they fled to the depths of the forest before this superior power. Siegmund learned to live far from all mankind, to regard human beings only as enemies with whom he must fight or be destroyed. . . . So they lived, his father and he, like wolves in the forest. . . .

Sieglinde follows his words with the deepest interest. In her imagination she sees them before her clad in coarse pelts, weapons fashioned by themselves clutched tightly in their hands, challenging any one who dares approach them. . . . Sieglinde loves this picture, her eyes are shining, she leans forward absorbing the story with wrapt attention.

Hunding searches his memory: yes, he has heard of the two wolves. . . . Something seems to stir within him, something dark and elusive which makes him wonder. . . . Who are the two wolves? There is darkness about them, but confused threads seem to come to him.

Sieglinde only half hears her husband. She wants to hear more of what happened, she would like to know how he came to their hut out of the darkness of the forest, so alone and lost, like an animal which is pursued. . . .

Sympathy, deepest compassion tremble through her voice as she asks him: "Continue, stranger, where is your father now?" She suspects some disaster, she feels that the answer will be one of tragedy, so she whispers the question in a trembling *pianissimo*. . . .

Siegmund is startled out of his somber reflections. Yes, he will disclose the tragedy of his life to this questioning woman. Pursued by his enemies he lost the trail of his father, he only found the pelt of a wolf in the forest, his father he never saw again. . . .

Sieglinde half turns away—she can scarcely bear to see these tragic eyes which stare into the darkness of memory. Siegmund's words: "I was driven to men and women . . ." break into her troubled thoughts. Through the orchestral music soars the blissful love motive, and Sieglinde, straightening up, listens with every fiber of her being. . . . I do not think that Siegmund's and Sieglinde's eyes should meet here. It is much more subtle and suggestive if she only half turns her head towards him, with her eyes looking into the distance in passionate expectation. What will he say—what strange confessions will she hear, what ties will take him far from her who is bound so miserably to Hunding?

- But no: it is a story of the most harrowing experiences which he tells. He brings misfortune to every one, there has never been a ray of sunlight in his life, he has never known happiness, no human being ever belonged to him, no friend, no woman. . . . "So I must call myself 'Woeful', only misfortunes do I know . . ." he says with deep resignation.

From these gloomy thoughts he straightens up and turns slowly towards Sieglinde, who leans towards him in oblivious devotion. She does not consider the danger inherent in Hunding, she does not realize that she is doing wrong in giving herself so completely, in giving her whole soul to this stranger. . . . She wants to help him. She wants to know that he is happy, wants him to learn to smile, just as she must learn to smile.

Hunding has watched Sieglinde sinisterly. He loathes the stranger who has come to his house to disturb it. . . . He hates this man who has been pursued by misfortune, for there is only one rule for him: the rule of brute force. . . . Siegmund seems to him a weakling. The Norns of fate must despise him to have woven such an evil lot for him. And, hating him, he says with harsh words that he cannot welcome any guest who seems pursued by misfortune.

Sieglinde has listened to him trembling with indignation. She who has always been oppressed like a slave, who has lived always in fear of Hunding, now develops daring and courage: for it is not a question of protecting herself but this stranger, whom she must save from Hunding's brutality. So she hurls her scorn at Hunding: "Only cowards fear one who is alone and unarmed. . . ." It seems strange that Hunding doesn't strike the woman to the ground at this moment. But it is the first time that Sieglinde has dared to oppose him, and Hunding is overcome with astonishment at her boldness. . . . He looks down at Sieglinde absolutely speechless, his slow-working mind cannot grasp so quickly what she has said to him, and before he knows how to react Sieglinde suddenly chains his interest with her question: "Tell, Guest, how you in battle finally lost your weapons!" so that he forgets what the woman has just done to him. . . . He, too, wants to know how this stranger, so young and strong, came to stand before him weaponless. . . .

But Siegmund's story opens his eyes: the man who fought to free a young woman who was to be sold by force to one she didn't love, is the same man whom he has to-day pursued over hill and valley. It was his own kin, his own family who would sell the maid just as Sieglinde was once sold to him. And the unsought rescuer had appeared. Quite alone he had fought against an unusually powerful force. He killed her brave brother, slew the suitor and the girl had died across the body of her brother, defended until the end by Siegmund. But with his weapons shattered he was forced to flee, pursued until his trail was lost. . . . And now here the fugitive sits at his enemy's table, a guest in the house of his enemy, delivered up to his revenge, his boundless hatred.

Hunding rises, sinister, threatening; he breaks the crushing silence which has fallen upon Siegmund and Sieglinde and seems to unite them. He stands there like a black monster, his voice is like rolling thunder when he tells the stranger that it is he who has pursued him, who hates him, who longs to destroy him. . . .

In a flash Sieglinde grasps Siegmund's hopeless situation: he is unarmed and delivered to Hunding's hatred. . . . He is lost unless a miracle saves him. . . .

Trembling, she creeps around the tree, concealing herself from Hunding's sight, sinuous as a snake, cautious as a cat. . . . She chooses the right moment to place herself suddenly and violently between the two men: thrusting aside Hunding's threatening arm she protects the stranger with her own body, the stranger to whom Hunding had sinisterly promised the rights of a guest until morning. . . . But in the morning he must look out for himself—with strong weapons must he defend himself, for he must pay for the dead for whom Hunding grieves.

In a wild rage Hunding shouts at Sieglinde: "Away from this

room, do not linger here! Prepare my evening draught and await me to rest."

Sieglinde inwardly collapses. . . . It is as if she is enchained; her hands are clutched together as if in a spasm. She stands there unsteadily, groaning in her helplessness, her futile hate. . . . In confused entreaty her eyes sweep from Hunding to Siegmund. . . . An angry gesture of Hunding, motioning her to leave, forces her to turn away. She stands with averted face—her thoughts work feverishly. Nowhere can she see any possibility of rescue for the stranger—nowhere any ray of light in the darkness of his fate. . . . Death seems certain for him when morning comes, if unarmed he must defend himself against Hunding's powerful weapons. . . .

Her sad eyes sweep up to the tree and fall suddenly upon the spot where the hilt of a sword shines out at her. The sword! The sword which a god, a father, a savior thrust into this trunk, the sword which will some day serve him who is able to draw it from the trunk into which it seems to have grown. . . . The sword—the only salvation! . . . With quiet decision she turns to the chest, and while carefully watching Hunding mixes a sleeping-potion in his drinking-horn. He likes to drink the sweet mead before lying down to rest upon the bear-skins. This drink will give him a long sleep and so allow the stranger time to draw the sword from the trunk and prepare for the struggle in the early morning. Sieglinde takes the full horn, and as she passes Siegmund tries with a glance to make him understand that she knows a way of helping him.

Siegmund looks at her questioningly—he cannot understand her expression of radiant confidence, his eyes follow her with great intensity.

Hunding, who stands looking gloomily in the opposite direction, makes a gesture of impatience at Sieglinde but she passes him with triumph in her heart. She will succeed in deceiving him! A smile hovers about her lips, as if the victory of the stranger has already been decided. She turns towards the door, and from it, after a hasty glance at Hunding, who stands with his back to her, she tries to draw Siegmund's attention to the tree trunk. There lies his hope of rescue—don't you see the glittering steel in the trunk? her eyes seem to say—but Siegmund does not understand. With an angry gesture Hunding frightens her from the room and she leaves, keeping her eyes fixed upon the tree trunk to the last second. She has taken the torch from the door, the white glow falls across her face—in her arm she holds the drinking-horn with the draught, like a precious possession which shall aid in the rescue which she is planning.

When she returns she finds the stranger stretched out upon the hearth as if he had gone to rest. With hasty steps Sieglinde goes to him—her glance sweeps back to the door, behind which her husband, sunk in deep sleep from the potion, is no longer a source of danger. Sieglinde has prepared for the night; her hair is loosened, she has removed her heavy fur and stands before Siegmund in a white garment. He looks up at her overwhelmed with delight.

She whispers hastily to him that she knows of a weapon which shall be his. A weapon! Siegmund springs up with new life and listens to her in great excitement. She tells him of the tragic marriage into which she was driven like a helpless animal. They all sat here in this room for the wedding ceremony—and she sat amidst them with grief and horror in her heart. They caroused and drank, paying no attention to her misery. Then a stranger entered the room—a strange, hoary old man. He wore a grey cloak, his hat was pulled down over his face so that it covered one eye, but the other eye glowed deeply and piercingly, and fear gripped all who met his glance—fear seized these coarse, dauntless men for whom battle and danger were as their daily bread. But they all sat stunned under the spell of the stranger's gaze. Only—strange and incomprehensible!—she alone had felt no fear. "For me alone his look awakened sweet and sorrowful longing—tears and comfort at the same time." When she looked into the shining eye of the aged man her heart contracted painfully. It seemed as if she must belong to him, as if she must go to him and fall down before him saying: "Father." But she could not. It was as if she were very close to him and yet utterly strange. There seemed an abyss between her and the man whom she would like to call father and whom with a shudder she felt as God. Tears had poured down her face, tears of pain and of release. For if he was father why should he seem strange to her? She wept because of this feeling of strangeness. Yet if he was a God he was closer to her than any God of whom she knew.... And her tears were sweet from this feeling of comfort. The hoary one swung a sword in his hand and thrust it into the trunk of the ash tree. The sword was buried deeply in it—and he gave his blessing to the one who would some day draw this sword from the tree. It would serve him in his direst need.

When he had gone away the guests tried to draw out the sword. But it had become a part of the trunk and no one succeeded in achieving this miracle. Until to-day it lies buried there—and with a great gesture Sieglinde reaches out her hand saying: "There the sword is buried."

Siegmund, standing very erect and with flashing eyes, looks at the sword in the tree trunk. Strangely, his father's prophecy seems to be confirmed: he had told him of a sword which he would some day find when in deepest need. . . . He is now in deepest need, he is defenceless. . . . And there is the promised sword! In a strange way threads seem to draw Sieglinde to him —she feels this bondage just as he does. Separating herself from him, she goes to the middle of the room and with wide open eyes says to Siegmund prophetically and with deepest feeling: "Then I knew who it was who, in my sadness, greeted me"—yes, he was *father*, he was *God*—"I know too for whom he intended the sword in the trunk." The God, the father has thrust the sword into the trunk for this stranger alone—now she understands, she knows that all this has been predetermined and decreed for her and him. . . . Her whole life seems to be a single road leading her to this man. With a cry of exultation she falls into his arms. Deliverance, atonement, freedom from outrage and disgrace—all this she sees in him: "Whatever I lamented would be won for me if I might find the blessed friend, if my arms might enfold the hero. . . ."

Siegmund, standing very erect, prepared for victory, draws her violently into his arms and stammers passionate oaths: he will kill Hunding, he will win this sad woman for himself, and happiness will come to both their lives—happiness and deepest contentment. . . .

Tumult surges within their hearts, tumult rages through nature: a wild spring tempest, the aftermath of the terrible storm in which Siegmund had approached the house, the premonition of a brighter, sunnier day, suddenly hurls open the door. . . . Sieglinde, frightened, flies from Siegmund's arms, suddenly fearful of new disaster. . . . But no: it is spring which has knocked at her door with its firm and releasing hand. . . . Outside, in the moonlight, the landscape is renewed with the eternal verdure of spring.

It always seems to me rather ridiculous that this landscape should seem so quietly undisturbed and still: a storm has thrown open the door—but generally the trees are absolutely motionless and there is in no way any illusion of the storm which fits so marvellously into the ecstasy of the action. Of course I don't mean that the trees should sway back and forth realistically—that would be just the opposite of what I should consider scenically artistic. But I believe that the feeling of the storm can be conveyed through effects of lighting. Flashes of light playing over the background of the scene should make this illusion possible in an artistic way. In any case the tranquil picture of the moonlit night which couldn't possibly produce a storm always seems to me very false and unreal.

Siegmund drawing Sieglinde down upon the bear-skins beside the hearth sings the lovely and ever-new song of spring. Sieglinde lies half leaning against him. From the fervent embrace which ends the song she raises herself, looking up at him with delight. She tells him how she has always longed for him. Everything around her has always seemed strange to her. But he is deeply close to her; he is no stranger, he is like a part of herself. Embracing him, pressing herself against him, she discovers in his face the "sacred light, which falls from his eyes and face and stirs her senses so sweetly". As if overcome with passion she half sinks against him—he draws her to him, looking into her face, enchanted. Her hands encircle his brow, she smoothes back his hair with a tenderly questioning gesture—she wants to absorb the wonder of this face as closely as possible. The wonder! For is it not a wonder? Like distant, half-forgotten memories, images return to her out of the buried past. Hasn't she seen him before? When? Where? She has seen this face before. And when he says that it may have been a dream, a dream of love in which he has seen her and she him, she denies it, looking into the distance with absorbed concentration. No, it was not a dream. It was reality. . . . And now as she remembers her eyes are lowered as if she sees before her the running brook whose waters had mirrored her face: and it was *his* face! It is the same face, hers and his —they are one. . . . Siegmund remains absorbed in the lovely dream in which he has sensed her presense: "You are the image which is concealed in my heart." But with a sudden movement she seems to want to hold fast the sound of his voice—her whole being drinks in his words. Yes, as a child—didn't she

know this voice as a child? Or is she confused—does the echo of
her own voice resounding from the forest blend with the sound
of his? Memory becomes more vivid—she presses against him,
peers feverishly into his eyes. . . . . These eyes—didn't the same
flame glow from the eye of the father, of the God who came to
her in her saddest hour and plunged into the tree trunk the sword
which will now free her? . . . And a name comes to her—didn't
the strange old man mention a name? Was it only an inner voice
which whispered the name he bore, the name which she will
perhaps hear from the mouth of this stranger, who is her own,
strange and yet a part of her as nothing else on earth? Turning
violently to him she asks with trembling voice: "Is Wehwalt
your true name?" But he, completely hers, wants only to bear
the name which she will give him—what is a name if it does not
come as a gift from her hands? Sieglinde wants to know. The
name of the father—tell the name of the father. Was it really
Wolfe? Siegmund remembers: Wolfe he was called by his
enemies—yet his name was Wälse. . . .

With a cry Sieglinde springs up: Wälse! That is the name
which glows in her heart like the sign of a God, to whom she
belongs, as Siegmund belongs to him. . . . Wälse! What gives
her the certainty that Wälse was the name of the aged man who
came to her? She knows it, she knows it: Wälse is her father,
he is the father of the stranger, they are both children of one
father. . . . And the sword which he drove into the tree trunk
was destined for his son, for the Wälse, who will be victorious
with this sword. Exultantly she now gives him the name which
he shall bear, under the protection of which he shall fight and
conquer: "So let me call you, as I love you: Siegmund—so I
name you."

With one bound Siegmund has leaped upon the table and
gripped the hilt of the sword. The hour of greatest need has
come—the promised sword seems to tremble under his touch.
With great strength he tears the sword from the trunk, the sword
to which he gives the name "Nothung"—which means: found
in need.

Sieglinde has watched Siegmund with breathless excitement—
her bearing is one of concentrated passion, of glowing expectation. Bending forward, she sinks slowly to her knees. This is a
gesture which until now was foreign to her: she has never
kneeled down before. It is as if the primeval woman kneels for

the first time, driven to her knees by the superior power of her passionate belief. Now she springs up, utters a cry, and as if in an ecstatic dance reels across the stage. Her arms are out-stretched, her whole body vibrates in the triumph of her victory. She sinks to the ground beside the table, her flaming eyes fixed upon Siegmund.

Siegmund has but one thought: he will take the sword and with Sieglinde will leave the house of her ignominy. Not another second shall she remain here—out into the forest, out into free-dom, into the fresh stormy spring! And to-morrow he will fight and win, and will make Sieglinde whom he has won through love his for ever.

Sieglinde throws herself into Siegmund's arms as leaping down from the table he clasps her to him in blissful oblivion, swinging the sword above her. Reeling, torn between laughter and tears, she calls to him: "Are you Siegmund whom I see here—I am Sieglinde who longs for you—your own sister have you won with the sword. . . ." Doesn't he realize that it is his twin sister, whom he believed lost, whom he holds in his arms, the sister with whom he shared his first years of life, whom he had thought dead?

His sister? And both united by love? What is the law of blood to them? The law of mankind? Wotan's wild blood flows in their veins, the blood of the father who detests the law, who knows no bounds, his blood rages in their untrammelled hearts. What do brother and sister mean? You Sieglinde, I Siegmund— and outside rage the tempests of spring. Out into freedom! Away from the narrow confines of human habitation with its rigid laws! Wotan's children are united.

They storm out into the spring—and amidst the wild tumult of the music the curtain falls.

Wotan, Fricka and Brünnhilde—their fates and conflicts I must pass over. Space is limited, the story of the *Ring* could consume a whole book in itself, if I am to penetrate into the depths of the characters I must content myself with Sieglinde. . . .

In the second act she comes running on to the stage, half collapsing upon the rocks, half supporting herself by them. She flies before Siegmund, who tries to hold her back. Her garment is torn, her hair dishevelled, her face is pale and distorted through suffering.

The portrayer of Sieglinde must look *changed*. She must not give the impression that she has just come from a beauty parlor and had a lovely new permanent. (Just as Brünnhilde should be the wild child of Wotan, not a well-groomed lady in an elegant dress and flying cloak.) For the second act I always had another costume made in exactly the same way as that for the first act, but it hung from me in rags. Siegmund says: "Scarcely could I follow your wild flight through wood and field, over rock and stone, speechless you sprang on. . . ." He holds her closely in his arms—and she hangs as if lifeless and unconscious upon his breast. When he says: "Siegmund is your companion," she looks up at him, awakening slowly: the beloved name has roused her. She first looks about her as if dazed—then she collects her senses—and turning around drinks in with wide open eyes the vision of her lover. Her arms are raised in ecstatic joy—she staggers to him with a suppressed groan and in blissful surrender sinks gently into his arms with a long passionate kiss.

But startled suddenly from the heights of joy she thrusts Siegmund from her. The miracle of the great love which she has experienced in his arms makes her shudder at the thought that she has once been forced to endure an abhorred marriage relation with a man whom she detested. Her body seems dishonoured and disgraced and unworthy of receiving Siegmund's glowing embrace. Oh that she could ever live beside Hunding! Oh that she had not preferred death to such a dishonorable life! Disgrace hangs over her; she feels herself impure, unworthy of Siegmund. Slowly turning her pale face to him she confesses how she has found fulfillment in his embrace, has known a bliss of which she had not dreamed, losing herself completely in the ecstasy of being one with him.

But thrusting aside this memory she rushes to the side of the stage: she is seized with horror as she thinks of Hunding. Shame and ignominy well within her—she brings disgrace upon her brother in the unheard-of union of brother and sister—disgrace to her lover in giving herself to him desecrated and profaned by another whom she detested and despised. Sieglinde collapses, but Siegmund raises her gently and holds her closely to him. He will avenge her disgrace with blood! Nothung, the sword of the father, shall pierce the heart of Hunding and through this deed she will be revenged. . . . But Sieglinde can find no comfort in this thought. She knows Hunding's savagery, knows his

immense power, surrounded by his friends and his brutal clan.
. . . They will force their way into this ravine—they will seize
her beloved and destroy him—for the law, the abhorred law of
marriage, is on Hunding's side—and the gods stand by the law,
protecting marriage as something sacred. She has broken her
marriage, broken her vow. Revenge will destroy Siegmund and
her—the revenge of the husband who has been robbed. Sieglinde
has sunk to the ground holding her hands pressed to her ears, as
if she hears the voices of their pursuers approaching. Her mad
gaze peers into the distance.

After a pause she raises herself with difficulty and with
trembling hands seeks for the hands of her beloved. "Where are
you, Siegmund?" she whispers groaning beneath a deluge of
tears—and with restrained passion, trembling throughout her
body: "Do I still see you? Ardent lover, noble brother" . . .
Her arms close about him, her hands grope for his face, her eyes
filled with tears seek his gaze. She implores him not to reject
her kiss, not to despise her who is disgraced. From the depths of
his love Siegmund kisses the mouth which is offered him.

There is a dull sound of horns in the music. Are they the
horns of Hunding, announcing his approach? Are they the confused and sombre tones of her own imagination? Again Sieglinde
is the victim of horrible delusions: she sees Hunding before her,
around him the howling pack of dogs ready to tear apart whatever he commands them to kill. Of what use is the sword? Of
what avail can it be against the onslaught of savage beasts? But
where is Siegmund? His image fades before her troubled eyes—
yet there, there she sees him. Oh dreadful face! With hands outstretched as if to push away the terrifying sight she stares into
the distance where she believes she will see Siegmund the helpless prey of savage hounds. They drag him to the ground, attack
him, tear him apart—the sword breaks in pieces, and there the
ash tree, the mighty tree which bore the sword within its trunk,
breaks and falls—burying everything beneath it. As if in a prophetic trance Sieglinde stands there gazing frantically before her,
her arms outstretched. . . . Then she falls slowly to her knees,
with her last strength calling her brother in despair—Siegmund,
her brother, her beloved.

Siegmund takes her in his arms and with tender care lets her
glide slowly to the ground, where in a deep unconsciousness akin
to sleep she rests from her torturing apparitions, cradled in his lap.

Naturally Sieglinde remains completely unconscious during the whole wonderful scene of the annunciation of death. She does not know what is happening around her, does not know how near her is death, how strangely the threads of fate are being knotted about her. Brünnhilde, telling Siegmund of his approaching death in battle—as Wotan has decreed it in order to please his wife Fricka—promises to defy this command. Siegmund's great love for the "poor woman who lies exhausted and grieving upon his lap" has touched her so deeply that she promises her help. With this help she will save not only Siegmund and Sieglinde but also the child who will be born to Sieglinde, Siegmund's son.

Only once in her sleep does Sieglinde stir, but without really waking. When Brünnhilde with mounting intensity explains to the defiant Siegmund that even his sword cannot help him since Wotan has withdrawn its magic power from this sword, Sieglinde raises herself as if in anxiety, but is immediately soothed through Siegmund's gentle protection and returns to sleep encircled in his arms.

I must mention here a very amusing incident: at one performance the Vienna opera had as its honored guest the reigning head of a duchy, and after the performance the duke came to us in the dressing-room to tell us of his appreciation. With excitement I waited to hear what the distinguished visitor would say to me. But he only looked at me with a smile as if he wanted to say: "I caught you"—and shaking his finger menacingly he said word for word: "I watched you in the second act when you sat with your head resting on the gentleman's knee, to see if you would move. . . . It was very good but you wriggled once. . . ." I was absolutely speechless and completely overcome by this deep tribute to my performance as Sieglinde!

Siegmund, hearing the sound of Hunding's horn through the threatening storm, springs up to prepare for battle. With great tenderness he lays Sieglinde down so that she may remain unconscious, lost in this strangely deep slumber. Her awakening will be a happy one, for Hunding will no longer live, having been killed by his sword, supported by Brünnhilde's aid, and life will begin for them in all its richness and beauty. He kisses Sieglinde's brow in farewell and leaves her.

Sieglinde groans, deep in her dreams. Flashes of lightning, the rolling of thunder and the blare of distant horns awaken her slowly from her deep sleep. She dreams she is a child—and her father is in the forest with her brother. What strange dark figures are pressing about us, Mother? They seem hostile to us. Fire surrounds us, dark smoke is choking us—help, Brother, Siegmund, Siegmund! And with the cry of "Siegmund" she awakens to find herself engulfed by sinister loneliness. Lightning flashes around her and through the rolling thunder she hears Hunding's voice.

The figures of both men, indistinct in the darkness, but often brilliantly lighted by flashes of lightning, are now visible on the rock above Sieglinde. She runs to the rock, gripping it in her anxiety.

"Stop, men, slay me first," she calls in despair, half out of her mind with fear for Siegmund's life.

A blinding light strikes her—she staggers back, the light is almost unbearably vivid: Brünnhilde appears beside Siegmund protecting him with her shield. But Wotan, seeing with fury that Brünnhilde has defied his command, the command of a god, appears beside Hunding and thrusts away Brünnhilde's shield. Siegmund's sword breaks—he falls dying, pierced by Hunding's weapon.

Sieglinde utters a shriek and falls to the ground unconscious.

She is scarcely aware that Brünnhilde raises her and carries her away in order to save her, the mother of the child which she has received from Siegmund. With a strong arm Brünnhilde carries her unconscious into the forest.

With a word of scorn Wotan has annihilated Hunding, whom he calls "knave". In a sudden outburst of rage he storms away after the disobedient Brünnhilde, his heart filled with revenge.

Amidst the raging tumult the curtain falls.

Brünnhilde has snatched Sieglinde and borne her along on her wild flight through the air. Grane, her noble charger, has carried her over clouds and storms—but Sieglinde has known nothing of all this. She has lain upon Brünnhilde's arm as if lifeless. Now her head rests upon the Walküre's shoulder as they enter the stage in the third act. Brünnhilde lets her glide down upon a mound which rises beneath the branches of the spreading fir tree. Sieglinde lies there half supported by one arm, like an image of stone. She stares before her seeing nothing. The world is dead for her, for Siegmund is dead: life seems extinguished since Siegmund no longer lives. She does not see the strange group of Walküres which flutter around Brünnhilde like excited birds listening with horror to her narrative. Brünnhilde dared to defy her father—she disobeyed the command of Wotan! Her punishment will be frightful—frightful will be the divine wrath!

But Brünnhilde is not concerned for herself: she pleads for help and protection for the poor woman at her feet. From afar a roaring tempest rages. One seems to hear the wild neighing of Wotan's charger through the soughing of the wind. Clouds gather —the god approaches, angry and destructive. The Walküres turn away from Brünnhilde: they cannot help her, they cannot all defy their father, they cannot all disregard his command. No one will help her—Brünnhilde goes from one to the other, pleading for help for the poor woman.

With a loving gesture she bends down over the afflicted one— and Sieglinde awakens through her nearness. She raises her head, her staring eyes meet Brünnhilde's gaze—her hand is extended in a gesture of definite rejection. She wants no help. She feels no gratitude to Brünnhilde for saving her life: "Who bade you lead me from the ravine? There in the storm I might have been struck down." How dared Brünnhilde take her with her? Sieglinde is ready to die, she longs for oblivion. What is life to her now that Siegmund no longer lives? If only the weapon which felled him had pierced her own heart, uniting them in death through the same blow. No, she cannot thank Brünnhilde. She must curse her unless she will thrust the sword into her heart and in kindness release her from this life, which is no longer life for her. . . . With outspread arms Sieglinde awaits the fatal blow.

But Brünnhilde calls to her: "Live, O woman, for the sake of love." This strikes Sieglinde like a blow: for the sake of love— for the sake of love she wants to die, doesn't the cold-hearted Walküre understand her?   Can't she see that it is because of love that she no longer wants to live? Sieglinde turns away shuddering. But Brünnhilde has more to say: "Save the life which you received from him—a Wälsung do you bear within your womb."

The message strikes Sieglinde as though a strong hand has torn the clouds asunder, and she looks upward into the blinding light of the eternal sun. Her face, at first distorted through a superhuman shock, is transfigured with divine joy. Tempestuously she rushes to Brünnhilde: "Save me, daring one! Save my child!" And turning to the Walküres, who have listened with great excitement, she entreats them too: "Shelter me, maidens, with the mightiest refuge."

The storm is nearing—Wotan approaches, dark clouds break in fiery flashes, the Walküres shriek with fear and listen towards the distance. With flying steps Sieglinde swings up the hill, listening with them, terrified, trembling. She falls upon her knees before Brünnhilde, embraces her with quivering hands—and her cry: "Save me, Maid! Save the mother!" is a fervent challenge.

With sudden decision Brünnhilde rises. She shows her the way through the forest. She will offer herself to Wotan, she herself will detain him, will hold him here, until Sieglinde is safely concealed.

Sieglinde scarcely hears that Brünnhilde is prepared to make this great sacrifice for her. It is not she who is worthy of the sacrifice, it is Siegmund's child! It must be saved! For this reason she loses no time in gratitude and idle words, she only trembles in readiness: "Whither shall I turn?" She follows the words of the Walküres with trembling impatience. There is danger everywhere, but can she not defy danger? Where is the danger which she does not dare to override for the sake of this sublime child?

There is another cry from the watching Walküres. "Raging Wotan rides to the rock—Brünnhilde, harken to the roar of his approach." Again Sieglinde rushes to Brünnhilde, again she falls upon her knees, is lifted up, stands with rigid bearing eager to hear what Brünnhilde will say. And it is a wonderful message which she receives from her: the son whom she will bear will be the most sublime hero of the world. In ecstasy, Sieglinde slowly and solemnly raises her arms—she stands there as if she were embracing the world, soaring beyond herself, mother of the most exalted of beings.

Brünnhilde hands her the broken pieces of the sword which Wotan had shattered in his rage. He who is to come will one day mend this sword and in the son the father will rise anew. He will complete what had to be destroyed. Deeply stirred, Brünnhilde solemnly lays the pieces in Sieglinde's hands, giving the child his name, the name which signifies happiness: "Siegfried". . . .

Sieglinde has received the pieces of the sword as if they were sacred. She leans her brow against the cold iron, and holding the pieces before her breaks out with the exultant words: "O most sublime wonder, noblest Maid!" The incredibly beautiful and noble music is a flood of harmony over which Sieglinde's voice soars in radiant purity. It is the intoxicated singing of her soul, a leave-taking from this earth, a union of herself with the gods, whose blood through Wotan, her father, courses through her own veins. The human woman rises into a goddess—and it is a goddess who lays her hand in blessing upon Brünnhilde's head in her parting: "Farewell! May the woe of Sieglinde be a blessing upon you...." Shuddering, Brünnhilde bows deeply before Sieglinde and receives her blessing. Sieglinde moves away with animated steps and disappears into the darkness of the forest.

Chapter VII

LEONORE—"FIDELIO"

THERE IS ALWAYS a somewhat childish pleasure in singing a rôle which ends before the rest of the opera. I was always very quick in dressing and removing my make-up, so when I left the opera house I could hear the despairing cries of the Walküres as they trembled before Wotan. I had the comfortable and satisfying feeling of having done my duty when I heard the others still working, and I myself, no longer the unfortunate Sieglinde deserted in the forest wilderness, could now as Lotte Lehmann go home to a fortifying meal.

But one's nerves are generally in too great an uproar after a performance to find refreshment in soothing sleep. The melodies just sung are replaced by those of the next performance; the after-effect has always faded away very rapidly, but the music of the coming day immediately takes possession of me. Half sleeping I am already singing the following program, at first with disturbing and torturing insistence, then gradually as a fading slumber song. It is strange: as I write I realize that through my whole life it has always been the music of the coming day which has accompanied and continues to accompany me in my dreams.

This process of continual self-transformation, this unceasing re-emergence in the most divergent forms, seems almost uncanny when one thinks about it. The interval between learning two new rôles was generally filled with rehearsals of other operas in the repertoire. When did I ever have time to live my own life? As I look back over those years their tempo makes me dizzy. Losing oneself completely in each rôle it seems as if something of each of the personalities with whom one identifies oneself must cling to one's own personality.

But perhaps I had better not indulge in this Hofmannesque conception, or I might begin to imagine that Elisabeth's purity, Elsa's transfigured dreaminess, Sieglinde's tragedy, Leonore's heroism, live on in me—whereas I actually see myself in private life as a simple human being—certainly without a halo or any heroic quality. I have never seemed courageous except on the stage—privately, I must confess, I am quite a coward. Perhaps it is for this reason that I especially enjoyed enacting Leonore's daring courage. How I loved to sing Leonore, this woman who in the garb of Fidelio follows her husband to his frightful dungeon, and braving death, saves him through her dauntless courage!

I have known unforgettable experiences with each conductor with whom I have sung *Fidelio*. Schalk, who first induced me to sing this beautiful rôle, imbued the opera with all the nobility of his being. Singing it with him I felt liberated from this earth. I am grateful that it was he who through many intensive rehearsals first revealed Beethoven to me. The Beethoven Centenary, in which I sang Leonore for the first time, in a new production of *Fidelio,* was a great event for the people of Vienna. There was scarcely a person who didn't take a vital interest in the celebration. Music was the very breath of life to the Austrians. They grew up with it and were so intimate with the treasures of their musical heritage that every one seemed to regard Beethoven and Mozart as his own personal property. Those days of the centenary festivities when even the bakers' boys delivering their rolls whistled Beethoven airs through the streets, painted Vienna in all its loveliest hues—a Vienna which perhaps may some day rise again from the rubble and ashes of destruction.

Bruno Walter gave his whole soul to this noblest of all operas. It was as if the whole gamut of human emotion from the depths of tragedy to the heights of joy pulsed from his heart.

And Toscanini? He made *Fidelio* flame through his own fire. There was thunder and lightning in his conducting—his glowing temperament, like a flow of lava, tore everything with it in its surging flood. I shall never forget the wave of intoxicated enthusiasm which broke from the Salzburg audience after the third Leonore Overture. There was something almost frightening in its storm—but the maestro let it break over him with his characteristic look of helplessness. It was as if he were saying: "You should honor not me but Beethoven."

I was always exhausted after the terrific strain of the prison scene and at first paid no attention to the music, but just sat waiting in the wings, grateful for a moment of rest after such drama. But the fire which flamed from the conductor's stand out to the remotest corners of the house always tore me out of my exhaustion. Even behind scenes we all joined in shouting enthusiastic "bravos".

To sing the Leonore is a wonderful but at the same time exceptionally strenuous task. At least, for me it was almost beyond the limit of my power. I never had a highly dramatic voice—it was for this reason that my longing to sing Isolde remained only a dream—and the part of Leonore made me feel that it demanded the utmost which I was capable of giving. But what a task it was! What joy to impersonate such a human rôle! I found in it the most exalted moments of my opera career and was shaken by it to the depths of my being.

Our performance of *Fidelio* at the Vienna Opera was ideal and our guest performance at the Grand Opera in Paris a triumph. Alfred Roller, the great stage designer, had created in his characteristic style a magnificent and somber setting. The broad gallery around the prison courtyard in the second scene of the first act was especially impressive. During the conversation between Pizarro and Rocco I could move around this gallery, and so convey the impression that I understood something of the fiendish plot which Pizarro was unveiling to the trembling Rocco but that the complete significance of the scheme was not entirely clear to me. A friend of mine once made a lovely remark about this stealthy listening from the upper gallery: "It is as if the soul of Leonore holds watch over the sinister threads which are being spun below as in a spider's web —as if above them her soul draws a protecting circle against these evil intentions and ill will."

Fidelio in Salzburg, Vienna, Paris, London, Stockholm, Hamburg, Berlin—was always the same tremendous experience. I could never become "accustomed" to singing Leonore—for me she was always new, always deeply exciting and utterly moving.

The part of Leonore imposes greater dramatic problems than any other rôle: she must be convincing as a man, while she is actually the most feminine of women. It must be clear that it is only through her great love that Leonore is capable of enduring the torment of her disguise.

One must picture Leonore as she was before tragedy threatened to destroy her life: she was the beloved wife of a man of high position in the political world. She was adored and honored. Then, through the clever intrigue of Pizarro, her husband was lured into a trap: he disappeared—she did not know where they had taken him. She has only known that he must be suffering in some prison and that his bitterest opponent in the political field, Pizarro, must be involved in his disappearance. But Leonore has not been contented to weep and complain in helplessness as would have been the average woman of her time. Where others would have given up in despair she *acted*. An evil plot has robbed her of her husband, a clever plot must bring him back to her—that is her decision. . . . She suspects which prison it is in which he is languishing. She knows the ways of Pizarro, she knows that he would only have taken him to the place from which there would be the least possibility of escape. She knows of a dark dungeon which would seem the most secure—no one could escape from it. Victims of political enmity—political "criminals"—have been thrown into this prison. How many innocent beings have suffered in this grave of the living! To reach it is Leonore's goal. But how? A woman could never accomplish this, and even if she did succeed in doing so without being recognized she knows that she would never be admitted. So she must disguise herself as a man. Secretly she learns to walk as a man, to make movements which until now have been completely foreign to her nature. She must be convincing if she wants to succeed. And she must succeed for she must free her husband. She practises carrying herself like a man until her bearing becomes convincing and natural.

She has the good fortune to be engaged as the helper of the prison master, Rocco. She has forged her way closer to her goal. But she has not found her husband among the prisoners to whom she must bring food. So, in her disguise, she serves here without really knowing whether her husband Florestan suffers within these dark walls. And now a distressing complication has arisen: Marzelline, Rocco's young daughter, has fallen head over heels in love with this handsome youth who seems so different from the young men whom she knows. Different from Jaquino, Rocco's helper, whose love until now had been quite welcome but now seems only a nuisance—for how could he compare with Fidelio's beauty?

Leonore—or rather "Fidelio", for this is the name under

which she lives here in disguise—sees that Marzelline is a spoiled daughter and that her father, Rocco, would gladly do anything to make her happy. If Leonore should seem to reject Marzelline's none too subtle indications of love, Rocco might in the end tell Fidelio that he must leave in order to save his daughter from a broken heart. That must be avoided! She must win Rocco's confidence, his *complete* confidence. . . . So she accepts Marzelline's advances and plays the lover. It hurts her to deceive these harmless and simple people who have been so kind to her. In moments of depression she hates herself for being able to do this. But the rescue of Florestan is everything to her. It is worth while to play an apparently unworthy rôle in order to achieve this goal.

The portrayer of Leonore must have a deep understanding of this whole situation and must know what she is feeling the moment she enters the stage. She is returning from a mission which has been a torture to her: she has had to fetch new chains from the blacksmith and knows that they may perhaps be placed about her husband—to make certain that he will never escape. She has suffered from this torturing thought and has also suffered physically from the weight of the chains, for never before has she carried so heavy a burden.

So she enters the door almost upon the point of collapse spiritually and physically.

She is pale—there are deep shadows beneath her eyes. She leans for a moment against the frame of the door as if to gather strength. . . . But her eyes search the faces of Rocco and Marzelline anxiously and questioningly: whenever she has been away she is fearful lest something might have betrayed her secret— she is always on guard, always anxious. But no—they both look at her with the same confidence as before.

I have always enjoyed speaking the dialogue very much and regret that it is now cut for the most part. I have never felt that the transition from the spoken word to the music seemed an interruption. On the contrary the spoken words seemed to make the drama, which in this particular opera is especially vital and powerful, even more natural and human. In speaking it is very difficult to find the right balance: it is so easy to make everything too pathetic—and I myself have never had the feeling of completely solving this problem. For example, when (after the heavenly quartet) Leonore asks Rocco if she may accompany him down to the lowest dungeon, and he tells of the approaching death of one of the political prisoners, there is the danger that Leonore may react so violently that it will seem unnatural. If Leonore should reveal her anxiety through the horror which it is almost impossible for her to suppress, wouldn't Rocco notice it and immediately become distrustful? Leonore almost betrays herself when she cries out: "Two years, did you say?" This victim who is about to die had been in this prison for two years —and it was two years ago that her husband was taken from her. Now she realizes that she is on the point of reaching her goal: it must be Florestan of whom the old man is speaking. She is overcome with emotion and with a superhuman effort tries to retain her composure. To make all this seem natural and sufficiently discrete is the task of a great tragedienne—a task which I certainly never quite fulfilled.

I once talked with Max Reinhardt about the problem of the dialogue and found that he had quite a different conception. He said that he would have the whole dialogue stylized, almost without any expression, more as a kind of melodious speech which flows out of the music back into the music. Very interesting, very original! It is a pity that he never produced *Fidelio*. It would certainly have been a very rich and revealing experience to portray Leonore in the light of his interpretation. Perhaps he would have opened for me an entirely new approach.

It is and has always been my highest goal to make every opera *as humanly convincing as possible*. Gestures, even if they must be stylized when borne by the music, must nevertheless always arise from genuine human feeling.

There are endless opportunities for subtle differentiations in acting Leonore: this very feminine woman must behave consciously as a man when she knows that she is under observation, but when she is alone she is feminine and soft. For example, the whole first part of the great aria (after the violently dramatic recitative at the beginning) should be sung with almost no movement—as if lost in prayer. Here she should be completely under the spell of her desperate struggle that she becomes Leonore and not at all Fidelio. In the second part she is overwhelmed by the immensity of her task and is so completely under the spell of her desperate struggle, that she becomes "Fidelio" from head to toe, even though she is alone. But she speaks of victory and success—and victory and success are dependent upon her own cleverness, her own skill in carrying out the plan which she has conceived: the excusable deception of these innocent people for the sake of her husband. . . . With the fanfare of trumpets she again becomes the man who in her absorption had given place to the loving woman.

In the following duet with Rocco, her strength almost leaves her. She will go with Rocco down to the dungeon—she will see the man whose death Pizarro has decreed. She will probably find that he is her husband. . . . But she must go down, for she must dig his grave that this murderous crime may be concealed from an avenging world. This task seems so superhuman that the mere thought of it almost crushes her; she loses herself in tears—tears which she, the man, must not shed in the presence of Rocco. . . . When, in his desire to spare the youth he declares that it is better for him to go alone she regains control of herself. With a violence which forces Rocco to yield she again offers to help him. For the moment the danger is surmounted. Rocco agrees.

The meeting with Pizarro brings new danger to Leonore. She sees before her the man who seeks to destroy her husband—she knows now that he is planning in cold blood to murder the being dearest to her. . . . Yet she must control herself, she must not yet draw the hidden pistol to point it at his evil heart. She must wait for the right moment.

It is important for the impersonator of Leonore to convey the terrible conflict of her emotions without unnaturally and over-obviously forcing herself into the foreground. Any striking gesture would attract the attention of Pizarro—and could she risk that? On the other hand it is absolutely essential that her inner trembling be perceptible. When at the end of the first act Leonore goes away with Rocco they pass in front of Pizarro whis is standing in the center of the stage. Leonore must not look up at him with a challenging glance or a conspicuous gesture as I have seen her do. The quieter, the more rigid and withdrawn she seems as she passes him, the more credible is it. She must move as if she were an automaton, as if she were obeying an inner command. The command is: "Pull yourself together, don't be excited, don't do anything which will make you conspicuous. . . ." She passes him slowly, with bowed head, her steps falter almost unnoticeably—but she moves on rigidly as if driven by an inner compulsion. And Pizarro, somewhat disturbed, follows the silent youth with his eyes as he disappears through the door on his way to the most tragic of all the dungeons.

In the first scene of the last act Leonore's task is made easier by the fact that Rocco is deeply affected by the sight of the poor prisoner who has been condemned to die at the hand of a murderer. He pays no attention to his helper whose emotion he readily understands, thinking it is only the expression of a sympathy which any one must feel in seeing such a pathetic half-starved being before him.

Leonore, now realizing that it is her husband who languishes here in chains, has momentarily but one wish: to make things bearable for him at least for the moment—to help him, to get him water, bread—anything which might revive him. When Florestan, grateful for the small piece of bread, touches her hand she again almost becomes the victim of her emotions: turning away from him she fervently presses to her lips the hand which his has grazed. Florestan had only caught a fleeting glimpse of her face, and with a sudden shock has asked: "Who is that?" A vague resemblance has gripped his heart, an improbable resemblance to his wife which he realized half unconsciously. But Rocco's explanation that it is his son-in-law has shattered every hope in Florestan, hope which he hadn't for a moment felt with any certainty.

Left alone with her husband—before the entrance of Pizarro —Leonore does not dare reveal herself to him. If he should give way to his emotion he might ruin everything—and so even though alone with him she has the painful task of continuing to play "Fidelio". She can only try to give him courage, to give him faith in providence which even at the last moment may still save him.

Like an animal ready to attack she creeps nearer when Pizarro discloses his cruel intention of murdering Florestan. She must jump between them at the very last moment, just at the instant when Pizarro, confident that everything has been prepared and that he is in no danger, is inattentive.

Of course the fact that she doesn't simply shoot him right away is one of the improbable things which have a way of happening in operas. . . . But how fortunate it is that because of this improbability the trio, mounting to a raging *presto*, introduces more exciting drama than could possibly have developed if the act had been logical and quick! For the dramatic signal of the trumpet, pronouncing freedom can, due to this delay, arise from the storm of the drama, flooding it with the radiance of salvation. The signal breaks like a ray of white light into the raging darkness. The quartet: "O you are saved, God be praised, God be praised" is almost unbearable in its divine beauty.

I have never been able to sing this without being stirred to the depths of my being—and my collapse after all had left and I was alone with Florestan was scarcely "acted". . . .

Until the last moment Leonore continues to be watchful; her pistol is constantly directed at Pizarro and it is only during the prayer of gratitude, "O you are saved", that the threatening weapon is lowered—for this is such pure song, so filled with the joy of deliverance and liberation that the pointed pistol would disturb the visual effect, and it is better to be a little illogical and forget that Pizarro might take advantage of this moment to put an end to his hated enemy, even though his plot has been defeated. The pistol drops from Leonore's hand at the moment when Pizarro goes up the stairs. He had hurled his murderous knife at her in an effort to kill the woman whose bold deed has ruined his life. But Leonore is quicker than he and has warded off the weapon with a quick movement—and now at last all danger has been surmounted. Without a sound she sinks to the ground unconscious.

At this point it is of the utmost importance that Florestan should not speak too soon. This prolonged moment of exhaustion should not be interrupted. And his voice must tremble, almost without tone—only not as is so often the case with pathos —the more simply, the more in a whisper he speaks, the better. Leonore's "Nothing, my Florestan, nothing . . ." is also a toneless stammering—and with these words she pulls herself out of her momentary loss of consciousness and staggers into his arms. The following duet is, if I may express myself so daringly, a reeling dance of ecstasy, a clinging together, separating, coming together again, feasting their eyes upon one another, being blissfully united—there is nothing to be found in any opera more exalted, more beautiful or more gripping. This duet is vocally very taxing and exposed, but through its inner surge one is borne over its dangers as if by the hands of angels—and I have scarcely ever had the feeling that this exultant hymn makes too great a demand upon one's resources.

When Leonore appears with Florestan in the last scene she must seem completely changed: to be sure she is still in the costume of a man—but she no longer assumes the behaviour of a man. She is absolutely feminine, soft, submissive. Leaning against Florestan, supporting and leading him, she has eyes only for him and scarcely takes any notice of her surroundings. She has achieved her goal: she has saved him, her task is accomplished, now she is ready to step into the background, to be nothing more than the wife of her beloved husband. Even when Pizarro, in the last throes of his despair, tries to involve Rocco in his sombre plot through his senseless accusation that he would have committed the murder with the help of Rocco, she only reacts with a languid defence. What he has done is clear and convincing. Rocco has only been an innocent victim of this cruel intrigue. The accusation is so senseless that it seems hardly worth while to say anything in his defence. Fernando, the minister who has appeared as their liberator, understands the situation completely and pays no attention to Pizarro's accusation. He orders him to be led away, and with his presence disaster disappears from the life of Florestan.

When Leonore is presented to Fernando as Florestan's wife she bows before him with the graciousness of a great lady. She is now again a woman of high position who is accustomed to receiving homage. So her bow of greeting should be one of equality, not humility.

The wonderful moment has come in which Florestan is to be freed of his chains. Bowing deeply before her, Fernando asks Leonore to remove them. Through her act she has brought about his release, and now she should be the one to remove his shackles.

This moment is so unspeakably beautiful that even in recalling it I feel tears coming into my eyes. From the breathless: "O God, O what a moment!" this prayer of gratitude soars with ethereal beauty; Leonore's voice rising above the chorus floats upward to God in inner transfiguration.

The opera ends with a great hymn of joy. Here one should not "act" too much. Here everything is music, ecstasy.

The arrangement at the end of the opera lies entirely in the hands of the stage director. At this point the individual must only be a part of the whole, for here the *ensemble* is everything. The less expected of Leonore the better. Much moving around, greeting Fernando, handshaking and nodding to the people, again savours too much of "filling out pauses". From the pictorial standpoint it is best if Leonore and Florestan remain in the center of the stage absorbed in one another. They scarcely notice the activity around them. Everyday life with its demands and duties does not as yet exist for them. Conventional greetings are still far from their thoughts. They are only aware of each other—of the union to which they have at last been restored, of the bliss of freedom which has now been granted them.

With a friendly and pleading gesture Leonore may turn once to Marzelline, who has quickly comforted herself for the loss of her supposed fiancé and has again bestowed her favour upon Jaquino. Leonore has been obliged to deceive Rocco and Marzelline and so she asks their forgiveness. Both bow deeply before her. But her gesture towards them should not be in any way conspicuous. Leonore remains leaning against Florestan: she only exists for him and probably has only thought of Marzelline fleetingly when she felt her eyes upon her. This almost unconscious apology must seem entirely incidental.

Though the whole gathering pays her homage for her courageous action, she is scarcely aware of it. She only lays this deed like a wreath at the feet of Florestan—moistened by many bitter tears for the harrowing experiences which they have endured and the streaming tears of overwhelming bliss.

I believe that for some time I overacted this final scene of *Fidelio.* The jubilation in the music, the power of the chorus, the idea of being free and of having given freedom made me just as overanimated as Florestan, who always seemed very suddenly to have developed amazing strength after two years of starvation in prison. . . .

Oh, these hours of happy sublimation! This pure ecstasy of artistic creation, of artistic bondage with the other personalities in *Fidelio,* with the conductor! The Vienna Opera—the Salzburg Festival Playhouse—London's Covent Garden—the Paris Grand Opera—in them there lies for me the whole wonder of years which have vanished, of beauty which has passed away. . . .

Schalk—Walter—Toscanini shine like a constellation of three stars in my memory. And ever again I say: "Thank you" to them in my heart.

"*Franz Schalk had always been a wonderful friend to me. In my memory his image merges with that of Hans Sachs. He was my guide. I looked up to him as to a father.*"

"*Arturo Toscanini: When I first began to lose my fear of him, realizing that he is always just and kind and that he does forgive, I became really free in singing with him. And then it was as if genius itself carried me with it in its flight . . .*"

"*Bruno Walter . . . is both conductor and stage director at once. I learned to understand him so completely that I wouldn't have needed a stage rehearsal for a new role: a talk with him about a role made everything so clear to the last detail, that the actual acting just took its natural course.*"

"*And now the distressing complication has arisen: Marzelline . . . has fallen head over heels in love with this handsome youth.*"

Lehmann as Leonore (Fidelio)—FIDELIO (page 121)

Chapter VIII

MANON LESCAUT—"MANON" (*Massenet*)

AS I RECALL the rôle of Manon my thoughts sweep back to a personal experience. Just as a performance was about to begin I received some very distressing news. I was so deeply upset that I couldn't imagine how I could ever get through the rôle that day. My life seemed ruined. Many women would have saved themselves by taking refuge in a nervous breakdown. But there was no time for any nervous crisis: *I had to sing*. I must be Manon—that frivolous, light-hearted creature who loved luxury more than her life or her honor, more even than her own happiness. I stood in the wings dissolved in tears—in a state which seemed to make any thought of going on the stage quite out of the question. But I heard the music for my entrance —I left the tortured and confused Lotte Lehmann in the wings and emerged on the stage as Manon Lescaut. . . . What a blessing is the profession of an artist! In no other is it possible to find such complete self-surrender. The transformation into another fate, the submergence of myself in the life of the character I was personifying silenced all my grief. I forgot. I was Manon; Manon as she quickly alights from the stage-coach and looks about her with curiosity, taking in for the first time in her life the exciting picture of a strange city.

Manon is very young, only sixteen. She has such an inordinate desire for pleasure and distraction that her family has decided to send her to a convent in order to save her from the fate to which her craving for excitement would surely lead her. So she has been put on the stage-coach and brought to Amiens, where a cousin, Lescaut, whom she has never seen, awaits her and will take her to the convent.

Manon is, of course, depressed by the thought of entering a convent, but she is thoughtless and so convinced that life is wonderful and beautiful and must turn out happily that she doesn't concern herself very much about her future. It will come out all right. The trip itself has been full of excitement. So many people—so many new faces. She found sitting in the stage-coach among strangers and listening to their conversation great fun. Now she stands amidst the people and looks about her with unabashed curiosity. She greets her cousin Lescaut without any trace of embarrassment. Her first words to him are: "Come, kiss me." Isn't he a relative? Why shouldn't he kiss her? He looks very nice—and she succeeds most effectively in enlisting his goodwill. He looks at her with delight—she is a credit to the family, a real Lescaut and a lovely girl. . . .

Manon begins to tell him of her adventures on the trip. She knows how to laugh and chatter with a childish coquettishness, and Lescaut listens to her with increasing delight, inwardly regretting that this charming child is so soon to be lost behind the forbidding walls of a convent instead of being given the opportunity to make the most of the pleasures of life.

He leaves her alone while he goes to look after her luggage. She obediently seats herself on a bench and seems engrossed in her little handbag.

Monsieur Guillot, a rich man who with three young ladies ("actresses" according to the list of characters) has been enjoying a pleasant and leisurely dinner upon the balcony of the hotel, now comes down the steps. Seeing Manon he is quite overwhelmed by her beauty and by the piquant charm of her child-like face. With quick decision, disregarding the scornful calls of his three companions, he addresses Manon. He tells her that a carriage will await her—and he will take her right to his arms and to the luxury which he is in a position to offer her. Manon is much intrigued by this first adventure—a real adventure, a proposal which doesn't seem exactly proper and which she won't accept, for Guillot is much too ridiculous. She will wait for someone whom she can really enjoy, who will give her a lot of fun. So with amazing boldness she has only hasty, quick-witted words of scorn for Guillot. Her cousin Lescaut interrupts them and frees her of the tiresome Guillot, but he again leaves her alone while he follows his friend who has insisted that he play and drink with him.

Manon, like a good child, again seats herself upon the bench. She has all the best intentions in the world. She wants to forget her mad ideas which always drive her towards seeking pleasure and forbidden joys. . . . She wants to stop dreaming and think seriously about the convent. . . . But—dangerously close to her, on the balcony—sit the three lovely actresses with Monsieur

Guillot—and it really isn't wrong just to look at their wonderful clothes, it is? Only from the distance, of course, only from the distance! She sees golden pearls shimmering about the neck of the loveliest of the women. Manon jumps up excitedly and approaches the balcony on tiptoe, peering longingly into a world which will soon be closed to her for ever. "O come, Manon, no more of this dreaming. Dreaming will not change your fate." But yet—isn't there laughing freedom somewhere in the world? Is there no way to escape to this alluring freedom, to a land where pleasure, enjoyment, luxury, would await her? But where is the road to this freedom? No one will help her. She is here alone and unknown, she must wait for her cousin who is a stranger to her, who will deliver her to the convent. It is the convent which will open for her, not the seductive world of enjoyment. . . .

Her resigned thoughts are interrupted: someone seems to be approaching—an elegant young gentleman—and Manon slips back to her bench and watches this fascinating stranger with the greatest interest.

The Chevalier Des Grieux has missed the time for the departure of the stage-coach. He is very indignant about it and must now still longer curb his impatience to see his father from whom he has been separated during a long trip.

Memories of the Viennese production of *Manon* come to me so vividly that I must speak of them. . . . It was not easy to sing *Manon* there—on a stage on which Marie Renard, the most capricious Manon before my time, had triumphed. Of course, I had not heard her, but I knew her very well and was bound to the old lady through a warm friendship. She must have been nearly eighty but she was still beautiful and piquant. I can imagine how enchanting she was in the days when she set Vienna afire with her charming Manon and Lotte in *Werther*.

And yet Vienna loved my Manon. It was a standard opera in the repertory and was always certain of a sold-out house. Alfred Piccaver was Des Grieux. I shall never forget his heavenly voice which had the quality of velvet! There are voices which are so beautiful that they make you oblivious of everything but their quality so that you don't even think of considering whether the singer is a good actor. Such a voice was Piccaver's. The more lyrically he sang the more unearthly the *pianissimo* in which he revelled, the more enchanting was the sound of this divinely blessed organ. The fact that he never made a world career was entirely his own fault: in spite of being English by birth he belonged absolutely to Vienna and never wanted to leave it. The wide world held no allure for him, and whenever, yielding to the pressure of his friends, he dared an expedition into the surrounding world he had only moderate success. He was only at home in Vienna, he only sang beautifully in Vienna and he only *wanted* to sing beautifully in Vienna. What a divine voice! I still revel in the memory of it!

No man has ever before made such an impression upon Manon as Des Grieux. He is young, he is handsome, he is elegant. . . . She sits trembling upon her little bench, awaiting an opportunity to attract his notice. When his glance falls upon her it is kindled to fire. Though pampered and accustomed to conquests he stands in confusion before the little insignificant country girl, Manon. He cannot find the smooth words which generally come to him so easily. Stammering he tells her how deeply she impresses him, stammering he asks her name. . . .

In spite of shyness Manon is more self-possessed. She accepts his ardent gaze with a childlike joy and finds coquettish words to convey to him subtly that he attracts her. . . .

He wants to know who she is, where she is going, what she seeks in life. . . . Sadly, yet chattering lightly, she tells him that she is on her way to the convent. The family—oh, they want to bury her there because she is much too interested in pleasure and frivolity.

Des Grieux is quite from head to toe the savior and liberator. So much charm, so much beauty can't be buried in a convent! It must belong to the world—to life, to love. . . .

Manon is shocked—really shocked. . . . She has been told so much about the punishment which sinners will receive in hell. God has shown her the way—so her family says—to atone for her dangerous desire for pleasure: the convent. . . . It is God's will. And besides even if she wants to how could she escape from the convent? Des Grieux knows how. She mustn't enter the convent—she must follow him out into the world. He will find a secret place—for her, for him—for them both.

Manon is overwhelmed. The gates of a world of which she has scarcely dared to dream seem to swing open before her.

Quickly and cleverly she makes her plan. She sees it all clearly before her: she will take the carriage which the silly old Monsieur Guillot has promised her. . . . The carriage which was supposed to take her to him will now carry Manon and Des Grieux far away—where no one will ever find them. . . .

Des Grieux, enchanted, whispers to her: "To Paris." In the rapture of the moment he even goes so far as to promise her that his name shall be hers. But he comes back to his senses. Oh, that won't be possible! The noble Des Grieux could never marry this little girl of whom he knows nothing more than that she is transportingly beautiful and attractive. Embarrassed, he asks her pardon. He doesn't want to arouse any false hopes within her, doesn't want to seduce her under any false pretences. But Manon understands this very well. She would never dream that she could be the wife, the lawful wife, of such a noble gentleman. She only wants to follow him, to belong to him "and yet perhaps it's wrong," she says as she turns away. Her family would never agree to it, the convent would throw her out. . . . But the magic word "Paris" which he whispers in her ear is the living present, the irresistibly alluring present. To Paris— we two! Tearing herself from his arms she looks up at the three richly adorned ladies who have again aroused her yearning desires—her longing for glamor and luxury Now everything will be hers—everything: glamor, luxury, love, bliss. Joy and delight await her. Laughing she rushes away with Des Grieux and climbs exultantly into the carriage. Never mind about Guillot—the world with all its bewildering gifts is opening wide before her. . . .

Lescaut, who hasn't watched over his lovely cousin very effectively, returns intoxicated. A suspicion that someone has gone off with her occurs to poor Guillot, who swears revenge.... Lescaut will find his cousin—he swears he will. . . .

Manon has lived for some time with Des Grieux in his apartment in Paris, and the second act takes place in the living-room of this apartment. Manon is very much in love with her tender lover, but her longing for luxury has not been quieted to quite the extent for which she had hoped. Des Grieux just isn't rich enough to fulfill all her extravagant wishes. She is happy in their hours of love, but she is not contented with the jewels, the gowns, the pleasures which Des Grieux is in a position to offer her. He would like to live only in his love for her—but she longs for a life beyond these four walls out amidst the gaiety of Paris. . . . Isn't she young and beautiful? Shouldn't Paris see how lovely she is?

Her neighbor, Monsieur Brétigny, seems only too willing to lay this world at her feet. It flatters her vanity to know that she has only to raise her little finger in order to win him—and to find through him the realization of her lavish dreams. But up to now she has loved Des Grieux too much, is too much under the spell of her passion for him to be able to leave him. Nevertheless her thoughts play with this possibility.

Des Grieux loves Manon deeply and sincerely. He has but one wish: to make her his wife, to give her through his name a position in society which he believes that he owes her. He has no idea that Manon's light heart dreams of anything more than his love. . . .

Having made his decision he is now writing to his father, telling him of his desire to marry Manon and asking his blessing and approval. Des Grieux lives as a well-to-do man upon his property—but if his father should withdraw his support he would lose a great deal—and that would be very unfortunate, for Manon understands how to spend money: it runs through her fingers like sand. . . . So Des Grieux is anxious to have his father's consent for practical reasons, as well as because of the filial affection and feeling of bondage which he has always felt for his father.

He is sitting at his writing-table busy with this letter. Manon comes to him and leaning over his shoulder tries to read what he is writing.

Des Grieux tenderly reads the letter to her. He describes his mistress in glowing colors and Manon listens with delight. Nevertheless she isn't entirely satisfied. While the fact that Des Grieux wants to marry her had for a time made her blissfully happy, it has ceased to do so. Marriage would mean living only for Des Grieux. Oh, of course she loves him! Loves him passionately. But she doesn't want to live here always—here in this little apartment, so near and yet so far from all the tantalizing luxuries of which Paris seems to be made. She doesn't want to be imprisoned here as the good and worthy wife—she, who more than ever longs for exciting adventures, longs to see the whole world at her feet. . . . Oh, she knows very well that she would succeed. Whenever she appears in public with Des Grieux she is followed by ardent glances. . . . She knows she is desirable and that greater joys may await her than Des Grieux is able to give her.

So with her face turned aside she asks: "Isn't it enough that we love each other?" "No, I want you to be my wife." It touches her that Des Grieux should love her so much. She knows that it will mean a struggle—he has often spoken to her about it. And this—this slight feeling trembles in her voice as she says: "Embrace me then." But with a gesture of impatience she immediately frees herself from his arms. Why does he stand there and look at her as if she must always lie in his arms. His adoring love gets a little on her nerves. He is always there, always near her. She is never alone. For example, she can never throw a flirtatious glance at their neighbour Brétigny without being observed. She must always be right at Des Grieux's side, virtuous and proper.

She says with restrained impatience: "Oh go and take your letter away." Des Grieux, already at the door, notices some extravagant flowers in a vase, flowers which he had not sent and which she certainly hasn't bought for herself. To his question Manon replies that she doesn't know who sent them. Someone threw them through the window and they were so lovely she kept them, but there is no reason for jealousy. Des Grieux takes Manon in his arms. Oh no, he doesn't distrust her—he knows that her heart is his. Manon, laughing, cuddles up to him like a coquettish little kitten. Oh certainly he can trust her. Her heart belongs only to him.

The maid enters the room and informs them that two guardsmen are outside demanding entrance in a very rude way. Pulling Manon towards the foreground as Des Grieux goes towards the the door, she whispers to her that one is her relative Lescaut—but the other—— Manon silences her. She knows who the other is: Brétigny. How shameful of him to force his way in here in a false disguise—but how clever of him! She is angry—and yet she has to laugh. She must also laugh over Lescaut who plays the morally indignant one and demands an accounting from Des Grieux to preserve the family honor. She sees through Lescaut. He, who once watched over her so carelessly, now knows how to make capital out of her. His intentions certainly can't be good if he comes here with Brétigny and in disguise is a party to introducing him who is not wanted. Manon isn't really annoyed by this bold game. It quite amuses her. How much Brétigny must want her, to resort to such methods just to exchange a word with her.

With amusement Manon sees how Lescaut draws the innocent Des Grieux to the side of the room, near the light, as he says, so that he can better read the letter which Des Grieux has handed him. It is the one to his father in which Des Grieux has made clear his honorable intentions.

While Lescaut reads the letter in a loud voice he gives Brétigny the opportunity he desires for a hasty conversation with Manon. Brétigny is very clever. He knows how to capture Manon's attention by telling her that this evening Des Grieux will be forcibly apprehended—upon the order of his father, to be sure. The father wants to put an end to this affair with Manon, and knowing that his son would only be obstinate and refuse to give her up, he seizes upon the most extreme method: force. Manon is beside herself and wants immediately to warn her lover. But Brétigny restrains her and tells her that this would only lead to her own arrest as well, on immoral grounds, and so—unhappiness and disgrace for both of them. On the other hand if she is reasonable and remains silent all the luxury of Paris will be at her feet. . . .

Manon is silent.

She is terribly excited and doesn't know what to do. Her heart drives her to stand by her lover, to remain at his side and share his lot with him, whatever it may be. However . . . however—she is young. . . . Why should she sacrifice herself? The voice of seduction is sweet in her ears. Luxury, joy, glamor, magnificence—Brétigny promises everything. . . . There can be no choice between misery and all he offers. She must obey her fate and abandon Des Grieux.

She gives Brétigny no promise—but he reads the promise in her eyes, in her expression of confusion. He knows that she will choose that which is nearest to her heart: magnificence.

When the two have left, the maid enters with the supper. Manon looks up bewildered as Des Grieux, about to leave with his letter, approaches her again. He has nothing new to say—only that he loves her, worships her. He feels instinctively that Manon's thoughts and feelings are not with him at this moment and asks her imploringly: "And you—do you love me too, Manon?"

Her answer: "Yes, my dear Chevalier, I love you," doesn't sound very satisfying. She is throbbing with impatience. He would like to hear more, would like to have a promise, an oath, something which would bind her to him for ever and ever. . . . But with resignation he takes his letter and goes away.

Left alone, Manon is plunged into the depths of confusion. . . . She is beside herself, helpless—she does not know what she should do. She tries to persuade herself that it is a sacrifice which she is making for the sake of her lover, when she abandons him. It is so easy to say to herself: if I were to go with him we would both be put in jail, but if he goes alone his father will free him. Perhaps this might even be true. But she knows that Des Grieux would be happier in prison in the consciousness of her loyalty and love than if he were free and she the mistress of another man. For that is what is before her: she must become Brétigny's mistress. It is as if she again hears the voice whispering in her ear of all the magnificence which will surround her. She cannot escape this voice. She will live like a queen, the queen of beauty. . . .

Oh, how weak she is, how helplessly the victim of this seduction. Tears pour down her cheeks—tears of sympathy for herself for having so easily succumbed to her greed for the luxuries the world may offer. Manon looks around the room, her eyes veiled with tears. She must leave all this, this room where she has been so happy, this little table at which they have sat, day after day, laughing, making love, happy in each other. . . . She says good-bye to these things—and her cry: "O my poor lover, how he loved me" is choked with tears. But not for a moment does it occur to her that there might be some other way out: for example to escape with him before the guards come to take him away. Escape? Into the unknown, perhaps to poverty and privation? She was not born to be poor.

She hears him returning and hurries to the window that he may not find her in tears. But Des Grieux sees by the moonlight the moist eyes of his love and asks why she is crying. Oh, it is nothing—just a mood. Supper is ready. Innocent and trusting, Des Grieux goes arm in arm with her to the little table. Manon moves slowly, leaning against him. She knows that this is the last meal which they will have together—everything is a farewell; she trembles and has difficulty in concealing her emotion.

Sitting beside her, Des Grieux tells her of a dream he had last night. She turns to him hesitantly, quite under the influence of her foreboding, and says with barely concealed bitterness: "Alas, who has not had a dream?" This dream is the picture of the deepest longing within Des Grieux's soul: a simple little house in the woods in a lovely unpretentious countryside. . . . Manon in this house. . . . Manon and he living by themselves, undisturbed, in perfect harmony. Turning her face away Manon says: "That is a dream, that is madness." But it is his longing that the dream should become reality: "There we shall find seclusion—if you but want it, Manon. . . ."

This well-known narrative of his dream is one of the most beautiful parts of the whole opera. Piccaver sang it so beautifully that the sound of it will accompany me for ever.

Nothing is more impossible for Manon than to be enthusiastic over this idyllic fantasy. She leans her head against his shoulder in order to conceal the expression in her eyes, for she cannot suppress the scorn which she feels mounting in her when she pictures to herself the boring loneliness to which Des Grieux would like to take her, who longs for all the joys of life.

A knock on the door spares her the necessity of answering. Manon straightens up in alarm. It is time. They come to take away her lover. He has not the slightest suspicion of it—and she? She is involved in this, is an accomplice: her knowledge incriminates her. Consumed with fear, she embraces Des Grieux who has risen to see what is the matter. Suddenly she feels that she cannot leave him, that she must stand by him and protect him and herself from the fate which threatens them if these men outside should take him prisoner. Des Grieux laughs at her strange behavior. He is happy that Manon is worried because it makes him feel that he really matters to her. But she is worried without any reason! He gently disengages himself from her arms and goes to the door. Before he has any idea of what is happening he is overpowered, bound and dragged away.

Manon has followed all this as if paralysed. She is even incapable of uttering a sound and looks on passively while Des Grieux is led away. When they have left the room she rushes to the window, and as she hears the wagon rolling away covers her eyes with her hands and bursts out sobbing. . . . But her "My poor Chevalier" is submerged in the overwhelming tumult of joy in the music. She turns around dizzily and stands in the

center of the stage with outstretched arms, triumphant, ecstatic.
. . . She is free. . . . Now the whole world will be hers. Now
there will be no quiet little hut, no narrow restrictions any longer.
Paris opens its magic portals. Manon has been victorious.

In the second scene of the second act Manon comes upon
the stage attired in ravishing beauty. This is a public holiday
on which she appears like a queen. She is now the mistress of
Brétigny, she is at the height of her power, her beauty, her artful
seductiveness. Brétigny spreads all Paris as a carpet before her
feet. However, he has refused one of her all too capricious
whims: she wanted the entire opera company invited to their
luxurious home to perform for her alone. She doesn't want to
go to the opera herself, it should come to her. Bored by the
fulfillment of even her most senseless desires she must now have
something which is unattainable. For once Brétigny has found it
right to play the master. A dangerous game! The story has
gone the rounds in Paris—every one is always interested in the
latest whim of the great courtesan Manon. And Guillot, whom
she as a country girl had scornfully rejected, has not relin-
quished his hope of winning this enchanting creature for himself. He hears of Brétigny's refusal and decides on his own
course of action.

A murmur of admiration rustles through the crowd as Manon
descends from her carriage. She is beautiful as a goddess! She
is lavishly adorned. Simple people ask themselves: "Who is
she? A princess? A duchess? Oh no, nonsense! . . . It is Manon
—Manon, the renowned courtesan. . . ."

Manon senses the admiration and envious glances of those
about her, and is delighted. She moves slowly on, surrounded
by cavaliers. Every one tries to come near her, seeking a glance
from her. Under her spell as always, Brétigny whispers to her:
"O most lovely Manon." She looks at him as she does at all the
others, with coldly coquettish eyes. That she receives the homage
of men is a distinction for them. Like a true queen she dispenses
her favor or disfavor—according to her mood.

Manon feels at the height of her success, at the height of her
power over men. The "world", for which she has longed so
fervently, is now hers. Her every wish is fulfilled before she
can make a demand, for Manon is not a woman who asks for
favors: she commands. . . . Monsieur Brétigny is like a slave to
the beautiful woman. All the arrogance of a heart intoxicated by

success sounds through the "gavotte" in which she extols youth as life's most precious possession. Yet a fleeting cloud shadows her radiance as she speaks of the time when her youth will fade, when her heart will be cold and her desires stilled. . . . But Manon cannot surrender to gloomy thoughts—why should one give a thought to the future, or the past, or the course of time? The present is sweet and intoxicating and she will live only in the present. . . .

Boldly she hurls the glorious "to-day" into the enigmatic face of "to-morrow". Even death is but a toy in her frivolous hands. Laughingly she challenges the dark enemy—in her last moment a conqueror and not a victim.

Then something catches her attention: a very distinguished elderly gentleman approaches Brétigny; she hears the name— "Des Grieux". As if struck by a blow she remains motionless, listening with the greatest intensity, but at the same time cleverly concealing her interest.

The old Des Grieux tells Brétigny that his son, whose life seems to have been ruined through a love affair, has withdrawn to a seminary and has expressed his unalterable determination to end his life as an abbé. He is at the Seminary of St. Sulpice —and will preach there.

Manon has understood the name of the seminary. She struggles to keep her composure. Brétigny points out to Des Grieux that the lovely young person over there is Manon.

Des Grieux observes her with cold disdain. She makes a gesture, and Des Grieux draws back thinking that she wants to speak with Brétigny.

Manon has made up her mind: she must know more of the man whom she once loved so passionately and whom she has never forgotten. The old fire leaps within her heart when she thinks of him. . . . Oh, she must see him, must speak with him, must win his forgiveness! She can't go on living like this any longer, so senselessly, so unhappily, the mistress of the boring Brétigny.

But in order to speak with Des Grieux she must first get Brétigny out of the way. So she calls him to her and tells him that he must immediately go and buy for her a bracelet just like the one she is wearing. It must be exactly the same. Brétigny goes away much concerned, for he knows how hard it will be to fulfill this wish immediately, but he is more than ever

"*Manon . . . only sixteen . . . has such an ominous love for pleasure and distraction that her family has decided to send her to a convent in order to protect her from becoming a victim of the fate to which her craving for pleasure would surely lead her.*"   •   MANON (page 129)

"This is a blow to Manon. Healed—his heart healed . . . It isn't possible . . ."

MANON (page 141

under Manon's spell to-day, and would gladly fetch the stars from heaven if she should want them. So he goes away—and Manon, as if in polite confusion, places herself in Des Grieux's way.

The old gentleman has observed this lovely young woman with interest. He finds her very beautiful and says to himself: "She is charming—I understand his loving her."

Manon has learned how to get around men. She knows that with some you must be bold, with others diffident. So she assumes a shy and confused expression, an exceptionally correct, polite bearing.

She excuses herself for having heard their conversation against her will—but Des Grieux interrupts her. He has no intention of talking with her. He detests the woman who has ruined his son's life. He intends to leave her with a cold and polite disdain. But Manon detains him. Hesitantly she tells him that she believes his son has once loved one of her friends. Des Grieux can only say: "Ah—indeed. . . ."

Again he starts to go—but Manon reaches out her hand with such a childlike imploring gesture that he remains against his will. Yes, what she would like to know is—and perhaps his father could give her this information—has his son completely overcome this love? Has his heart been healed?

The Count Des Grieux does not give a clear answer. He speaks of the fleeting summer, of the withering roses—and isn't it better not to ask too much?

Manon is dismayed. She has not been prepared for such clever smoothness. She must know, she must find out. Has he forgotten her? Is it possible that her beloved Chevalier no longer thinks of her?

With a gesture of despair she begs him to remain. She only wants to know if he is still angry? If he has suffered? If he— if he—still loves her?

The count looks at her fixedly and says with decision: "His heart, with strength sent him from heaven, is whole. . . ."

This is a blow to Manon. Healed—his heart healed. It isn't possible. He loved her too much for that. But his father knows better: "He has done as his faithless beloved has done: forgotten. . . ." And with polite formality he bows to her and leaves Manon, who says to herself with pale lips: "Forgotten. . . ."

Guillot and Brétigny come to her and a quarrel develops

between them. Guillot has engaged the ballet of the opera to dance for Manon. It is costing him a fortune, but he would venture anything for her. Wrapped in her thoughts, not heeding what is taking place around her, Manon goes to the seat of honor, which has been quickly arranged for her. The ballet dances across the stage—but Manon has no eyes for the artists. She sits quietly, lost in her thoughts, and pays no attention to her surroundings. Her brain is working feverishly—she must see Des Grieux. She must go to St. Sulpice—she must try to tear him away from the cloister, back into her arms, back to her thirsty lips. Suddenly she loathes and despises the splendor around her—all these false, empty joys. . . . She wants only him, Des Grieux. . . .

Lescaut watches her with increasing concern. Her fine cousin has attached himself to Manon and enjoys a questionable life at Manon's—or rather Brétigny's—expense. He wouldn't like to see Manon leave him and go back to the very honorable but only moderately well-to-do Des Grieux. For Des Grieux could offer neither Manon nor Lescaut the luxury to which they have become accustomed. But knowing Manon's impulsiveness Lescaut is very much worried. Again and again he tries in vain to draw Manon's attention to the ballet, but she only turns away impatiently.

With sudden decision she turns to Lescaut: "My carriage—immediately. . . ." Suspecting the worst, he says to her: "To where do you insist upon driving?" Her answer, "To St. Sulpice" makes him completely lose his composure. But he must obey, for he is so to speak the servant of Manon and his fate rests in her hands. So he hastens to do her bidding.

As she is leaving Manon is detained by Monsieur Guillot, who expects her to express her gratitude for the surprise he has prepared for her with the ballet. But he is mistaken. He has overestimated Manon's gratitude. And when he asks, confident of his success—"Now, queen of my heart, what do you say to this surprise?" she turns towards him very ungraciously, saying over her shoulder: "I have seen nothing . . ." and goes on, leaving Guillot behind, dumbfounded and angry.

The next scene takes place in the reception room of the Seminary of St. Sulpice.

Des Grieux has preached for the first time and has been very successful. Every one has been delighted by his deep religious feeling, his penetration, the quality of his voice and his well-constructed sermon. Without question he will become the favored abbé of this seminary, to which people will crowd in order to find wisdom and comfort in his words.

For the last time his father implores him to return to the world. He speaks of the good, normal happiness which he will surely find through marriage with one of his own social position. He could be so happy, if only he would follow his father's advice. But with determination Des Grieux rejects all his promises and all his artful persuasion. The world has too deeply disillusioned him. Manon was "the world"—the only thing which made life seem worth living. Now he wants to retire to this cloister and live only with God. Nothing can alter his decision.

The old Des Grieux can see nothing but weakness in this determination, for he knows that it has been no inner urge towards religion which has driven his son to the shelter of the cloister, but a very worldly reason—Manon. He can see no good in his son's future as an abbé. It would be better and more honorable, he thinks, for his son to marry and through his children continue the name of Des Grieux. That is his duty, not this false surrender to God. So he leaves his son with a heavy heart, but as he doesn't want to feel that his beloved son is unhappy or in financial embarrassment he tells him that he will send him thirty thousand francs, the inheritance from his mother. . . .

This sum, which was certainly plentiful at that time, became in our Viennese opera the subject of a never-ending joke. The singer who played the old Des Grieux always varied the amount of this gift. Sometimes he was incredibly generous and promised his son a fantastic income—sometimes it was only a few francs. This nonsense reached such a point that we all waited expectantly in the wings, eager to hear what Papa Des Grieux would give that day. In the orchestra they made bets as to the amount. Of course, the father Des Grieux was the focus of interest, and he knew this and enjoyed it. He always made a dramatic pause before he announced his decision to the world. It wasn't easy for poor Piccaver, who sang the rôle of young Des Grieux. He stood with his back to the audience and struggled, generally in vain, to keep his composure. This scene finally became so amusing and so hilarious that the director of the opera took it in hand and decreed a fine for every repetition of this nonsense. But this was difficult to enforce and I don't remember whether it was ever effective.

When Des Grieux, touched by his father's generosity, wants to embrace him in gratitude he holds him back with a gesture of coolness: "Farewell—remain in prayer," he says sadly and somewhat scornfully as he leaves him.

Des Grieux remains behind alone. He gathers his thoughts to pray, but through his prayer Manon's image pursues him, confusing and disturbing him. He urgently implores God to dispel this image. "Fly, O fly, sweet image, too dear to my soul." With all his might he struggles against the love and longing within his heart, and leaves the reception room to seek in the chapel new strength with which to battle the tumult raging within him.

Manon appears with the lay brother who has admitted her. A cloak of dark lace covers her glamorous gown, her behavior is shy and confused. She feels very much out of place within these walls. Imploring the lay brother to call Des Grieux she wants to offer him a tip as she is accustomed to do, but he refuses it with dignity. Left alone she looks anxiously about her. She doesn't think of this cloister as a place in which one may serve God. She has only the impression of a prison. The walls seem so dead, the air so cold—his heart must have changed. He must have learned to condemn. . . .

From the chapel comes the sound of devout singing, and Manon moved against her will wishes that she might be able to pray as these people do—surrendering themselves completely to their ecstasy of devotion. She falls upon her knees and impetuously implores the Holy Virgin for one thing: the heart of Des Grieux. It doesn't occur to her that her plea profanes Des Grieux's surrender to God. What is the cloister to her? What is an oath to God? She wants her lover back again—and if the art of seduction doesn't succeed perhaps the help of the Holy One will. . . .. Her prayer is deeply felt and sincere—she has no awareness of the immorality of her plea.

Des Grieux, summoned by the lay brother, appears in the doorway. Seeing him, Manon impetuously throws off her cloak. She is so sure of her impression upon him—she knows that he must find her beautiful in this wonderful gown. It will awaken memories, the sweetest of memories. She stands very erect before him in all her triumphant beauty.

But Des Grieux's answer is not the one which she had expected and hoped for. He staggers back terribly shocked, but immediately regains control of himself and in a severe tone orders her to leave the cloister. . . .

Manon immediately changes her tactics: it won't be so easy to win him back. She is deeply affected and now approaches him with shyness and humility. But her words of self-reproach seem to make no impression upon Des Grieux. He repeatedly interrupts her and again orders her to leave. He takes refuge in the faith to which he clings so desperately: Heaven will not tolerate this love—it can only be a dream, never again reality. Turning to her filled with bitterness he cries: "Faithless woman. . . ." Interrupting her imploring pleading he tells her that her image has vanished from his heart and from his thoughts for ever.

As if collapsing, Manon leans upon the confession bench— her voice is trembling and childlike. Oh yes, she knows that she is bad. She is like a little bird who sits imprisoned longing for freedom. But doesn't he feel how often in the night her soul comes to him and knocking at his window begs for admittance? Oh, can't he forgive her? With his face averted he thrusts out a "No." . . . She sinks to the ground and embraces his knees in passionate pleading. She will die, she will pass away, if he doesn't forgive her, if he doesn't love her as he did before. Clinging to him, she whispers with feverish passion of the ecstasy which they have known together. . . . She weaves her net about him, seeking his eyes, awakening his memory. . . . Isn't it her hand which he has loved? Isn't it her voice which once intoxicated him? Her eyes which even through tears shimmered so brightly and beautifully—isn't she the same as before—isn't she Manon? . . .

Des Grieux flies across the room but she follows him, places herself in his way, embracing him, forcing him to look at her. Des Grieux struggles superhumanly against this seduction which shakes him to the depths of his being. In vain he turns to God, in vain he pleads with Manon to leave him, to understand that it is sacrilegious for her to touch him who is dedicated to God. Yet half unconsciously he already stammeringly repeats her words—and as she sinks again at his feet in a gesture of complete surrender, he succumbs: he no longer knows what he is doing. Out of the torment of his heart he calls to her: "No, I will fight against myself no longer. . . ." Manon utters a wild cry of triumph—and he draws her into his arms. Even if the wrath of heaven should destroy him, here in this heart which beats against his own in feverish passion—lies his life—in these eyes which sear him—his fate. . . . "O come, Manon, I love you. . . ." They rush away, clinging ecstatically to each other. . . . This scene is incredibly effective and quite carries one away. It is the climax of the opera.

The next scene is in a gambling-room of the Hôtel Transylvanie in Paris. It is by no means an elegant group which has gathered here: mostly professional gamblers who are not bothered by the fact that the game is illegal and they may be arrested. Lescaut is among the gamblers. He has followed Manon—Manon and Des Grieux. Some time has elapsed; Manon has spent a second period of passionate bliss with Des Grieux—but her extravagance has made his money flow away like sand into the sea.

Manon has persuaded Des Grieux to try his luck at gambling and he has given in to her. He is so weak where Manon's wishes are concerned. She always wants something new—extravagant gowns and anything which she sees, without ever asking whether he can afford it. So he must try to win some money through gambling.

Manon is surrounded by her friends and adorers as she enters the gambling-room on Des Grieux's arm. The atmosphere here doesn't disturb her at all. She finds it exciting—adventures hover about her, danger and rolling gold. That is her life, her joy!

But she sees with distress that Des Grieux stands aside—his face troubled. He seems to abhor the gambling-room. Guillot, who is sitting at the same table as Lescaut, watches Manon with hatred. There is the ravishing woman who has escaped him, whom he would still like to possess but who has always treated him so disgracefully and made him seem so ridiculous that it would be sweet to take his revenge. . . . Revenge on her and the handsome young man who is again her lover. Guillot plays on, his teeth tightly clenched—and Manon, without noticing him, approaches Des Grieux. "Am I still the mistress of your heart?"

she asks coquettishly. Des Grieux answers with a violent outburst of passion. Yes, she is—to-day and always. . . . He loves
her and he hates her, but he belongs to her. He now sees her
clearly, just as she is with all her faults. . . . "Thrice womanly
heart," he calls her—"with insatiable desire for pleasures and
money—yes, a crazy spendthrift . . . but I can't help loving
you. . . ."

Manon makes the most of this moment when he is completely
under her spell, for very often he hasn't found her extravagance
"charming": he has reproached her violently, they have quar-
relled, he has threatened her—but to-day she holds him fast in
her hands. She feels it. Clinging to him, she promises to love
him still more—oh, beyond all measure, if he would dare to
gamble, if he would win gold with which to buy her gowns,
furs, brocades and silks. . . .

"I have given you everything," Des Grieux says sadly. "And
what will you give me if I agree, obeying your madness?"

"My life, my whole being, my eternal love," Manon swears.

A short trio of mounting grandeur terminates this game of
question and answer. Yes, he will do as she wants. He will give
her the last thing he is able to give: his honor.

While he goes to the gambling-table at which Guillot
challenges him to a game, Manon looks about the room with a
dazzled and intoxicated expression. Oh, up to now she has been
happy in spending alone—but this is more fun: this game, this
foolhardy, daring game for money! While her friends cluster
about her she sings of the joys of the present moment. Who
knows if to-morrow will still see her alive. To-day is to-day—
let us enjoy it. . . .

Des Grieux wins with the disconcerting luck of the beginner.
Money piles up before him, and Manon rejoicing in all this
wealth throws her arms about him and whispers to him: "How
I love you. . . ."

With increasing scorn Guillot watches the apparent harmony
of the two lovers. He rises pale with fury, ends the game and
accuses Des Grieux of having cheated. Des Grieux is beside
himself and is on the point of striking Guillot. The latter leaves
the room hurling a threat at Des Grieux and Manon. All feel the
danger of the situation: if Guillot should make a formal accusation of cheating, he—"the stainless one"—would be believed
rather than Des Grieux, who had fled from the cloister and who

has established a bad reputation through his life with the frivolous Manon. But Des Grieux refuses to escape. He has done nothing to warrant punishment, he has just had good luck in gambling. He will stay and let the matter take care of itself.

Suddenly there is a violent knocking at the door. Most of the gamblers escape over the roofs—but among the few remaining are Manon and Des Grieux who resolutely rejects any thought of flight.

Police enter the room led by Guillot. With a scornful glance at Manon he says with cold politeness: "I infinitely regret this, madame, but I told you that I would take my revenge. I have revenged myself and hope that you will be able to console yourself."

Des Grieux, awakening from his somber brooding, springs at Guillot. But Des Grieux's father steps between them—Guillot has fetched him at the same time as the police. It is less important to him to ruin Des Grieux than to ruin Manon. He knows very well that it is she who has enchained the young man—as Guillot has longed, in vain, to be enchained. She shall be punished, she shall be ruined because she has not been willing to become his. He looks at her with deep satisfaction and with all the hatred into which his passion for her has been transformed.

The old Des Grieux turns with kindly austerity to his son. His first words are: "Yes, I have come to rescue you from the disgrace which is increasing for you daily."

Manon stands very erect and listens in flaming rebellion. A disgrace, to live with her! A disgrace to be the lover of Manon Lescaut! But her head is slowly lowered: she realizes that she has now lost Des Grieux irrevocably. There can never again be any return—any return for her from the misery into which Guillot has plunged her in this moment. For she knows what awaits her: imprisonment, exile, poverty and misery—and therefore death. . . . For she could never live in misery.

The old Des Grieux, stepping to his son, whispers hastily to him: "You will be freed later. . . ." But Des Grieux does not ask about his own liberation. "And she, Manon?" he asks tremblingly.

His father has no mercy for the woman who has brought all this misfortune upon his son. "She will be taken where she belongs." Amidst despairing pleas for mercy, which no one heeds, Manon is led away.

The last scene pictures a deserted country road which leads to Le Havre. Manon has been convicted of immoral behavior and is about to be deported along with other degraded women. Lescaut has tried in vain to bring about Manon's release. But without influential help this is impossible and there has been no one willing to help Manon, who has been universally condemned for her heartless extravagance and the frivolity with which she has brought ruin to an honorable man like Des Grieux. Through a bribe Lescaut has at last persuaded a guard to permit Manon a moment of freedom that she may speak once more with Des Grieux.

With despair her lover awaits her. His hope has risen again, since it was possible for Lescaut to arrange this last meeting. In spite of Lescaut's warning he cherishes the hope that he will be able to save Manon and take her with him.

With dragging steps Manon comes over the dusty hill—her dress is ragged and torn, she looks deathly ill, her beauty is destroyed, her health ruined. . . . The time which she has spent in prison amidst frightful surroundings, amongst criminal women, has broken her spiritually and physically. She has reached the end of her strength, the end of her life. . . .

She moves forward reeling, half unconscious. She has been told to go this way—so she goes on without any expectation. She moves like an animal going to its slaughter in dumb torture, knowing nothing of what is taking place. Slowly she raises her tired eyes—and there before her stands Des Grieux! With a smothered cry she falls into his arms. Deeply shocked, Des Grieux looks into the ravaged face which had been once so radiant and his stammered: "Manon, O Manon . . ." is choked with tears. Leading her gently and lovingly to the foreground he raises her head to kiss her, but seeing that her eyes are flooded with tears, he asks tenderly: "You are weeping?" Manon is changed. It is not only outwardly—she is not only sick and miserable. She has come to realize all of which she has been guilty. During the long period of her imprisonment she has brooded and succumbed to melancholy introspection. Her whole life has been spread before her like an open book. And this has not been gay reading. Everywhere she has seen guilt—

everywhere sin, everywhere heartless and cruel egotism. . . . She is bowed down by the weight of her guilt. For the first time Des Grieux hears her accuse herself: "Yes, I weep over myself for disgrace and over you for grief. . . ."

Des Grieux believes her. He believes that they will again find happiness—he begs her to forget the past and to think only of the good which lies before them. But she turns away filled with bitterness and says: "Why should I deceive myself?" Des Grieux draws her gently down upon a mound of sand. A miserable resting-place—hard and unaccustomed for one used to luxury, but she leans against him and listens to his voice, listens to his promises of a better time to come.

His kindness overwhelms her and she lies in his arms, weak and pale. Into his ear she stammers burning self-accusations. She wants nothing more of life than his forgiveness. . . . That she should have caused him even one day of trouble would have been sin enough. But that she has ruined his whole life—can he ever forgive that? Beneath tears such as she has never wept before she struggles for his forgiveness. Embracing his knees she lies sobbing at his feet. Des Grieux is moved to the depths of his being. Raising her tenderly he says to her: "What should I forgive? If only your heart is again mine!"

Manon experiences a last deceptive happiness. At these words she straightens up, plunges into his arms and in an outburst of joy sings with him the lovely duet: "O I feel a pure flame." Des Grieux finds the right words: "Heaven itself has forgiven—and I love you." Trembling, Manon lies upon his breast and whispers in sudden weakness: "O, now I can die. . . ." Die? Des Grieux speaks of life and happiness. Her fainting soul is strengthened by his faith, and staggering across the stage she sinks slowly and as if with blissful thoughts upon a rock by the wayside. While the orchestra with the most delicate *pianissimo* plays the theme which has accompanied her through her exciting life—the same theme with which she has clung to him, tearing him away from the cloister—she says softly and half unconsciously to herself: "Yes, I can still be happy. . . ." Her thoughts wander back to the past. She sees again before her the little hotel where she first met Des Grieux, the coach in which they escaped, the dark country road which witnessed their first kisses. . . . She sees the letter which he wrote to his father, the little table from which she left, to dare her foolish flight

into the treacherous world, the solemn abbé's role in St. Sulpice. . . . Softly and unnoticeably her voice floats back into
song: "O I remember well . . ." But Des Grieux tears her away
from her dreams. Time is pressing. He still believes that he
can take her away, still believes in the realization of his hopes.
But she collapses, incapable of going any farther. . . . A shadow
falls across her eyes, wiping out everything before her. She feels
that it is the shadow of death. Desperately and feverishly Des
Grieux tries to hold fast the life which is ebbing away. There
is no time to lose. Already night is approaching, already the first
star shines above them. Manon looks up as if dreaming and
weakly stretches out her hand in yearning to the star: "O lovely
diamond . . ." And with a half-sad smile: "You see I am still
vain . . ." Des Grieux is very worried that they should be wasting
so much time here. "Someone is coming, Manon, let us go . . ."
is an urgent plea. But she knows nothing of the present now—
she kisses him, her tears welling anew . . . kisses him in a last
farewell.

Now it is Des Grieux who implores and pleads. With the
same music to which he has wrung his hands in the cloister he
tries to shake her back to consciousness, to call her fading soul
back to him. In vain. Manon, who with her last strength has
raised herself, now falls back into his arms, and with her last
breath sings of love and hope, of past happiness and renewed
bliss. . . .

Manon dies. . . . Sinking to the ground she breathes out her
life, stammering almost inaudibly what she had once said to him
when she was still half a child at the hotel in Amiens: "And that
is the story of Manon—of Manon Lescaut . . ." Des Grieux,
sobbing, throws himself over Manon's body from which her soul
has fled.

The curtain falls.

Chapter IX

MARGUERITE—"FAUST"

IN VIENNA WE of course gave the French operas in German, as it was customary throughout Germany and Austria to give opera in the German language. But how much is lost when a language is used other than that for which the music was written! Well as I understand the desire in America and Britain to make opera more popular by giving it in English, my artistic feeling is nevertheless disturbed by this violation. The elegance of the French, for example, can never be conveyed in a translation into the much more cumbersome English or German. Our Viennese performances of their operas must have sounded anything but smooth-flowing to the ears of the French.

With *Faust* it is different. Of course, so far as the music is concerned it is typically French—but the text is a translation from the original German of Goethe's *Faust* which is a part of the life of every German. *Faust* is almost like the Bible to a born German—from earliest childhood he is accustomed to quotations from it. No book was so important to me in my youth as *Faust*.

It seemed like sacrilege to hear *Faust* translated into French. In the opera this immortal tragedy of the struggle for knowledge is changed into a rather commonplace love story—and the beginning of the original *Faust*—the desperate search of Doctor Faust for truth and the meaning of life—becomes only a graceful introduction to this love affair. But one must try to unite the French charm with the essence of Goethe, to be as true to him as possible within the frame of the French music. This is certainly difficult but not impossible.

The personality of Margarete—Marguerite—is always associated for me with that of the Salzburg Margarete: the actress Paula Wessely. Her innate simplicity, her quality of the old German burgher maiden, her poetic charm devoid of sentimentality, made her unforgettable. She was a real child of the people. Even outwardly her round face, which was not actually beautiful, became so through its inner animation; her natural gestures, her way of speaking poetry as if it were everyday prose, made her ideal for this rôle.

To carry this quality of naturalness over into the operatic rôle is the task which confronts the portrayer of Marguerite. The whole personality of Marguerite must be indicated in her first entrance in the second scene of the first act. She comes out of the church and crosses the scene absorbed in her devout thoughts. Faust places himself across her way, and asks if he may accompany her home. You must consider clearly just what this meant in those days. There was a great difference between the classes of nobles and burghers. There was no bridge between them, as the noblemen had never considered the burghers of equal position. For a young nobleman to address a simple child of the people meant an unheard of deviation from established custom. Faust addresses her as "Fräulein"—a title which is not fitting for one in her position. Marguerite has every reason to be offended by the unconventional behavior of this young man. But she clothes her refusal in a friendly tone. She has wit and understanding. She is not at all shy and helpless. Usually the first phrase which she sings is made too sentimental—or too coquettish. *Both are absolutely wrong.*

Marguerite has only had a hasty look at the stranger but he attracts her. Quite against her will she finds him interesting and would like to know who he is. She thinks him rather impudent to address her as "Fräulein, my beautiful Fräulein"— but is nevertheless flattered by it. So she listens to him, and holding herself very erectly says quietly with lowered eyes: "No, no, sir. I am neither a Fräulein nor beautiful, and can go home alone." With her last word she looks up and meets the eyes of the stranger. Now for the first time she is overcome by shyness, and with a gesture of wanting to run away, turns and moves quickly on.

When she appears in the second act she comes slowly, lost in thought. One must realize that she is just returning from church and has had the strange experience of being approached by an unknown nobleman. Really she should be cross, but he looked so handsome that he attracted her very much. A dreamy smile plays about her lips, and stepping to the foreground she says softly to herself: "I would give something to know who that gentleman was to-day . . ." This should be sung without any sentimentality, as if she were saying it to herself—her eyes are shining as she looks into the distance, as if seeing the image of the unknown youth before her.

Trying to banish these thoughts she goes to the spinning-wheel. She puts it in order, arranges the thread and begins to sing to herself. This song of the "King of Thule" must at first be sung without any expression, so that she gives the impression of singing unconsciously. Her thoughts are not in the least on this song, they are still with the stranger and can't escape from him. Leaning backward a little, she says with a smile: "He has a noble bearing, I felt that immediately." With a sigh she turns back to the spinning-wheel. How foolish she is to think about him! How could she have anything to do with such a distinguished gentleman? She will forget about him quickly, very quickly. . . .

But between the verses of her song her thoughts return to him, and she remembers how hotly her blood mounted to her cheeks when she felt his eyes upon her. . . .

She sings the end of the song with real expression. The beauty of the verses must have touched her, so that she finishes the song with genuine feeling.

But then her thoughts return to the nobleman . . . "Only great noblemen go about so proudly and so benevolently . . ." Yes, he was condescending and friendly—it was almost as though he were of her own station; he was so kind and intimate—and yet he spoke with a certain distance. . . . He was definitely a nobleman and not just an ordinary person—she realized that immediately.

Suddenly brushing away her thoughts she puts the spinning-wheel aside and goes across the garden path to her parents' home, where she now lives alone. Her mother is dead, her brother—a soldier—away on the field of battle. (Here the opera differs from the drama of Goethe: in the drama the mother lives and is later put into a deep sleep through a sleeping-powder which Faust has given Margarete for this purpose, so that she can receive her lover in her room undisturbed. In the opera this rather brutal incident is simplified: it isn't necessary for Marguerite to resort to any such unsympathetic means, for her mother simply is no longer living.)

Marguerite feels a great longing for her distant brother—perhaps for the first time she is aware of the danger, as a young girl, of living so completely alone. . . . There is, to be sure, Siebel, her boyish friend, who has promised her brother Valentine as he was leaving that he would watch over Marguerite. There is her friendly neighbor, Marthe Schwertlein, who while she has the best of intentions doesn't have quite the right influence over the lonely child in her flower garden. Marguerite has a dull feeling that no one would have dared to address her so boldly, with so little consideration for customary convention if her brother were beside her as guardian and protector.

Upon her threshold she finds a wreath of flowers. From Siebel—she often receives flowers from him and knows that she is his first romantic and reverent love. It is a love which she can only return with a sisterly feeling. But the flowers over which she has rejoiced fall from her hand, as leaning against the door she discovers a richly ornamented little box. How has it gotten there? She has a strange feeling of apprehension, and hesitates before opening it. But it isn't a sin, is it, just to look into it? Opening it she gives a cry of delight: it is filled to the brim with costly jewels which sparkle in the sunlight and glow with a strange and seductive magic.

It is the magic of hell which radiates from them. Mephistopheles, the devil who has assumed a human form, has attached himself to Faust in order to win his soul and has touched the jewels with his foul magic. For Marguerite they are only bright stones—she has no idea of their value, but she rejoices in their beauty and splendor like a playful child.

At the beginning of the well-known "Jewel Song" there is the danger of being too coquettish. It seems to me rather unnecessary to mention this—the personality of the innocent Marguerite is so clearly indicated that I can't imagine any one could play this coquettishly and with conscious vanity, but I have seen such fundamentally false conceptions that I want at least to mention it. Marguerite sings this whole aria with childlike joy in the glittering playthings which is all the jewels are for her. Certainly this aria is as remote from Goethe as the whole personality of Faust in the opera is from the Faust of his drama. However, the actress must find a way to preserve the character of the Marguerite which Goethe created: the innocent child who plays with the bright colored stones.

In placing the heavy chain about her neck a sudden apprehension sweeps over her: it is as if the hand of evil has touched her, threatening and oppressing her. She gasps in sudden fear,

but her glance falls upon the mirror which she—how con-
veniently!—has found in the box, and her sigh again changes
into an expression of joy.

During the postlude of the aria she kneels again before the
box, gazing with astonishment upon the wealth of jewels.

Her neighbor Marthe now comes to her—as she so often does
—to chat with her. She immediately sees the wonderful jewels
and when Marguerite tells her that she has found them on her
doorstep, she declares that, of course, they belong to Marguerite.
The young girl shakes her head laughingly. Not for a moment
does she think that the jewels could be intended for her or that
she could ever keep them. She only half listens to Marthe's
chatter. The old woman has again many complaints about her
husband who has been missing for some time. Oh, he was never
so gallant—he never gave her expensive presents like these
marvellous jewels. Marguerite scarcely pays any attention to
her. She is accustomed to Marthe's complaints and has only an
indulgent smile for this weakness.

Faust and Mephistopheles enter the garden—but Marguerite
does not notice them. She is much too occupied with the
jewellery, too overcome with delight to pay attention to the
visitors. Marthe has perhaps often been called away by her
numerous friends, so Marguerite only turns around when Marthe
gives a startled cry on hearing the amazing news that her
husband is dead.

A somberly mounting *tremolo* from the orchestra accompanies
this further meeting between Faust and Marguerite. It is not
joy which she feels when she sees the handsome stranger again—
here in her garden—the stranger who has absorbed too much of
her thought. He stands in the gateway to her garden, erect and
silent; his eyes are humble yet they look at her longingly, and
evading them with difficulty Marguerite turns away, pressing
her hand to her throbbing heart. Dark and fateful clouds are
forming around her; she has a deep sense of foreboding from
which she cannot escape.

The little verbal comedy between Mephistopheles and Marthe
slips by her unnoticed—she does not hear them: she is oblivious
of the others and only conscious of the presence of Faust.

He offers her his arm but she shyly draws away from him, and
in a short quartet her voice floats over the others like a trembling sigh. Marguerite should sing no vocalizes in the delicately

flowing and sustained phrases—"Pray keep me no longer"—she should sing with great warmth and inner animation and give to the coloratura line a breathy quality of trembling expression. The fear within her heart speaks through this music—it conveys her shyness, her surrender in spite of her own determination. The scene is left to Marthe and Mephistopheles, as Faust leaves with Marguerite, hesitant and uncertain, at his side.

When they return she seems to have overcome her first shyness. Faust has been kind and friendly to her. He has seemed like an old friend—perhaps there was no reason for all her anxiety? He is so sweet to her—she feels confidence in him and no longer sees why she should have been afraid. She had taken off the jewels when he came into the garden and he did not stop her. She is now quite her old self again—the good, innocent child, Marguerite. . . . He has asked so much about her life here: he wants to know about all that concerns her, and she tells him everything gladly.

Yes, she is quite alone . . . her mother is dead, her brother in the Army. Her little sister whom she had loved so dearly has died. With great feeling and an unconscious charm she tells of the child whose death was such a terrible loss to her.

But when Faust tells her that the child must have looked like an angel if it resembled her, she is seized with fear. He is laughing at her—this strange nobleman, who speaks to her with such friendliness. Perhaps he thinks that she is a stupid child and is making fun of her?

At his words: "I love you . . ." she shyly runs away. He quickly follows her into the garden.

During the humorous little scene between Mephistopheles and Marthe, Marguerite is seen running across the stage pursued by Faust. I must confess that I have always detested this scene, a rather silly nuance which seems traditional everywhere, strangely enough. . . .

When they both reappear upon the stage Marguerite seems very much disturbed. She moves quickly, with flying steps, she attempts to escape from Faust. She whispers hastily: "It is already late, farewell," and tries to run up the steps to her door, but Faust tenderly restrains her. He draws her into the garden which is flooded with moonlight, and her childish game of questioning the flowers: "He loves me, he loves me not" receives the glowing answer: "He loves you . . ."

In the soft moonlight, with his arm about her, Marguerite leans against Faust in an oblivious surrender. She listens to his words of love, replies to his oaths with similar oaths, whispers the eternal but ever-new longing for death of one in love. . . . His kisses become more ardent, more demanding. And she awakens to a new reality, of which she had never even dreamed.

Her imploring plea for consideration touches Faust deeply. The purity inherent in Marguerite's words awakens his sense of chivalry. Controlling his desire he bows before her, and lets her approach her home alone. He only craves one word, one last word of love. . . . Marguerite, melted by his look of longing, at once fearful and blissful, would like to rush back into his arms. But instead she calls a hasty farewell and hurries away. . . .

Faust would now have left the garden, would have gone away in order to avoid temptation, but Mephistopheles—the embodiment of evil—whispers to him to remain. So, as if under a spell, Faust stays and sees Marguerite throw open her window. He hears the words of love with which she addresses the stars above —the wonderful confession: I love him. With tender desire she spreads out her arms to the beloved, whom she believes far away, and with a suppressed cry of delight he rushes to her, drawing her to him with a passionate kiss to which she surrenders helplessly.

The curtain slowly falls.

I remember a performance in Vienna in which Chaliapin sang Mephistopheles. He followed Faust to the window with a cat-like leap, and during our embrace stood leaning over us, his long body pressed against the wall beside the window like a great spindling spider. A shudder of horror ran through me as I saw this tall, strangely grotesque figure above me, his long hands stretched out towards me like greedy tentacles, and the grey veil of his fantastic costume spreading out like a shroud of mist. What a master of the theatre he was—and what incredibly thrilling effects he produced!

In Vienna the next scene was cut and I do not know whether it is given in America. It is neither important nor especially lovely. The conversation between Siebel and Marguerite, the song at the spinning-wheel, seems to retard rather than illuminate the action.

The next scene is laid in the church. Marguerite approaches with heavy dragging steps—her lover has deserted her and she knows that she is pregnant. Bowed down by her feeling of guilt she moves among the people who seek to avoid her. Hesitantly she starts to kneel, but some women beside her, shocked by Marguerite's immorality, get up with the usual indignation of the narrow-minded. Marguerite moves a few steps farther and sinks slowly upon her knees before the image of the Mother of God.

This image of the Holy Virgin hangs upon a column, within which Mephistopheles is concealed. Often one sees him, and always, when he begins to speak, his face is illuminated. Personally I don't like this over-obviousness. It seems to me much better if one only hears the voice sounding its sinister threats from above Marguerite's head but does not actually see the face of Mephistopheles. Here, as so often, what might seem *less* is actually *more*.

Mephistopheles forbids her to pray, demons call her name. . . . Deathly fear consumes Marguerite; with horror she cries: "Is this already the Day of Judgment?" The voice of Mephistopheles is now quieter; he speaks to her in the voice of reminiscence, and she listens to his words leaning her head against the pillar, her eyes closed. Mephistopheles speaks of her childhood, her innocence, the purity of her every thought and act. The voice swells threateningly—sombrely the terrifying present breaks in upon the image of the past . . . sin, guilt, abandonment, imminent destruction are before her. Despised by the world, forsaken by her lover, her mother dead, her brother away in the field, she is left alone and unprotected, abandoned to a cruel fate. Feverishly Marguerite tries to pray—her pleading, filled with fear, mingles with the solemn chorus of the people, but the evil voices will not let her pray. . . . She tries to rise, staggering; she plunges to her knees, ringing her hands in fervent prayer; her voice soars over the chorus in a cry of despair. But God does not seem to hear her. It is only the voice of the Devil which answers her, damning her to everlasting perdition. Turning, senseless with fear and despair, Marguerite looks into the frightful eyes of Mephistopheles, whose figure has suddenly become visible. With a cry she sinks to the ground.

The action of the following scene is continuous with this one. The soldiers have returned home. While Marguerite has been in the church her brother Valentine has learned of her tragic fate. His faith in Marguerite's unassailable purity is destroyed, his pride as her brother too deeply wounded for him to be able to forgive her. In a duel Faust has wounded him fatally—and Marguerite, coming from the church, hurries on to the scene at the moment when her brother lies dying upon the ground. Here, whoever portrays Marguerite must act very realistically. She has only one or two phrases to sing, but nevertheless she must remain the center of the action. Her plea for his forgiveness is without words but she must not be passive in her participation. Valentine sees her as an immoral person, one who in the future will give herself to whoever may cross her path; he sees her demoralized and on the brink of ruin.

Marguerite is so shattered by his harsh and cruel words that she can say nothing, but the crowd pleads for her. The same people who before have despised and forsaken her now shudder before Valentine's hardness, and implore him to be merciful to his sister. But Valentine's last word is a curse: "Though God may forgive you—be cursed upon the earth . . ."

Valentine dies. The shock of all this has been too great for Marguerite. Her mind begins to be confused—she has no idea what the people around her mean, she stares blankly into the void which stretches before her. . . . At last she becomes aware of Valentine's body at her feet—and sobbing, collapses over him.

In the last act she lies upon straw in a prison cell. In her madness she has killed the child who was born to her. She has been condemned and will be put to death the following morning. Faust comes to save her. He approaches, led by Mephistopheles, who has told him that he himself with human hand must open the cell. Faust stands before Marguerite deeply shaken. His voice arouses her from sleep—swaying, she rises and plunges into his arms. But her joy in seeing him, her delight in being near him are madness. She does not hear his pleading, she does not realize his presence. Her thoughts sweep back to the day on which she first met him—and she re-enacts this scene as if it were the lovely present. . . . She is both Faust and Marguerite, she pleads and smiles, with trembling words she paints the scene of their first meeting before the church. Faust's pleading becomes more pressing, but she leans against him begging him to remain.

Mephistopheles beats impatiently upon the door warning them

to come. With gruesome realization Marguerite sees Mephistopheles as he is: the *spirit of evil*. She stands there very erect,
with her hands extended towards the evil one in repudiation, and
nothing can induce her to follow him—and with him Faust.
Beyond—freedom awaits her; beyond—the way lies open which
will reunite her with Faust, but she remains here, falling upon
her knees in fervent prayer, deaf to all pleading, deaf to all
desperate entreaty.

Faust, determined to save her, tries to tear her away from her
prayers; his manner is violent, his voice rough—he will force
her to follow him. . . . But Marguerite, with the superhuman
strength of one insane, frees herself of him, and with the cry:
"Away, away! I shudder before you . . ." falls dead.

In an apotheosis one sees Marguerite, redeemed and purified,
floating towards heaven, amidst a group of angels. This last
scene endangers the effect of the opera: the scene is always
rather falsely sentimental, and I much prefer having the transfiguration conveyed by the dawn, which, breaking through the
little window in the cell, casts its rays upon the body of
Marguerite.

Everything which is made too definite is inartistic in its effect.
The imagination must be given opportunity for play, one must
be allowed to conceive what will not seem sufficiently subtle in
an exact reproduction. For that reason I come more and more to
the opinion that *a stage scene should be as little realistic as
possible*. Opera, which to begin with is unnatural—for isn't
it unnatural that all speech should be sung?—should never try
to reproduce reality. All scenes set amidst nature should be
stylized. Isn't a painting more convincing and effective when it
conveys the mood, the atmosphere through great lines than when
it seeks to reproduce nature with photographic exactness? We
had a performance of *Ariadne auf Naxos* in Salzburg many years
ago with settings by the stage designer—Oscar Strnad. I
remember that through a lack of understanding I found the
grotesque stylized designs of the Baroque sets horrible. To-day
I realize what he intended and regret that I cannot again see the
same setting and have the opportunity to appreciate it with
understanding.

Of course, it is very difficult to make the splendor and magnificence of the Rococo convincing in a stylized form. The

impression of great costliness must always be retained, so that the stylized setting does not give the impression of being cheapened. The material should be luxurious, the lines simplified, indicated, drawn in a sketchy way. The costumes should be worked out in the same manner: costly brocades cannot be avoided, the colors should melt into one another as in musical harmony—but with details omitted.

Chapter X

GLIMPSES OF LATIN OPERAS

IT IS OFTEN difficult to retain the mood of the performance when something funny happens on the stage. I remember a performance of *Lohengrin* in which one of the supers in removing his helmet during the prayer removed his wig with it. When the prayer ended and I stepped back into the row of ladies-in-waiting, I should have followed the struggle between Lohengrin and Telramund with great intensity, but I noticed the despairing efforts of this poor man in trying to replace his straw blond wig on his dishevelled black hair without attracting attention. . . . I really suffered with him. Of course, he had the feeling that the eyes of the whole audience were riveted on him. One saw unmistakably the beads of sweat on his forehead as with furtive side glances he tried again and again to raise the hand from which swung the long-haired wig, only to let it fall again. Finally he gave up: he stuffed the wig into his helmet and slapped it onto his head; but this didn't exactly save the situation, for the helmet was now much too small and swayed threateningly over his dishevelled hair . . . I didn't know where to look and tried to think of all that was sad in order not to lose my composure completely.

At a stage rehearsal one is really like a child in school, and I believe this feeling of continuing to be, so to speak, under the rod of a cross teacher, helps to keep singers young. There is the conductor, of whom one is generally a little afraid (at least I was) and the stage director who often takes it as a personal affront if the singer has her own ideas which may perhaps conflict with his. There is the discipline of rehearsals and at the same time the ever-alert and roguish humor of the happy-go-lucky artist. Every conductor is annoyed if concentrated attention doesn't prevail in each rehearsal, but one just can't work and be ecstatic all the time . . . one has a sense of humor, and funny little things are always happening which cause suppressed laughter, just as in one's school days. This reached its peak when Leo Slezak was on the stage. One could write books about his humor, his ever-ready play on words and his boyish delight in them, but it was not always pleasant to be right on the stage when he made one of his irresistible jokes. The last act of *Meistersinger*, on the festival meadow, was often an absolute torture. He would stand with his back to the audience and make us laugh so much that I often thought the curtain would have to fall and that we would all be heavily fined for our lack of seriousness. But no one could ever be angry with him. He was the typical "bad boy" from head to toe, and probably remained so until his Elsa—his wife whom he adored above everything else—died. Shortly before his death I had a very touching letter from him. A deep loneliness spoke from every line, a loneliness which even the great love of his daughter who lived with him could not make him forget, for without his Elsa life seemed over for him. He had only one desire: to see his son Walter again, and his grandchildren. He wrote very touchingly of his eagerness to come to America and of how he would visit me in Santa Barbara and how we would lose ourselves in our memories. "We will cry a little and laugh a lot," he wrote. But we could no longer cry and laugh together, for he died. His loss moved me very deeply. He was a wonderful and sincere artist, an incomparably good colleague and a fundamentally kind human being.

Perhaps it may seem strange that I appear to have no associations connected with the Metropolitan Opera. That is true. I came rather late to the Metropolitan—surprisingly late. Although I was well known throughout the international world the Metropolitan seemed to take no interest in me. For many years this disappointed me very much and I had a burning desire for an engagement with this renowned opera house. Americans had heard me in Salzburg, Vienna, Paris, London—but never in New York. Yet when I was finally engaged there it came as a sort of "anticlimax". I never really felt at home on this longed-for stage, and always felt more as a guest than a member of it. The great singers to whom I was bound by many colorful and wonderful memories had all been my friends through many appearances together in Europe and in every possible festival throughout the world. And I, who in Vienna was accustomed to consider the ensemble effect of the opera as the highest goal from the strictly artistic standpoint, was surprised and disappointed by the production of many of the operas in the repertory. I had pictured the Metropolitan as something breathtaking, had dreamed of it as an unattainable ideal. But the "box office" plays too great a rôle here. Opera must be subsidized in order to be so managed that it may serve Art, and Art alone. Why shouldn't this be possible? It was in Europe, why not in America? In America I have scarcely sung any but German operas, and for some time was announced in concerts as a "Wagnerian" singer—a designation which I hate, as I hate every limitation and restriction. I sang Tosca a few times here, but did not have much success with it. I never really made this rôle my own. Perhaps because its very superficial theatricalism is entirely foreign to my being. It always seemed to me "too much". One must have another kind of temperament to do justice to it—a flaring and nervous temperament which is capable of throwing things around, stamping the feet and tearing the hair, perhaps. . . . That I don't have at all. My own lack of discipline, which has now almost disappeared but in my youth was really catastrophic, expressed itself quite differently. Little things never irritated me very much, and I never took out a bad mood on my good old helper in the Vienna opera house—Adelheid— as many others did. But when someone tried to make me do something I didn't want to do or expected subordination from me, then I became obstinate as Shakespeare's Katherine.

So with Tosca—it must have been this lack of flashing temperament which made me always feel foreign to the rôle. Certainly it was not the Italian music itself. I have sung and loved singing many Italian rôles, and Puccini, who heard me several times in Vienna, seemed quite satisfied with me. I remember especially a performance of Bohème which he attended, and his kind words at the end of the performance.

I always enjoyed singing Mimi very much, and it would give me great pleasure to consider this rôle more in detail if it did not develop so obviously. But the limits of this book prevent my considering all the rôles of my repertory. All the rôles: good heavens—it would take me ten volumes to go into them all, so diverse and varied was my repertoire! Because of this limitation in space I have naturally selected the rôles which are most interesting psychologically in order to analyse them. Mimi is not one of these, and so I can only touch upon it fleetingly— although this is no indication that I haven't sung it with great joy.

In appearance I was, of course, far from the ideal Mimi—I always looked very healthy, not just the type to represent one who is fading away from the ravages of tuberculosis. But recently I came across some old pictures taken at this time, and was surprised to see how much I had conveyed the outward impression through make-up—and still more through my bearing.

It is important that Mimi should give the impression of a certain frail delicacy. I don't mean that she should convey a painfully clinical picture of her illness through continuous coughing, but she should give the impression of a kind of fragility which would make one want to help and protect her. She must seem to be surrounded by poetry—the somewhat morbid poetry of one who is fatally ill. As she stands in the doorway at her first entrance she must be immediately a picture of delicate helplessness. She should not stand very erect but should lean against the door-frame as if needing its support.

Mimi has often watched the young poet Rodolfo from her little room. She is warm-blooded and craves love. A lonely Parisian *grisette* who takes from life whatever it may offer— feeling perhaps unconsciously that life will be short and one must make the most of it while one is still able to do so.

It is no shy young girl who comes by accident to Rodolfo. He attracts her. He belongs to a circle, the delightfully lighthearted Bohème, of which she is a part. So she seizes upon the excuse that her candle has gone out, to make a detour past his room on the way to her own. She stands in the doorway a little embarrassed, smiling in charming confusion. But the first impression which she is forced to give is not the one she would have chosen: her illness is more compelling than her desire to please Rodolfo: climbing the stairs has made her out of breath, and her inner excitement at seeing him, whom she secretly loves, before her, at speaking to him and being near him, has not helped to quiet her fluttering heart. So she falls into his room, exhaustedly gropes her way to his table and faints. . . .

Rodolfo is deeply touched by the fragile beauty of this girl, and what her loveliest smile might not have succeeded in accomplishing immediately, her fainting has achieved: he immediately falls head over heels in love with her. The delightful little comedy of the lost key, the searching on the floor, Rodolfo's quick success in finding it and his clever concealment of it, must all be played with great charm. When Rodolfo tells her who he is, what he does, she listens enchanted. Oh, she knows all this, she has known for a long time that he is a poet, she has known him from afar, has known his friends. But she listens to him with shining eyes as if it were a fairy tale which he is telling. Yes, his soul is one with hers! He lives in his dreams as she does, he builds castles in the air in his poems just as she weaves them with delicate fingers when she embroiders flowers on silk —and forgets that doing this is her profession. Oh no, she does not feel that she is earning her bread when the flowers which bloom so beautifully on the soft silk give her the illusion that they are the flowers of her garden—flowers which bloom in the wonderful park of which she dreams, though she has only seen it from outside, from beyond the iron railings of the well-to-do. She tells Rodolfo of these dreams—and he understands her.

They are young, they are alone—alone in an attic room flooded with moonlight, which is transformed into the most beautiful of palaces when they look at each other, enchanted, rapturous, transported. They fall into each other's arms—and the call of his friends from outside the door, which, as every night, lures Rodolfo to the Café Momus, scarcely disturbs them. . . . Rodolfo would like to stay here alone with this charming girl who has so taken his heart by storm. But Mimi isn't satisfied with love alone, she wants fun and distraction too. So she leans against him, and her whispered "I want to be close to you" is the sweetest of promises; but now she would like to go with Rodolfo and his friends to the Café Momus and plunge into a whirl of amusement, taking part in a life for which she longs passionately —but which is endangered by an insidious illness, which she recognizes but tries to disregard.

The second act is a gay and colorful sketch of bohemian life. Mimi is part of it all—she is youth and laughter and a resonant part of the joyous symphony: fun, enjoyment, love. . . .

In the third act she enters the stage broken by the illness which is consuming her. It has not been only joy which life has offered to Mimi and Rodolfo: both are ardent human beings, both divinely independent. And so their hours of blissful surrender have been mixed with wild conflicts, scenes of senseless jealousy, outbursts of violent distrust. After one such quarrel Rodolfo had left Mimi—and broken in body and soul she has come to their mutual friend Marcello, seeking his advice. Sick and miserable she has dragged herself through the snow to him.

She has told him everything, and her despairing words have often been interrupted by violent and harrowing fits of coughing. She has come to the end of her strength, the end of her patience. . . . Knowing that there can never be any cure for his frantic and tormenting jealousy she sees no escape for herself and Rodolfo. Into this tragic scene of hopeless confession comes Rodolfo—and Mimi hides herself, feeling incapable of seeing him or speaking with him. From her hiding-place she hears the devastating truth: it is not jealousy which makes Rodolfo act as he does: it is worry over Mimi's health. He cannot offer her anything which might cure her desperate illness. He is bitterly poor. For this reason she should separate from him and take another lover who could offer her money and comforts which might help her to recover. Mimi breaks down sobbing. It is not only his willingness to sacrifice himself which bowls her over—it is the horrifying realization that she must really be on the verge of death. Her secret fear has found cruel confirmation: she is ill, deathly ill. This torturing cough is not just a passing infirmity as she has so often persuaded herself—no, she is the victim of a creeping death—and in her cry: "O my life!" she sobbingly clings not only to Rodolfo but to the warm, sweet life which she must soon give up, so soon. . . .

In Rodolfo's arms she tries to understand that it is best for her to follow his advice. And her touching farewell is sung with restrained tears—with the greatest tenderness. Yet her farewell is actually a reunion after their quarrel of that evening, as they now go together to Rodolfo's miserable little room—back to its coldness and poverty. It is too difficult for them to part when the world about them is so dark. It would make their solitude still more harrowing. Only when spring comes again will they separate—only when the world again laughs in all its radiant colors. So they leave arm in arm, vanishing into the darkness of the night, while the lightly falling snow weaves a veil about them.

In the last act Mimi's entrance into the exuberant group of his friends in Rodolfo's room breaks like a somber discord into a gay song. She has come to die. She wants, when she dies, to be near him whom she has loved so deeply. Leaving him could not save her life. Now feeling this pitiful existence ebbing from her she comes home to him, to the only one whom she has ever really loved. . . .

At this point the portrayer of Mimi should be as realistic as possible. She must really give the illusion of dying, no movement should have enough vitality to make her seem healthy or in any way vivid. The only forceful outburst—vocally—"I am born anew. I feel life returning to me here" must be borne by ecstatic delight, from which she falls back in utter weakness.

Their friends now leave the two lovers alone. The last hours of her life are filled with memories of a lovelier time. She remembers Rodolfo as he was the first day she came to him— the whole charming comedy which they had both played: the lost key, the pretended search for it—and the finding of each other's hands. . . . All this lives again for them and casts the last rays of a setting sun over her ending. . . . Surrounded by their friends who have returned, burying her hands in the muff which they have brought her to warm them, she dies, extinguished like a fading light. One must see Mimi die: one must see the muff falling from her hand, see how she stretches her body, how her breast is raised in a last sigh. Her last words, whispered almost soundlessly, words of delight over the warmth of the muff, must be half spoken. It is a toneless singing, bright and empty, as if a child were speaking. . . . The dying words fade away in a faint murmuring.

The aria plays a very important rôle in Italian opera. It often becomes so much the center of interest that some singers seem only to be concerned with this climax and not to bother about the development of the character as a whole. . . . I have sometimes seen singers, without any concern for their fellow artists, turn to the audience and blast out the aria right beside the footlights, as effectively as possible—in this way seeking the greatest applause! I don't need to say that this is inartistic. *The aria is always part of the whole*: it arises from a situation, it gives a surging musical line to the dramatic action. Therefore the singer must forget the public. There only exist the figures of the opera who must be vital and convincing, as convincing as possible within the imaginary realm of opera.

My Italian repertory included a large number of rôles: Madam Butterfly, Madeleine in *Andrea Chénier*, Manan Lescaut by Puccini, and his Sister Angelica. I sang this beautiful and gripping rôle in Vienna at a memorial performance for Puccini after his death. I have even sung Turandot, which climbs vocally to such giddy heights that it amazes me to-day that I could ever have sung it. . . . But I never really enjoyed impersonating this princess with a heart of ice.

Santuzza in *Cavalleria Rusticana* interested me much more, but I never actually undertook it. Perhaps it was the same question as with Tosca: this figure should possess a wild and theatrical temperament—perhaps I should never have done it justice. Here I think again of Maria Jeritza's Santuzza, which made a great impression upon me. Not because Jeritza with her acrobatic dexterity rolled down from the top of the church steps —that I liked less . . . but I remember her entrance. In a flash the whole personality of Santuzza was indicated: the poor, harassed woman, broken in body and soul. Plunged into misery through the unscrupulous Turiddu—her dragging labored movements gave the impression of her being pregnant. I call that very great art: to be able with a few lines to make clear the whole character of a rôle.

Ruth Draper, whom I admire very much, has in her repertory a scene in which she represents an Italian who enters a church, sees a painting of the Madonna and kneels before it. That is the "story"—she does not say a single word, but her wonderfully expressive face speaks in all the languages of the world. As she enters one knows immediately it is an accident which has led her to this church, she has come through it only as a short cut from one street to another. She is pregnant. She is desperately unhappy. She wants to put an end to a life which has become too burdensome for her. She wants to destroy herself and the life which dawns within her. Without really seeing it her troubled glance falls upon the painting of the Madonna. Then slowly this picture of the gentle Mother of God grips her (the picture, of course, is not really there—it exists only in the mind of the actress, but she makes the audience see it as clearly as she sees it). She slowly turns more directly towards the picture as if guided by a supernatural force. Her face is transfigured by her emotion—she drinks in the beauty of the painting, she sees the Holy Mother—she sees the child Jesus in her arms. Such an infant she bears within her and nourishes with her own life—and yet she wants to kill it. One feels that the eyes of the Madonna look down upon her pleadingly; one feels how she changes, how she softens, finding her way back to life. Slowly

TURANDOT (Puccini)

SUOR ANGELICA (Puccin

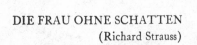

DIE FRAU OHNE SCHATTEN
(Richard Strauss)

she falls upon her knees, her eyes are veiled by tears, and a fervent and heartfelt promise rises to this mother of all mothers: yes, I will live—I will live for the sake of the child. . . .

I sat there breathless when I saw this the first time. I had only one fear: if only she would not say a word—would not shatter this reverence with a sound! . . . But no: there was only the expression of this blessed face. I was infinitely grateful for this experience.

Above everything else Santuzza must be a woman of the people. There must be something primitive and unbridled in the expression of her grief. The Sicilian blood within her is fiery—there are no subtle transitions between love and hate— there is only the passionate pulse of flaming life. When she first speaks to Turiddu's mother, Lucia, her humility is like the abject cowering of a tormented animal. She accepts with submission and apathy the fact that the church has ejected her as a sinner, she who has sacrificed her honor in order to bring happiness to a man who had been deceived and deserted by another. . . . She doesn't consider what may be right or wrong. Before the steps of the church she falls back trembling—for she is not worthy of entering it. . . .

Turiddu's mother despises Santuzza—she sees her only as the mistress of her son, who has given herself to him without honor, without the blessing of marriage. But Santuzza succeeds in touching her heart. In simple words she tells her the tragic story of her love: how Turiddu, deserted by the fickle Lola, was gripped by a morbid desperation from which her love released him, perhaps saving his life. She knows that it was only desperation which drove him into her arms—that for him she was only an escape from the threatening labyrinth of his misery. But she loves him so much that her only concern is his happiness, his peace. To help him is her joy, her mission. . . . But Lola, now the wife of the well-to-do Alfio, again tries to weave her spell about him. She is not pleased that he can seem to find forgetfulness in the arms of another. So she places herself in his path, and he, only half recovered from his love, again succumbs to her. His mother, Lucia, is deeply shaken. Santuzza has aroused her compassion and won her motherly heart.

Santuzza remains waiting for Turiddu. She will once again

seek to convert him. Once again struggle to win his love, his devotion.

The scene between Turiddu and Santuzza is rather disturbing in its bare brutality. What does pride, or honor, mean to Santuzza? She is determined to win back Turiddu, to lure him again to her arms through her pleading. Upon her knees she drags herself to him, embracing him in spite of his resistance, begging, pleading, imploring. Suddenly the voice of Lola, her rival, is heard—and Santuzza, torn by jealousy, sees how Turiddu is attracted by this lighthearted charming voice, how he wants to be free of the embraces of Santuzza, whose passion it was sweet to enjoy but whose tenacious love has become a bitter after-taste of the time in which she made it possible for him to forget. . . . Lola enters the stage coquettishly and with complete self-possession—a worthless little woman who seeks for pleasure and grasps it wherever she may find it. It amuses Lola to irritate the brooding Santuzza, and without any pretence of concealment she flirts with Turiddu, who is now completely under her spell.

When I was just a beginner I had to learn the part of Lola rather quickly and substitute for a fellow-singer who was taken ill. It was one of the first rôles which I had to "portray". I was so clumsy and so horribly inhibited that I could scarcely move or stand on the stage, and the self-assured Lola was the very last person whom I was capable of representing. In deathly fear I stared at the conductor, possessed by the single desire to sing "correctly", fearing that otherwise I would never be given another rôle. Why under these circumstances I had any desire for another rôle is not clear to me, for the tortures which I endured I wouldn't wish on any enemy. I really must have been something catastrophic, for after this performance even a very good friend advised me to give up the stage for ever. In any case it was a long time before I was entrusted with any other rôle. I am quite convinced that no Turiddu would have remained with me after this performance—and certainly winning him back would have been very easy for Santuzza.

Lola utterly enrages Santuzza by her cool contempt, her graceful nonchalant arrogance. As she was about to enter the church—as befits a "pious and virtuous woman"—she has thrown a flower to Turiddu, which he, delighted, wants to catch, but Santuzza like a cat springs between them and thrusts the flower aside with her foot. Again she pleads for his love. Again she falls at his feet embracing him, holding him fast, until he, deeply disgusted, hurls her to the ground. This brutal and wildly realistic scene must be acted with the utmost passion. Turiddu strikes her because he can no longer save himself from her. Plunging to the ground, in a paroxysm of fury and despair she shrieks her curse upon him as he storms away. . . . (This was the moment when Jeritza rolled down the church steps. It was breathtaking and terrifying, but to my taste too much calculated for theatrical effect.)

At this moment Alfio, Lola's husband, appears. Perhaps if she had been more composed Santuzza would never have done what she now feels compelled to do: to reveal the love affair between Turiddu and Alfio's wife. But this revelation breaks from her like an avalanche which cannot be halted. She scarcely knows what she is saying—a burning desire for revenge sears her tortured heart, blinding her to any consequences, to the frightful fact that through her betrayal she has perhaps endangered the life of her love. She only wants Alfio to know that Lola should be punished, that Turiddu should be punished and an end put to this affair.

Alfio bursts out with a violent oath of vengeance. Only Turiddu's life can pay for this deception. Now Santuzza awakens to the realization of what she has done. She would gladly take back all she has said. At the bottom of her passionately loving heart she doesn't really want Turiddu to suffer. . . . She turns to Alfio pleading and imploring: there is only one thing which she wants now—Alfio's forgiveness. But he breaks away, certain of his revenge. Santuzza follows him in a vain attempt to restrain him, to make him change his mind.

The part of Santuzza really ends here—she returns only once more at the very end of the opera, when Turiddu, slain by Alfio, dies behind the scene. Santuzza, sobbing, throws herself into the arms of his mother.

The development of this rôle is too obvious, too lacking in complications to touch upon it more than fleetingly in this book.

Cavalleria Rusticana was repeated regularly in the Vienna repertory and not treated with very much respect. I should have loved to hear this opera under Toscanini—how the old hackneyed melodies would have bloomed with new beauty through his inspiration! I once heard him conduct the prelude to *Carmen* over the radio and felt that I was really hearing it for the first time. For me there is a challenge in giving new life to melodies which have become overpopularized, in freeing them from the curse of becoming hackneyed by infusing them with vitality.

It is strange that I never sang Santuzza! She and Carmen were among the most coveted rôles in the Vienna opera. I believe that every singer at least once in her career dreams of singing Carmen. But I personally can't remember ever approaching that point of madness, for I could never have been a credible Carmen. One must be born for this rôle, and of the many Carmens whom I have seen none has entirely satisfied me. I read with great interest what Bruno Walter says of this rôle in his autobiography—*Theme and Variations*. He wanted Fritzi Massary—the enchanting queen of light opera, the Yvette Guilbert of the German stage—for Carmen, but she refused. She was very wise not to have succumbed to this temptation: not only because the timbre of her voice does not seem quite right for Carmen, but because what is fundamentally essential for this rôle was wanting in her—a primitive quality. Fritzi Massary was supreme in her field, with the charm of a born Parisienne (she was German) she knew how to bring out piquant points in her *chansons* as no other. Her temperament was breathtaking— she could be a graceful devil, could laugh in flashing cascades, could sing and play the champagne song from *Fledermaus* ravishingly. She was a very great comedienne and I would believe her capable of anything—comedy and tragedy. But I do not believe that she would have been right for Carmen. For the fundamental theme of Carmen's nature is a somber and savage passion which must blindly possess whatever it may desire, even if it costs her life. Everything else is but the superficial garment which shrouds this demonic flame: the pulsing temperament, the lust, the urge to excite men, the fickleness of her feelings—all this is but superficial. She is just a rather vulgar woman, Spanish to the last drop of her savage blood. As a gambler may be possessed by the gambling table, a drinker by alcohol, so she is possessed by her desires. Limitations and restraints do not exist for her. In her first song, the well-known "Habanera", she says: "And when I love, take care!" She says it playfully, laughing carefreely. . . . But in the second verse, standing at Don José's side, she repeats this threat somberly and terrifyingly: she trembles with desire for this man who scarcely notices her. She must possess him, she will possess him. She would like to darken with passionate craving the innocent clarity of these eyes which rest upon her devoid of all desire— to destroy the comfortable quietness of his dull imperturbability. "But when I love, take care". . . . That is the true Carmen—here her whole nature is revealed. Whatever she may covet she makes her own, only to turn to something else and forget what she has wanted before. But just as her going ahead and forgetting are honest and elemental, so is her momentary love honest and elemental. She would challenge death in order to possess Don José, just as in the last act she runs blindly to her death because she is driven to Escamillo. "Very well, kill me, but free the way"—she cries to Don José who blocks the entrance to the arena, the way to Escamillo.

Savage with the savagery of an animal—a heartless child, a demonic woman shrouded in tragedy—that is Carmen. Fritzi Massary could have made everything credible through her great art as an actress—but the fundamental quality would, I believe, have been missing in her: the somber, compulsive passion which drives her to possess, to destroy, to die.

Instead of longing for Carmen, my unfulfilled desire was for years Isolde. A dream which to-day I only remember with a smile, for my repertory was so rich in personalities even without this rôle. The Ariadne which through its stylized form gave me new problems to solve, Desdemona, Lotte in *Werther*, Butterfly and innumerable short-lived modern operas. Oh, and I mustn't forget Tatjana in Tschaikowsky's *Eugen Onegin*: Bruno Walter directed a wonderful performance of this opera in Vienna—and as always had the supervision of the stage direction in his inspired hands. I was on a protracted concert tour in America when he cabled me to return with the rôle completely learned. It was absolutely impossible for me to study during the tour. And so on the trip back to Europe I sat at the piano in the dining-room of the ship, every day after lunch, learning the Tatjana, while the stewards with much clatter cleared away the tables around me. It was the only "undisturbed" time to use the piano. But I did it and knew my rôle when I arrived in Vienna.

Chapter XI

TATJANA—"EUGEN ONEGIN"
(*Tchaikowsky*)

WE HAD a wonderful stage setting for *Onegin* in Vienna: the first scene conveyed all the soft melancholy of the Russian landscape, the peacefulness of this country home and the dreamlike atmosphere which surrounds Tatjana.

The first duet between Tatjana and her sister Olga, which is heard from behind scenes, soars above the friendly conversation of their mother, Mme Larina, and their old servant Filipjewna, as they sit busy with their housework in the shadow of the great tree.

Tatjana has developed from a quiet child into a young girl, absorbed in dreams. She is like a part of the surrounding landscape: one feels about her the expanse of the Russian steppes, the glowing sun turning to gold the far-spreading wheat-fields, the winter snow which buries them, the wind which on autumn days roars about the house as if it would raze it and tear every living thing on its wild course into the vastness of unknown space.

Tatjana has always been a dreamer. Books are her only friends and it is through romantic novels that she experiences the glamor of a world foreign to her and so distant as to seem unapproachable—a world which this country girl will probably never know. She is surrounded by servants, respected and honored, but how far she feels from anything which to her imagination seems desirable and worth living for.

She comes slowly out of the house with her vivacious sister Olga, who is always in high spirits. Even as she walks she is immersed in her book. She pays no attention to her surroundings but immediately seats herself, absorbed in her fascinating novel. Only the approach of the harvesters brings her back from the world of her imagination. She stands on the terrace steps with her mother, her sister and her old nurse Filipjewna, to receive the homage of the peasants who are celebrating their harvest. She looks upon them with a friendly, far-away expression. She loves this colorful picture, loves the sound of the folksongs, the rhythm of the rough dances in which the people swing so happily.

When the harvesters have scattered for the refreshment to which they have been invited by Mme Larina, Tatjana goes slowly to the other side of the garden and seats herself upon a bench to enjoy her reading. She moves with a lazy swing and a gentle rhythm, giving the impression that she is scarcely in contact with the earth. She is so completely withdrawn from reality that even her bearing must convey the impression of being withdrawn. She is pale and looks as if she has known suffering, but it is a vicarious suffering which comes from identifying herself with the characters of her romances and making their fates her own. To-day, as always, her heart is absorbed in the romance before her. Its characters are far more real to her than the people who actually surround her.

Suddenly she is disturbed: a visitor has arrived. Visitors rarely come to Mme Larina's. The farm is situated in a lonely expanse and few neighboring farms border its widespread fields. But their nearest neighbor, Lenski, comes to them as often as possible: he has lost his heart to the gay carefree Olga. To-day he brings a guest with him: Eugen Onegin. Onegin is a man of the world. He has travelled widely and his polished manners convey a worldly elegance. For the first time there enters Tatjana's life a man who resembles the characters of her novels. Her dream seems to have become reality. . . . It is as if she is under a spell. She is too timid to lift her eyes to him, but the fleeting glance with which she has taken in his appearance has overwhelmed her and pierced her heart.

Onegin takes little interest in Tatjana. His friend Lenski has told him of her—of her shy romantic nature, her unworldliness —but he has described Olga in glowing terms, revealing his secret love to his friend. Onegin doesn't see anything exceptional in either Olga or Tatjana. Olga is too uncomplicated, too obvious for his taste—Tatjana with her pale beauty is quite attractive, but she is so immature, so unawakened and shy. Onegin only loves women who are surrounded by glamor—sophisticated women of the world, who know life and are eager to explore it in all its facets. He has no interest in the romanticism of young girls. . . . While Tatjana (in the lovely quartet) confesses to herself the love which has so suddenly flamed within her, Onegin coolly appraises the two girls. In any case his judgment is in favor of Tatjana. Of the two he finds her more attractive than the rough country girl Olga. Unfortunately, however, he is far from feeling any deep interest in her.

While Lenski talks with his beloved Olga, Onegin with cool politeness approaches the dazzled Tatjana. His words are banal —yes, they show the abysmal gap between the man of the world and the dreamer Tatjana. But she does not sense this. She is lost in admiration of him.

They go into the garden and Lenski takes advantage of their absence to declare his love to Olga.

When they return Onegin gives the impression of being rather bored by the shy child at his side, and of making conversation rather condescendingly, but she appears quite intoxicated, she almost staggers, she seems to be walking on clouds. She can't take her eyes off his face, she listens to his empty words as if they conveyed revelations.

Watching them, the faithful Filipjewna is touched by Tatjana's timidity. She says to herself with a smile: "Can it be possible that she is interested in this young man?"

Tatjana does not follow Onegin as he enters the house, where a hearty meal is to be expected. She can't yet come down to earth—she can't descend so quickly from her rapturous world to one of banal conversation. She doesn't realize that Onegin is anything but romantic, she only senses the great and shattering experience of first love. . . . So she remains alone on the terrace, and slowly sinking upon a seat throws her arms over the railing, looking up into the dreaming light of the moon in devout ecstasy.

Very slowly the curtain falls.

The second scene of the first act finds Tatjana in her bedroom, which is furnished in an old-fashioned, comfortable style. There is a writing-table, a madonna, and there are books everywhere. Tatjana's personality is reflected in this room: she has arranged it just as she wanted it, and loves it, living amidst the books and flowers, and the writing-table at which perhaps she secretly composes poetry. . . .

When the curtain rises Tatjana is sitting before her simple dressing-table. Filipjewna has done her hair in braids. There has been much to talk over. The harvest festival, the visitors, Lenski who is now to marry Olga—yes, and Eugen Onegin. . . . Tatjana does not fully open her heart to her old confidante. Her love is a sacred secret. It is something entirely her own—no one else shall know how her heart is budding and singing. Hesitantly she goes to her bed and lies down. She knows that it will be a sleepless night! The dreams which before have never had any reality now have a name: Onegin. . . . This name will keep her awake—every word he has spoken will become poetry in her intoxicated thoughts. She longs to be alone with her dream—yet she wants to talk, she is restless and helpless. The room oppresses her; it seems stifling and humid between these walls which before have been so dear to her. She would like to know how Filipjewna experienced her first love. The good old woman was once young, her heart was once filled with dreams, wasn't it? She urges Filipjewna to tell her how she fell in love and married. . . . Was it the way it is in novels? Was it romantic and wonderful? But alas, it is a very commonplace story which the old woman tells. Tatjana can't even listen to it. She doesn't want to hear about boring reality, about marriages which parents have arranged as they saw fit. She wants to be told of passionate adventure and sweet fulfillment. She sinks back into her own world. Filipjewna is very much astonished that she doesn't listen and reproaches her gently, but Tatjana in a violent outburst of passion and confusion throws herself into Filipjewna's arms. The old woman can't understand such behavior. She no longer recognizes her "soft little dove", Tatjana. Perhaps she is ill? Concerned about her, she wants to sprinkle her with holy water, but Tatjana shakes her dark curls: no, she isn't ill. She is in love, in love. . . . With an expression of half comical despair she throws herself back upon the bed: "I am in love . . ." The miracle, for which she has waited all the years of her young life has now come to her, but she doesn't seem to understand it. What has happened to her? It is something so absolutely extraordinary that no one could really understand it, for there never could have been any such feeling on earth before: "I am in love . . ."

This outburst, which is the last thing she would have expected of this shy child, makes Filipjewna feel quite helpless. Trembling, she says distractedly: "It isn't possible. . . ."

Tatjana composes herself. She knows what she must do. She can't wait—she can't be like Olga who plays with being in love as one would play with a brightly colored ball. Fate has ordained this, a fate which she must make her own, which she must obey, to which she must surrender. . . .

She asks the old servant to arrange the writing-table and promises that she will soon go to sleep, but first she must do something which she feels compelled to do.

She waits until Filipjewna has left the room, pretending that she is now quiet and ready to sleep. But as soon as she is alone she rises with passionate decision.

The stormy prelude to this solo scene, the letter scene—the loveliest and most effective of the whole opera—is the reflection of her violent excitement. The music roars like a hurricane, for it is as a hurricane that love has gripped Tatjana's soul. She is the helpless victim of a raging passion which, emerging from her dreams, from something intangible, has now become a glowing reality. The image of her dreams has at last taken form, has become a reality to whom she may speak, to whom she may reveal herself. . . . Boundless is her confidence, boundless her confusion, to which she finds no alternative but unabashed confession. It doesn't occur to her for a moment that this very experienced man to whom she turns might not take such a candidly passionate confession seriously, that he might consider her just an immature, hysterical dreamer and might even laugh at her. . . . She doesn't doubt for a moment that he will understand and will know how to bring peace to her restless heart. In the novels in which she has lived she has read so much of ardent passion— now she feels glowing desire pulsing through her and surrenders to it helplessly, unwilling to fight against it.

So she begins to write: in a letter she wants to lay everything bare before the man who without realizing it has in such a short time captured her whole heart and awakened her senses. The pen races over the paper, but she is not satisfied with what she has written and begins all over again. The first senseless torrent has ebbed. Her thoughts now begin to take form—she has found the composure which is necessary to write this letter as she imagines it should be written. She tells him of her "sad fate"—for she feels herself misunderstood by all around her. For one little more than a child, life in this strictly orthodox Russian household is very narrow: she knows that her mother will soon select a husband for her—and she alone rebels against this infringement of her rights. She is not like her contemporaries, not like her carefree merry sister. She is consumed by an unquenchable thirst for freedom and free will, but she knows that she has not the strength to struggle against the world of tradition. Eugen Onegin has appeared as a savior. He must help her, he will free her, will bring her the happiness for which she longs. He must be aware of her love, must know that it was his and her fate which has led him to her, to this remote isolated estate. All this she writes to him. She writes that if he had not come she might yet have done what her mother would some day demand of her: marry the man whom her mother would select for her. Marry another? Tatjana jumps up impetuously. Under the spell of her almost prophetic imagination she fancies that Onegin has been sent by God. Out of dreams he has come to her, has become a living figure, a being close to her. From dreams he will draw her into the sweet reality of his glowing embrace. . . . Tatjana sinks upon a chair as if overcome by weakness at the thought of such fulfillment.

But have there not also been unfortunate complications in novels? Has she not read of men who, coming in the guise of a noble person, have yet planted evil in innocent hearts? Could it be possible that Onegin might be like them? "The face I dreamed, was that delusion? Art thou a dream of fancy?" Her anxious questions are borne on the most entrancing music, floating lyrically. A fleeting doubt passes over her—but the melody of her heart is one of love and confidence. Suddenly, with the certainty of one who walks in her sleep, conviction again takes possession of her. In an outburst of renewed passion she breaks into the wonderful surging phrases: "O can't thou see I've none but thee? With none to understand and cherish, lone and helpless I must perish, unless my savior thou wilt be." Sobbing with wild excitement she sinks down upon the bed—but she rises again, and brushing back her dark curls from her fevered brow goes with determined steps to the writing-table and closes and seals the letter. "To thee, my vision face divine, to thee, thine honor I confide me . . ."

The end of the letter scene has great dramatic power, the music is transporting and the action convincing. Any half-way credible Tatjana will have success with it, for the scene carries the actress. It moves me deeply to remember the storm of applause which always broke over me when, passionately excited after the heroically dramatic ending, I collapsed upon the writing-table. The rôle of Tatjana, as far as I am concerned, has become so distant, so much a thing of the past that perhaps I may mention this success without seeming too boastful.

Consciousness slowly returns to Tatjana. She straightens up and notices with astonishment that day has already dawned. The warm gold of the sun streams into her room—she goes to the window and drinks in the peaceful quiet of the landscape before her, like a quieting medicine. But no sunny morning can take away the tender melancholy which she feels. Only Onegin's answer to the letter upon her writing-table—only that could dispel it, or on the other hand plunge her into the depths of despair. So the charming melody from beyond, played by the shepherd upon his flute, only makes her sadder. "Unhappy creature," she sighs softly to herself.

She scarcely hears Filipjewna entering the room. She comes to awaken her for the Holy Mass and is very much astonished to find Tatjana already awake and dressed. The good old woman thinks that the night's soft slumber has done her darling Tatjana good. She notices her rosy and glowing cheeks, and does not suspect that it is inner excitement rather than sweet refreshment which has colored them.

Tatjana is happy that Filipjewna has come so early: she can now take care of the letter—secretly so that no one may see it. . . . It takes quite a while for the old woman to understand what it is that Tatjana wants. She lives in a pleasant equanimity and is disturbed when anything so unusual is asked of her. But readily and obediently she takes the letter which is thrust at her so impatiently, and leaves the room. Tatjana with quick steps flies across the room in order to watch Filipjewna. She knows that her fate will now soon be decided. The question of life or death, it seems to her, lies entirely in the hands of Eugen Onegin. She is overcome with anxiety but recovers herself with the faithful and ecstatic determination: "Be it life or death, I am prepared . . . I do as God has ordained for me . . . He will help, He will change everything." The curtain very slowly falls.

The third scene of the first act is laid in the garden of her parents' home. Tatjana has suggested this garden in her letter. She wants to meet him here, wants to hear his answer from him himself. . . . It all seemed so obvious and natural in the ecstasy of the night. But to-day, in the bright light of the morning, she can no longer understand how she had the courage to write him so openly. To-day she is again the shy young girl, ignorant of the ways of the world, wrapped within herself, living in dreams which are far from crude reality.

She comes running breathlessly into the garden as if she were running away from something. She is running away from herself, from the moment which will bring Onegin to her and with him the judgment for which—oh fantastic, indiscreet child, she has asked him. . . . Unconsciously she realizes the impropriety of her behavior. Why should Onegin be interested in her? Why should he love her? How could she have dared to write to him? But it is too late . . . Onegin is approaching. She moves a few steps towards him and stands before him with bowed head, confused and overcome.

Onegin has been very unpleasantly surprised by Tatjana's letter. It is very embarrassing to him that this half-child in whom he hasn't the slightest interest should have confessed her passionate love for him. As the guest of Mme Larina he feels compelled to agree to this enforced rendezvous and put sense into the child's head. . . . He must give her a lesson—for how dangerous it is to behave in such an uncontrolled way. She might have turned to a man who would have acted less correctly than he intends to—or a man who might have been interested by this kind of immaturity which leaves him cold—yes, even repulses him. . . . But naturally this is an uncomfortable moment for him. It isn't pleasant for a man to have to say "no" to a young girl, so his feelings regarding Tatjana are definitely unfriendly and unsympathetic.

He regards her with chilly politeness and motions to her to sit beside him on the bench. He tries to clothe his refusal in friendly and condescending words. But the singer who plays Onegin must be very careful here—not for a moment is he *kindly*. Kindliness would make his rejection bearable for Tatjana. That she suffers so bitterly—suffers throughout her whole life from it—can only be due to the way in which he has spoken to her. Onegin cannot be blamed for rejecting Tatjana's confession of love—he is only to blame for the heartless way in which he rejected it. Through his smooth words one must feel his inner aversion. One must feel that he does not take this childish passion as a precious open-hearted confidence, but as the hysterical behavior of a badly brought up girl for which he finds no excuse.

Naturally Onegin knows how to use clever words—he is polite, experienced, conventional. But Tatjana feels his impatience, his scarcely concealed aversion beneath his smooth words. His philosophy of life is something so foreign to her nature that she can barely grasp what he is saying. . . . He does not want to marry, because married life would bore him. He must be free in order to enjoy life. And the imagined love within Tatjana's heart—oh, it is just a silly trick of her imagination. . . . Tatjana listens, her head bowed deeply. She has no answer to his words. She knows no answer to his banal advice that she should learn to control herself. He gets up; for a moment he looks down at Tatjana, knowing nothing else which he can say to her, then in sudden impatience he shrugs his shoulders and leaves her.

Not until he has gone does Tatjana rise, and then with a gesture of childlike helplessness fall to the ground, burying her head in her arms.

The second act takes place in the ballroom of Mme Larina's home. There is a large ball, there are many guests and the atmosphere is charged with excitement. With her mother and sister, Tatjana must do the honors. She goes about with a charming but absent smile, greeting and speaking with friends and acquaintances quite automatically. She is pale and looks very much like a child seeming rather lost, in her dress of white tulle, with her dark curls falling over her shoulders. It is apparent that she tries to avoid meeting Onegin. But he, as a polite guest in her home, invites her to dance. She dances with him without ever raising her eyes to his, and very soon excuses herself, leaving the ball hastily. Dancing in his arms and enduring his cold impersonality has been too much for her.

Onegin is exceptionally bored. These few days of country life have been more than enough for one so accustomed to the distractions of city life. He can find no pleasure in these young geese here. The old-fashioned formality which surrounds him makes him nervous and scornful. The only one who seems at all worth considering more closely is Olga, Tatjana's charming sister. She is by nature a coquette and, like himself, does not seem to belong in this circle. She is the fiancée of his friend Lenski—and nothing is farther from his thoughts than wanting in any way to alienate her from his friend. Not for a moment does he feel any serious interest in her—but he is bored, and it amuses him to return Olga's coquettish glances. . . . A little flirtation should be permissible.

Above: *"Not until he has gone does Tatjana rise, and then with a gesture of childlike help-lessness fall to the ground, burying her head in her arms . . ."*

EUGEN ONEGIN (page 184)

Below: *"She urges Filipjewna to tell her about how she fell in love and married . . . Was it the way it is in novels? Was it romantic and wonderful? . . ."*

Tatjana—EUGEN ONEGIN (page 179)

"*A struggle develops between Tatjana and Onegin—a struggle between passion and the resolute decision not to break her oath of loyalty to her husband . . .*"

EUGEN ONEGIN (page 292)

"*Tears of sympathy come to her eyes . . . sympathy for the man who has been destroyed by his own nature; tears of sympathy for him and for herself, for the life which has been denied them, the happiness they have lost.*"

Tatjana—EUGEN ONEGIN (page 191)

But Lenski, observing this flirtation with mounting jealousy, takes it very differently. He is deeply annoyed by Olga's fickle behavior and reproaches her violently. She really hasn't meant it badly. She has no feeling of guilt whatsoever. . . . Good heavens! One should be able to flirt a little with a man as fascinating as Onegin! What has that to do with being the fiancée of Lenski? She loves Lenski and wants to marry him. But she doesn't want to bury herself just because of this marriage. After all, she is young, exuberant, and loves to flirt without thinking anything of it. . . . So she just laughs at Lenski and is amused by his groundless jealousy. She is on the point of giving the cotillon, the most important dance of the evening which she promised to Onegin, to her fiancé, but Onegin steps between them, reminding her of her promise. He really hasn't the slightest intention of separating Olga and Lenski. It is only his burning impatience, his concealed scorn for all the formality which surrounds him, that makes him act in a way which gives Lenski the impression that his friend wants to betray him. Onegin has never had great respect for women. He has always so quickly won anyone whom he wanted to win that he has become cynical and unwilling to credit any pretensions of virtue. Now he has just had the unpleasant experience with Tatjana. Even this shy child, who seemed the personification of innocence, has offered herself to him in a surprisingly revealing way. And this Olga flirts with him—as he would never allow his own fiancée to flirt with anyone else. Is the whole world false and rotten to the core? Is there a worm beneath every lovely shell?

From impatience, from an inner revulsion, from the contempt of a heart which has lost its faith, he acts as he now does: he takes the all too willing Olga with him, leaving his friend standing alone. As she is leaving, Olga throws a jesting word at Lenski: "You shall have a lesson, you jealous creature . . ."

Tatjana has been an unwilling witness of this scene and is deeply disturbed by it. What has become of her romantic figure: of her ideal? For the first time she has a glimpse of "the world" for which she has so longed—timid and hurt she wants to run away, but a crowd of young girls who appear with the renowned French composer and singer, Triquet, intercept her. Triquet adores Tatjana and has written and composed a song for her. Now he wants to sing it to her who is for him the queen of the

ball. Against her will Tatjana is pushed into the center of the
hall. She has to sit down and listen to Monsieur Triquet's
song. He kneels before her, and in homage offers the music.
She thanks him with a heartfelt warmth she rarely shows,
but feels more than is generally suspected. Triquet is quite
overcome by her friendliness and enthusiastically kisses her
hand.

The mazurka starts and Tatjana is torn along into the whirl
of the dance. While it is going on a scene of violent jealousy
develops between Lenski and Onegin. In vain Onegin tries to
bring his friend to reason. Blind jealousy makes him appear to
Lenski as a dangerous seducer, who has only come here with the
most evil of intentions. Lenski does Onegin an injustice, but he
can no longer see any way to regain their old friendship or his
former confidence. The scene reaches such a climax that the
dancing is stopped, and all those present, much to the horror of
Mme Larina, watch the battle of words between the two friends
who have suddenly become enemies. The act ends with Lenski's
challenge to Onegin to meet him in a duel. The guests leave the
house in confusion, and Tatjana hastens to the sobbing Olga.
She is utterly repulsed by Onegin's apparently evil intentions—
with a single blow the image of her dreams has been shattered.
Onegin is not only cold and cruel, he is unscrupulous, frivolous,
sinful. . . . And Tatjana is awakened to a reality from which
dreams will be banned in the future.

In the second scene of the second act the duel takes place
between the two friends. In spite of the fact that they both feel
the tragic senselessness of this duel, they feel that their honor
does not permit them to be reconciled. They must fight it out.

Onegin kills his friend. His honor, which had been challenged,
is redeemed. In despair Onegin leaves the home in which he
has brought misery to everyone as well as to himself.

With the third act, years have passed. Tatjana has never again
found her way back to the dreams of her childhood. . . . She
has gone through the years almost lifelessly, indifferent to her
surroundings, indifferent to her own fate. She has obediently
given her hand in marriage to the man whom her mother has
chosen for her: the Prince Gremin. He is older than she, a man
highly respected and honored, who loves her sincerely and with
whom, in the eyes of the world, she has known an ideal marriage
through these years. Tatjana has not been really unhappy in

this marriage. She has great respect for her husband and is grateful for his love and considerate kindness. She has a warm affection for him. But her pulse never stops at the sound of his footsteps, her heart never races with that wild fire which she but once experienced—in that dreamlike night, when, still a child, she wrote her impetuous letter of confession. . . . She has locked this night within her memory as within a secret shrine. She does not often think of it, she does not want to think of it. Sometimes it seems to her as if she only really lived in the time when she lived in her dreams—in the time when a figure of her dreams appeared before her in reality and then broke upon the earth like a deity with feet of clay whom a storm has dislodged from his false throne. . . .

In all these years Tatjana has heard nothing of Onegin. He seems to have vanished from the face of the earth. She knows nothing of him and is glad that she doesn't. She wants to know nothing of him. Her peace has been hard won. She wants now to preserve it.

Onegin in the meantime has raced through the world—restless like the Flying Dutchman. The fact that he has killed his only real friend in a duel gives him no peace. His conscience tortures him, for he knows that he alone was responsible for this tragedy —he alone, through his frivolous flirtation with Olga. Certainly he hadn't meant anything seriously. He had not the slightest intention of hurting his friend. But he should have taken the sensitiveness of Lenski's nature into consideration. He should have realized that Lenski could never take things lightly as he did; he should have known that, what meant for him only dis-traction and amusement, was for Lenski the holiest thing on earth. Through all these years he has searched everywhere for this distraction and amusement, but it has given him no peace, he has not been able to forget To-day, after his long travels, he returns to St. Petersburg and attends a great official recep-tion. He stands—lonely as always—between the merry and apparently carefree people with whom, since this tragedy entered his life, he has felt nothing in common. . . .

All the nobility of Petersburg society have gathered together in this reception. Among them are Prince Gremin and his wife Tatjana. As always Tatjana excites attention and admiration when she appears in all her splendor on the arm of her husband —a great lady from head to toe. She has learned during this time to represent her position in society, she has learned to be the princess of whom in her girlhood she has so often read, the jewel-adorned princess of her dreams. . . . She moves with dignity and grace towards the place of honor which has been reserved for her, and receives the many people who throng about her eager to exchange a greeting with the beautiful and fascinating Princess Gremina who sits there in all her loveliness, like an image of alabaster and gold.

With increasing astonishment and interest Onegin has observed this strikingly lovely woman, whom he feels he has known, without immediately realizing that it is Tatjana, the shy little country girl, who was once in love with him.

Prince Gremin comes to him and engages him in conversation, but over his shoulder Onegin's eyes continue to seek the Princess.

Tatjana has seen Onegin. She cannot believe that he must again cross her path and steels herself against the possibility that it may be he. He had vanished—unattained and unattainable. Is it possible that he is here, close to her? Can what has seemed to be buried past suddenly become living reality? Turning to the acquaintances who surround her she asks as if with polite interest: "Pray tell me who is that who stands beside the Prince?" She receives the confirmation that it is Onegin. Suddenly the blood pulses feverishly through her slumbering heart, and with horror she feels an awakening within herself—the wild and terrible awakening of her senses which have so long seemed dead. But she struggles to compose herself and from her lifeless face no one can suspect the tumult of her emotions.

Onegin asks the same question of Prince Gremin and learns that Tatjana is the Princess, his wife. . . .

What has happened to this child of the wide prairies? How could a girl, who seemed so lacking in all attraction, become so changed, how could she have flowered into such beauty that she seems to place every one else in the shade? How is it possible? How can he withstand this sudden overwhelming feeling which like lightning has struck his heart to flame?

He must pull himself together—the Prince leads him to his wife, but not without first telling him of his great love for her, his deep devotion, his indestructible and infinite happiness in her love.

Onegin is presented to Tatjana.

Through the music trembles the motive of Tatjana, the motive of turbulent love. With this motive she has once risen from her bed, stumbled to her writing-table and with trembling hand begun to write the stammering confession of her love to the man who is now bowing deeply before her . . . the same man who had rejected her with hard words, devoid of kindness, devoid of any friendly understanding. . . .

Tatjana does not betray her excitement through any gesture. She greets Onegin with a friendly but condescending politeness as she would greet any stranger, for she is a great lady accustomed to homage. She says with cold formality as if searching distractedly through her memory: "It seems to me we've met before . . ." They are inconsequential remarks which they exchange, but in his words tremble concealed allusions—in hers, a cool and negative rejection. When she asks: "Since when have you returned from your travels in foreign countries?" and he answers "This morning", she shudders: on the very day of his return she meets him. And she will have to meet him again, will be again the victim of this strangely altered look in his eyes, the eyes which once regarded her so coldly and scornfully.

She feels no longer capable of enduring this comedy, so she rises and, with the excuse of being tired, leaves on the arm of her husband, without giving Onegin any parting glance or the courtesy of a friendly word. She does not want to be friendly, does not want this man to enter her home, to cross her path. . . .

The scene ends with a violent and passionate outburst from Onegin, who has fallen head over heels in love with this wonderful woman who once seemed so undesirable. Now Fate has led him back to her, a Fate which he will challenge, tearing away all obstacles. The obstacle is Prince Gremin. But Onegin knows no consideration. He must possess whatever he desires to possess . . . and he is confident of his seductive power, confident of his hold over Tatjana. She cannot have changed so completely, that dreaming, ardent child. Be it life or death, he will drink the sweet poison which is called love. . . . The scene ends with the musical *motif* of Tatjana.

The last scene of the opera takes place in the reception-room of Princess Gremina's home. Tatjana has received a letter from Onegin, asking her to receive him. He must speak with her. She doesn't want to deny this request, for she is unwilling to betray the fact that his presence could in any way have any

importance for her—either in the past or in the present. But
she has overestimated her inner strength. Now that she awaits
him the same consuming restlessness, which she had felt when
she was still a credulous and trusting child who believed that she
had found the ideal of her dreams, sweeps over her.

Tatjana enters the room in great excitement, holding his letter
in her hand. The letter was late in reaching her, Onegin will
follow it immediately, so there is no possibility of refusing him
even if she had wanted to. In confusion she sinks upon a chair,
in the same helpless confusion as of old. She does not hear that
Onegin has already entered the room and is looking down
at her with deep emotion, sensing her inner conflict. With
quick steps he hastens to her and sinks down at her feet. Tatjana
rises.

She has regained her composure now that he is actually before
her. She again takes refuge in the rôle of the great lady conscious of her superiority, for whom there can exist no problem,
since what she must do is self-evident.

With cool politeness she asks him to be seated. She wants to
speak with him quite sincerely—everything should be clear between them—so she says. With quiet irony she reminds him of
the time when as a helpless young creature, the victim of her
passion for him, she had come to him offering him all the richness of her heart, ready to receive her judgment at his hand.
Onegin is now painfully moved; he regrets bitterly his cold and
unsympathetic behavior, for it has denied him the greatest
happiness he could have known: the possession of this wonderful
woman whom he now so ardently desires. . . . His fervent plea
to spare him the cruel punishment of remembering has weakened
Tatjana's hard-won composure. The painful suffering which
she endured because of him returns to her heart, and with
mounting feeling she speaks of his coldness, his cruel coldness.
. . . She sees herself again as she was: a good, pure child, who
wanted to offer him her whole soul. She sees herself as she is
to-day: a woman who knows bitterness, who has forgotten how
to believe, who has lost the most beautiful thing which one can
possess—the innocence of an untouched heart. . . . But this
woman is surrounded by glamor, the fame of her husband,
riches which overwhelm her, the adoration of the people—it is
this which has now changed Onegin's feeling for her. She sees
it all very clearly. She expresses it in a forceful challenge:

"Why do you pursue me now? Because you have found me in high society, surrounded by pomp and show?" Now she has become desirable for the man who didn't love the innocent girl whom he could have possessed so easily, without any intriguing obstacles. But now . . . to steal this woman away from the great Prince Gremin—that is enticing, isn't it?

Onegin has never before met a woman who has seen through his heart so clearly and with such cruel accuracy. He is very much taken aback, but is excited to the utmost by his single glowing desire to possess this woman who can never belong to him, who will never *want* to belong to him. With passionate words he rejects her cold reasoning. Pressing against her he says that he wants nothing of her, nothing more than to be able to lament, to tell what he feels, to weep beside her. . . .

Onegin is very clever. Words of sensual passion would have offended and repulsed Tatjana, but this fervent repentance grips her heart and makes her tremble. Tears of sympathy come to her eyes—of sympathy for the man who has been destroyed by his own nature; tears of sympathy for him and for herself, for the life which has been denied them, the happiness which they have lost. Her life at Gremin's side is good and correct. But only here, in Onegin's eyes, glows the fire for which her senses have languished so long.

With delight Onegin sees the tears in the eyes of the beloved woman. He knows that they are tears for the past, and his mood seems in tune with hers in the lovely short duet: "Ah happiness was once so near us . . ."

Tatjana suddenly tears herself from this dangerous mood of tender memory back to the threatening present. "Destiny has wrought otherwise for us! I am wedded now, you must go, it is your duty to leave me . . ." Duty? When has Onegin ever listened to "duty", when his heart spoken with wilder words? Instead of leaving he sinks upon the sofa beside Tatjana, and passionately seizes her hand. His wooing is unchecked, wild, without restraint. Moved to the depths of her heart by his overpowering ardor, Tatjana tries in vain to tear herself away. Pursued by him she reels across the stage, calling to him repeatedly in the anguish of her heart that it is his duty to leave her immediately.

But overwhelmed by his passion she turns to him crying in self-forgetful ecstasy: "Of what use are lies, deception? Yes—

I love you . . ." Against her will, against her conscience, she has
said it—for the first time confessing to herself, what she has
tremblingly concealed within the depths of her soul: her love
for this man, whom she has meant to hate, has meant to make
herself despise. . . . Half fainting she falls into his arms. Onegin,
thinking that he is now upon the threshold of fulfillment, receives
her tenderly as she yields to him. She will be his . . . she will
follow him, will leave her husband. The happiness which was
"once so near" has now become actuality—sweet, intoxicating
nearness. From now on it shall be indestructible for them both.
The mask has fallen from Tatjana's face—she is no longer the
glamorous princess, she is Tatjana the charming child, Tatjana
the flaming, passionate woman. His lips seek hers—but Tatjana
awakens from the confused tumult of her emotions. She awakens
to the consciousness: I am no longer Tatjana, I am the Princess
Gremina.

A struggle develops between Tatjana and Onegin—a struggle
between passion and the resolute decision not to break her oath
of loyalty to her husband. Tatjana is on the edge of succumb-
ing. In a wild prayer she seeks strength from God as she feels
her own strength ebbing from her. Onegin, knowing everything
is at stake, forces her into his arms, forces his kiss upon her. But
she tears herself away from him—and storming across the stage
cries: "Farewell for ever . . ." With a harsh finality the door
closes upon him. Onegin stands defeated. He cries: "Repulsed,
dishonored—O how hard a fate."

That is the end of the opera.

It seems like a kind of anticlimax. The ending is abrupt and
surprising. In spite of this highly dramatic scene it lacks a
really effective release from the electrically charged atmosphere.
Pushkin's story ends in the same abrupt way. Here, as well as
in the opera, I found the suddenness of the end disturbing.
Tschaikowsky describes his opera as "Lyric scenes in three acts".
Scenes which apparently are not intended to give a complete
story—just as the figures of this novel live on after the novel is
ended and the reader is left uncertain as to their ultimate out-
come. But the reader and the hearer remain a little confused:
one has rather the feeling of seeing dark and threatening clouds
on the horizon which make one believe the end of the world is
approaching, so menacing are the mountainous clouds. . . . Then

there is a brief clap of thunder, a fleeting flash of lightning and the heavens clear. . . .

But actor and audience should picture the ending in their imaginations. They should see how Tatjana becomes resigned, how she lives on in quiet contentment beside her husband for many years. She often thinks, with a half smile, a half sigh, of the unfortunate Onegin who has disappeared and no longer crosses her path. Her wounds have healed. The scar within her heart no longer gives her pain.

And Onegin? He storms again into a world which can give him neither happiness nor contentment. The only great happiness which might have enriched his life he has sacrificed through his own folly. He knows that nothing can ever take its place, that nothing can ever silence the angry voice of reproach which torments him through sleepless nights.

His figure, enveloped in drama, vanishes into the darkness of the times. . . . Adventure lurks abroad in the world into which he has flown. Perhaps he will find his grave beneath the waves through which his ship glides in its restless course. Perhaps a shot will find him, even as a shot found and killed his friend. Perhaps a war may bring him adventure, and honor for his valiant heart—and death. . . . Oblivion closes over his grave. A grave at which there is none to grieve, over which there is only the occasional flutter of an angel's wings: the dream which Tatjana may dream, but of which she remembers nothing in the bright light of morning. . . .

Chapter XII

SINGING WITH STRAUSS

IT IS LATE AT NIGHT. The clock strikes in warning—I should stop writing and sleep. But through the starlit sky beyond my window, faces—familiar, half forgotten—float before me . . . the masks of many rôles which I have impersonated in my long opera career float towards me out of the quiet night. The dreamy murmur of the Pacific Ocean as it breaks upon our beach becomes music, and surging phrases which I have once sung seem to resound and ebb away with the surf.

I feel impelled to hold fast these figures to which I once gave life—to be again transformed into the personality of whatever rôle I was creating.

But this book is drawing to its end. The frame is almost filled —and these other faces must fall back into the opera scores, captured within the colorful confusion of the music, the printed words, until another shall come who will awaken them to life through singing and acting.

There is, however, one rôle which I have saved for the last: The Marschallin. She has always been one of my favorite rôles, and she is the only one who still lures me back to opera. But besides this she has meant for me the fulfillment of my dream: to be completely an actress. I hope Richard Strauss may pardon me—his *Rosenkavalier* music is wonderfully beautiful, and I believe immortal—but even without his music Hofmannsthal's libretto would still have been a delightful comedy. I have always longed for an opportunity to act freely without being tied down by music. In this opera the music is completely interwoven with the words. The music never says to the words: I am more important than you. The words never say to the music: I would have expressed this differently. Together they form a complete and perfect unity, and the Marschallin, however divinely she may sing, will never be a Marschallin if she is not a good actress.

In another opera, *Intermezzo*, Strauss has also brought the union of word and tone to realistic perfection, but the music in itself does not have the charm of the *Rosenkavalier*, nor its immortal worth. I sang the rôle of Christine in *Intermezzo* at Strauss's special request at its *première* in Dresden, and found much pleasure in this gay comedy-like part. Here the character of the singing conversation goes so far as to make the transition from the sung to the spoken words unnoticeable—a very new approach which delighted me.

It is a pity that this opera is never given in America. It would in any case have to be translated into English, as the flow of conversation, the play of words, is in this case of utmost importance.

Opera as a form of art will perhaps only become really popular in America and Britain when the text is completely understood through being performed in English. Personally I do not like this idea at all. I have been delighted to find opera produced here in its original language. The music is written for the words of the original text, and any translation generally seems a very awkward substitute. But if opera can only become popular with the mass of people when it is possible for them to understand its language then it is probable that this argument is more important than the purely artistic standpoint. Of course, this takes for granted the ideal condition in which the diction of every singer is so perfect that every word may be understood, which unfortunately is often not the case. However, in Austria and Germany every opera is sung in German. I sang the Italian rôles Mimi, Butterfly, Manon Lescaut, Tosca, Sister Angelica, Turandot, Madeleine (*Andrea Chénier*), as well as the French Manon, and Lotte in *Werther*—in German. The Viennese, musically cultured in the highest sense, took it as a matter of course that every opera would be performed in German. So perhaps the same concession should be made elsewhere in order that opera may be brought closer to the people. But even if this should be practicable there will always be one exception—*Der Rosenkavalier*. The typically "Austrian aristocratic dialect" of this opera seems absolutely untranslatable and is an inherent part of its charm—like the enchanting waltz which floats through it. This dialect cannot be translated with slang, because it is not a dialect of the people but a somewhat affected, graceful and refined speech which is essentially Viennese, and which the aristocracy still speak to-day.

In *Intermezzo* the conversation runs in a very different way.

In this case it is the everyday speech of the average person and so will not lose its characteristic quality in translation. Realism reaches such a point in this opera that Christine says many a harsh word, holds amusing telephone conversations, quarrels with her maid, etc. In this opera Strauss has really described a scene from his own home life. He himself is Robert Storch, and his wife Pauline, famous for her sharp tongue and violent temperament, Christine.

There are many legends which circulate over the world about Pauline's unbridled temperament, and Strauss has immortalized her in his *Intermezzo*. Describing her with humor and kindly wit, painting the fiery devil, he confesses his great love for her in every word and every tone. (He also wrote the libretto.)

Pauline Strauss was a well-known and excellent singer and met her husband when singing under his direction. The story of how they became engaged is very amusing and quite typical of their relationship. Strauss himself told me of it—with the radiance with which he always spoke of Pauline. She sang Elisabeth in *Tannhäuser* under his baton, and in a rehearsal made some mistake, or dragged or hurried the tempo (the latter seems more probable to me in view of her temperament!). In any case an argument arose between her and the young conductor, which finally reached its climax when she threw the piano score from the stage on to his head, shrieked some frightful insults, and leaving the rehearsal, rushed to her dressing-room.

Strauss, terribly annoyed, laid down his baton, interrupted the rehearsal which had been so violently disturbed, and without knocking entered Pauline's artist's room. Those waiting outside heard through the closed door wild shrieks of rage and fragmentary insults—then all was quiet. Turning pale each looked at the other: who had killed whom? A delegation of orchestra members approached the threatening door. A shy knocking. . . . Strauss opened the door and stood in the doorway beaming radiantly. The representative of the musicians stammered his speech: "The orchestra is so horrified by the incredibly shocking behavior of Fräulein Pauline de Ahna, that they feel they owe it to their honored conductor Strauss to refuse in the future to play in any opera in which she might have a part. . . ." With this boycott they wanted to prove to Strauss how eager they were to take his side and to what extent they condemned Pauline de Ahna's unheard of behavior. . . .

Strauss regarded the musicians smilingly.

Then he said: "That hurts me very much, for I have just become engaged to Fräulein de Ahna. . . ."

"I want to have life and temperament around me," says Conductor Storch in the opera. That Strauss found to the limit in Frau Pauline.

I myself have experienced many somewhat disconcerting evidences of this. I remember a lovely afternoon in Garmisch—we had coffee and cakes in the garden, and were enjoying the *gemütliche* coffee hour very much (a somewhat heartier German version of the English afternoon tea) when a sudden storm descended upon us. We had scarcely time to gather everything together and get ourselves and the cakes under cover, before there was a terrific deluge of rain. Pauline took this violent interruption of a pleasant hour as a personal insult. Giving vent to her anger a very special thunderstorm poured over Richard's head. He let all her accusations pass over him with the greatest meekness. Only when I dared to say: "But Pauline, how can your husband stop the rain——" he turned to me anxiously: "Don't defend me—that always makes it much worse."

Frau Pauline came from a distinguished officers' family, and from the inborn adoration of the officer class she once confided to me that she had made a *mésalliance* in marrying Strauss. "I should have married a dashing lieutenant," she said, sighing deeply at the thought of all she had missed in life. I laughed at her and said that with the best of intentions I couldn't waste very much sympathy on her for being the wife of the greatest living composer.

It is strange that I never really came close to Strauss as a conductor. His immobile face, his apparently complete coldness (which was perhaps only the result of excessive self-discipline) was like a barrier which kept me from approaching the great conductor Strauss. Only in rehearsals did he open up a little. I studied the dyer's wife in his *Frau ohne Schatten* with him, and lived for fourteen days with him and his family in his very lovely villa in Garmisch. One should not see a king in the bosom of his family—one loses one's respect. Strauss's wife Pauline was the real master of the house and I learned to admire one quality in him—his angelic patience and adaptability. He played many of his Lieder for me at this time, in between intensive rehearsals for *Frau ohne Schatten,* and I often saw tears shadowing his eyes—and Frau Pauline would embrace him sobbing in one of her violent outbursts of tenderness: all the old Lieder seemed to awaken so many mutual memories. In such moments I loved Strauss.

Once in Vienna in a performance of *Walküre* I saw Strauss making furious faces from the conductor's stand, which I thought were directed at me, for my conscience was never entirely free where exactness in singing was concerned. When Strauss came on to the stage after this act I deluged him with one of my uncontrollable outbursts, and at the end of a violent tirade tore off my wig, declaring that I would sing no more. Sobbing, I ran to my dressing-room, leaving Strauss standing there unable to say a single word. The amusing part of this affair was that he hadn't meant me at all but a member of the orchestra, who had achieved the distinction of making Strauss's face expressive. However, I was quickly quieted down when he came to me laughing and shaking his head, and explained the misunderstanding. He wasn't angry at all—he had infinite understanding for such temperamental scenes and took them with a kind of amused grin. It seemed to please him that not only his Pauline indulged in such senseless frenzies.

After the performance Pauline came to me with an absolutely radiant expression: "Fine, that you gave it to him, that raging devil . . . that imp of Satan. He got it that time . . ."

To my objection that he hadn't meant me at all, and that my attack was quite senseless, she replied laughing with delight: "Didn't do any harm. Anyway he got it for once."

Of all the conductors with whom I have sung, Strauss was the most magnanimous about forgiving mistakes. The complete effect was much more important to him than absolute exactness. For example, in *Intermezzo* he permitted me every conceivable freedom—and when someone remarked to him ruefully: "It is a pity that Lehmann is so frightfully inexact in this rôle. She positively flounders through the whole opera!" he laughed and replied: "When Lehmann flounders she is still preferable to others who sing exactly."

As Ariadne I once made an almost incredible mistake, due to a moment of absentmindedness which is generally quite foreign to my nature. When Bacchus appears on the rock and greets Ariadne, who believes that she sees in him the Death for which she longs, she must sing to him: "I greet you, messenger of all

messengers." In the performance Bacchus rose and I bowed
deeply before him. The prompter whispered to me: "I greet
you——" But I was perfectly convinced that Bacchus was supposed to sing this phrase and not I—how, why, I have no idea!
I have never been able to imagine how this could be *possible*.
Hearing the words repeated by the prompter I thought: "What
is the matter? Why doesn't Bacchus sing this phrase?" After
the performance we had forgotten about this incredible scene,
but the next day Strauss sent me the following line: "Because
the ⟨♪⟩ was so beautiful, Lottchen's penalty is
diminished so at the next performance of
Ariadne the lines 'I greet you, messenger of
all messengers' need only be sung twice! But in spite of this it
was *very beautiful!* In gratitude, your most faithful admirer,
Richard Strauss."

His sense of humor was always alert. In an *Ariadne* rehearsal
at one place in the trio of Dryade, Najade and Echo, he said:
"I certainly stole that, that is from Schubert." He was obviously
amused.

He was accustomed to being treated with great deference—
and this he didn't like at all. I don't for a moment believe that
this was a pose—I am convinced that he honestly disliked any
obsequiousness. Perhaps for this reason he liked me personally
very much (so far as one can ever assume that Strauss is capable
of any personal interest), just because I didn't always bow down
before him but found an actual pleasure in arguing with him.
I have often written him rude letters of which I was a master in
my uninhibited youth, and have a very amusing letter from him
—an answer to an apparently strangely charming one from me.
He says with Beckmesser: "A letter from Lotte [a letter from
Sachs] that means something . . ." And then he goes on to say
that upon receiving the letter he immediately thought: And now
what have I done? She has written me another horrible letter.
And upon opening it was pleasantly surprised to receive such
nice lines from me.

This open naturalness is one of Strauss's pleasantest character-
istics. Yet I cannot imagine that any one outside of his family
was ever really close to him. In some strange way it seems as
if the world never really touched him at all: he is egocentric in
the extreme and to such an extent that his indifference often
borders on cruelty. If a singer well known to him—a so-called

friend—should die, I imagine that Strauss would only say: "Pity
—he or she sang this rôle very well. Who can take his place?"

Strauss has been criticized for his lack of character in political
affairs—and I don't want to defend his dubious conduct. But
I would like to say this: he lives so completely within his own
personal world that the world of politics—yes, "the whole world
constellation including the universe"—doesn't concern him at
all. For this reason he has no political convictions, as I see
him. World events do not touch him—they are not at all a
part of his life. He certainly is no dreamer who lives his ideals
withdrawn from the world: he has a sharp business sense,
and where finances are concerned has both feet very firmly on
the ground. His "unworldliness" is due to a lack of *interest*,
not *ignorance of the ways of the world*. I am convinced that he
was never a Nazi at heart—that would be quite contrary to his
whole nature. It would be quite impossible for him to be
fanatical about anything political. He was probably quite indifferent as to who was in power and in what way this power
was used. It was not his world, not the world of his art, not the
world which surrounded him and his family. But when a
member of his inner circle was threatened he immediately
seemed sympathetic to Nazism in order to save the situation—
I can picture all this very well. As I have said I don't want to
defend what seems quite inexcusable from a human standpoint.
But a man who has given such glorious music to the world may
perhaps be considered less harshly. Strauss is a genius—and
a genius always goes his own way, even if others cannot understand and approve it. But there is something in geniuses which
is beyond understanding: the divine spark which can never be
touched by "good or evil", which lives within itself and creates
and speaks in its own language. For the sake of this divine
spark, which Strauss certainly possesses, let us not seek to judge
or despise him. Strauss as a human being is not as interesting as
his creations. Let us think only of the beauty he has brought
us, and look upon his person as the shell from which speaks the
divine voice of music.

I have enjoyed singing all the Strauss rôles which were entrusted to me: Sophie, Octavian, the Marschallin, Arabella,
Christine, the Composer, Ariadne, the Dyer's Wife. From the
colorful play of these rôles only one has remained for me—the
one opera rôle to which I have remained true: the Marschallin.

"*I have enjoyed singing all the Strauss roles which were entrusted to me: Sophie, Octavian, the Marschallin, Arabella, Christine, the Composer, Ariadne, the Dyer's Wife.*"   Lotte Lehmann as Octavian in ROSENKAVALIER (1); the Composer in ARIADNE (2); Sophie in ROSENKAVALIER (3); and as she appeared in Beethoven's FIDELIO, with Richard Strauss (4)

"But the Marschallin is too great, too wise. She turns to him, and her eyes say —farewell . . ."
ROSENKAVALIER (page 255)

"Her own girlhood rises before her. She sees herself just out of the cloister sees herself in a marriage into which she had been 'ordered' . . ."
The Marschallin—DER ROSENKAV-ALIER (page 228)

Chapter XIII

MARSCHALLIN—"DER ROSENKAVALIER"

AFTER THE STORMY PRELUDE which describes most expressively the love night of Marie Thérèse and Octavian, the curtain rises upon a happy and peaceful scene. The Marschallin sits relaxed upon the sofa, her youthful lover kneels at her feet, his head resting upon her knees as she strokes his hair. . . .

This is the picture on the stage. But Hofmannsthal intended it quite otherwise. He wanted the Marschallin to be still lying in bed with Octavian kneeling beside her. I am not sure whether it has been prudery which has everywhere changed this setting so completely, or whether the fact that such an arrangement makes it difficult to project tones so that they are understandable has been responsible for the change. The bed cannot be in the immediate foreground, it must be pushed more to the side at the back of the stage in order not to be too dominating. It wouldn't be advisable to have this first scene so far removed from the audience. I sang the Marschallin in Berlin when the young and modern stage director Gustav Gründgens directed it. He placed the bed in the center of the stage, where it was later concealed by a screen. But during the levee and the scenes with Octavian it always seemed to be in the way, so that I didn't find this arrangement any solution of the problem.

When *Rosenkavalier* was first presented it was still the period of the Empire, and I remember that the court had ordered as "moral" a version of the opera as possible. Many of the priceless allusions of Baron Ochs were omitted or altered in a so-called "improved" version. Perhaps it is due to the tradition established by this first performance that the more conventional sofa has been retained until to-day, instead of the all too obvious bed. However, in that case the prelude should have been rewritten! Fortunately the court didn't quite understand the boldness of its descriptive music.

The Marschallin has fallen in love with a charming youth and has taken him as her lover. She is "between ages"—and although Strauss, as he once told me, saw in her a woman of about thirty-five, a woman of that age seemed much older at that time.

In that period of the eighteenth century it was not at all astonishing that Marie Thérèse should have a lover in spite of being the wife of the Prince of Werdenberg. Under the strict eyes of that exceedingly moral Empress Maria Theresa, the nobles of the court behaved quite scandalously. To have the right tone it was almost necessary to have an affair. They tried to imitate the frivolous French court—and the Empress, alone among the ladies of the court, was incapable of wiping out this moral laxity.

So the Marschallin is a woman with much experience in affairs of love. . . . Married to the Field Marshal at a very early age, she has known through her illegitimate affairs the joys which were denied her in her conventional marriage. Now at the threshold of that period when resignation is just around the corner she finds pleasure in the boyish Count Octavian, who has found with her the first adventure of his seventeen years. Of course, Octavian (like so many young men who have their first affair with an older woman) is head over heels in love with Marie Thérèse.

The past night has seemed to offer a promise of many nights to come, and in his youthful exuberance he dreams that he is the only one who really knows the woman in his arms, that he is the only one who has been able to awaken in her the passion which he has enjoyed. The Marschallin smiles at such *naïveté*. She has had a number of lovers. . . . For her, Octavian is a charming plaything, an enchanting youth, whom it has been a priceless experience to teach of love.

To-day she is a little tired. This passionate youth has wearied her. So her manner and bearing must be the result of this pleasantly relaxed and tender weariness. She teases him playfully: "Does he complain about that, Quinquin, does he wish every one to know it?" This is her answer to his exaggerated entranced tenderness: "How you were, how you are, that no one knows, that no one suspects." She already uses a conversational tone, already addresses him with the distant "he", while Octavian, oblivious of this, continues to use the intimate "thou". Again he assures her that he is the only one to whom she has devoted all her fiery passion, he is the only one who really knows "how she is". . . .

From the glowing embrace which the Marschallin receives rather passively, Octavian drawing back with his characteristic

impetuosity begins to philosophize, half lying, half resting upon
his elbow. He speaks of the thoughts which have run through
his head in these confused days of his first experience. "What
do they mean, the words 'You and I'? Oh, you and I are one,
are we not? And yet—I long for you, long to be yours, you,
who are I . . . What am I: you? Your boy . . . But if we are one,
one in our embrace, then who am I? Am I still a boy who
belongs to you or am I a man who possesses you?" The Marschallin has listened with a half-smile. She is pleased by this
charming boy who not only has all the virtues of his youth—
beauty, freshness, bold impetuosity—but who can also be in-
tuitive and poetic and who can talk as if he were a philosopher. . . . She draws him closely into her arms, and nestling his
head against her breast sings softly, rising to a broadly floating
forte: "You are my boy, you are my treasure! I love you."
The motherliness which a mature woman feels for a young
person is in her tender: "You are my boy." But there is more.
There is the lover: "You are my treasure," and from this mixture
of feeling rises the sweet and very warm: "I love you." They
linger in a prolonged and tender embrace.

Octavian rises when he hears from beyond the twittering of
birds, whose song runs through the orchestral music in an enchanting illustration. For a moment the Marschallin seems
slightly bemused. She covers her eyes with a delicate gesture,
as if she were feeling faint, but again looks at Octavian and laughs
lightly as he draws the curtains across the window to shut out
the daylight which means separation for them. Octavian, a little
hurt (for he is always aware of the superiority of his beautiful
adored one, and is fearful lest she be laughing at him) remains
standing by the curtain, and asks reproachfully: "Are you
laughing at me?" But she reaches out her hand towards him
and says tenderly: "Am I laughing at you?" a teasing question
to which Octavian reacts exaggeratedly: "Angel . . ." He runs
towards her, but his impetuosity is abruptly restrained by the
Marschallin, who suddenly hears something. There is a disturb-
ance outside—this sweet morning idyll seems about to be interrupted. But Octavian will have nothing of the outside world and
only answers: "I won't listen." The Marschallin's attention is
drawn to a tinkling sound, the funny harmonious clinking of bells
which dangle from the turban of her little black servant boy.
But she listens without fear, for no one would dare to enter this

room without being admitted. Octavian makes the most of this
opportunity to tease his beautiful sweetheart about all her
admirers: "It might easily be messengers with letters from
Saurau, from Hartig, from the Portuguese envoy?" He is
jealous of them all and has feared them all, feeling that they
might be preferred to him in the competition for the favor of
the Marschallin. But at this moment he can afford to scorn
them. Now he is the victor, and feeling this can fold his
arms proudly and say: "No one shall enter here! Here I am
the master."

The Marschallin appreciates the humor of the situation, and
her—"Quick, hide yourself! It is the breakfast," is sung laughingly and with a gentle scorn.

Octavian quickly vanishes behind the *portière* which suggests
a little alcove or dressing-room. In his haste to disappear he
forgets his sword which lies revealingly beside the bed. A little
annoyed as she sees it the Marschallin calls out: "Throw your
sword behind the bed." Of course Octavian immediately obeys.
She goes behind the screen and puts a mantle over her thin
négligée, while the little negro, dancing elegantly, enters with
the breakfast and sets it upon a small table. The Marschallin
does not step out from the background until he has left the
room. There is really no reason why she should conceal herself
from the little negro. He is her servant, her page, her obedient
shadow. He has often brought breakfast to her in bed. So why
shouldn't he see her in her dressing-gown? It isn't necessary
for the Marschallin to put on her mantle behind the protecting
screen (as I have seen it done). She goes to the back of the
stage simply because her robe happens to lie there spread out
upon the bed. When the little negro has gone she gives a sign
to Octavian. He eagerly emerges from behind the curtains and
wants to take her in his arms. But she pulls his ear, and with
a tender reproof draws him jestingly to the front of the stage.
This boy has to learn how to meet such emergencies. He must
learn not only to think of love, but must also know how to conceal this love from the world. So she scolds him: "Does one
leave one's sword lying about in a lady's bedroom? Doesn't he
have any better manners than that?" Octavian doesn't appreciate
the joking in this reproof. He only realizes that he has acted
badly and awkwardly. All the men over whom he has been
victorious to-day—Saurau, Hartig, the Portuguese envoy—

would have known how to behave and wouldn't have caused their loved one a second's annoyance. He goes quickly to the other side of the stage and says defiantly, hiding his misery and shame behind this attitude of defiance: "If you think that I behave so stupidly, and if it annoys you that I am not experienced in such things, then I don't at all see why you like me!" She has listened smiling. Yes, it is true: he certainly is not experienced in "such things"—but that is just his charm. She finds this boy enchanting, his youthful awkwardness is such a charming exception to the sophistication of which she has become so tired. So she says with great tenderness: "Stop philosophizing, dear sir, and come here!" and with piquant emphasis: "Now it is time for breakfast—everything has its proper time." For he has yet to learn how to wait, how to know which is the right time for passion and which is the right time for comfortable chatting. He has yet to learn that the pauses can also be exquisite, that prelude and postlude are important parts of the great comedy love. . . .

At the moment she wants nothing so much as this contented relaxation. She has no desire for any more storm, she is tired and wants to start the day with a fresh mind. The past night is now a delightful memory. . . . Octavian enjoys this breakfast *tête-à-tête*—his first experience of the kind. He serves his beloved with a roguish tenderness, but in his impatience even this breakfast seems to be too long. He takes the cup from her hand and again embraces her. They whisper endearing words into each other's ears. He calls her "Bichette", she calls him "Quinquin". Through it all is a light playfulness, the banter of those in love. Overwhelmed that it is he, not much more than a boy, who is the lover of this most attractive woman, he straightens up and says with youthful pride: "The Field Marshal is in the Croatian forest and hunts bear and lynx. And I—I am here—and hunt what? I have good luck . . ." The boy is rather tactless in his pride over his victory, and the Marschallin is annoyed. As he mentions the Field Marshal she gives a sudden start and turns slightly away, frowning. It is not right that the boy should mention her husband in a way that is almost scornful. Certainly she doesn't love her husband, but she respects and even fears him. For he, with his great pride, would be deeply distressed if he knew that his wife betrayed him with a young boy. Loyalty, to be sure, is a virtue which is little thought of in this circle. The whole court would understand if it knew of it. But one shouldn't "know". One should have the grace to conceal it. And the young lover should have the delicacy not to mention her husband at this moment. In any case, what does he know of the Field Marshal? He should not dare even to mention him. She herself, yes—she may say, loudly or softly, that she is anything but happy in her marriage—but he, the lover, should be quiet. He should have the tact to remain silent. For this reason her "Leave the Field Marshal alone!" is a rebuke. And the dream comes back to her which secretly tormented her through the night: "I dreamed of him." She is disturbed and distracted. For a moment she is overcome with fear. If he should find out, if he should come now, the young man's tactless scorn would be quickly silenced.

But Octavian takes her remark very differently. She has *dreamed!* He does not understand that one can have dreams of anxiety, for him there can be only dreams of love. . . . She has dreamed of the Field Marshal, she has dreamed of another man —last night—in his arms! He is hurt and shocked, he cannot understand it. The Marschallin, amused by his naïve interpretation, says smilingly: "My dreams are not made to my order." It amuses her to see him jealous, jealous of the very man of whom he has just been so scornful. His even more excited question: "Last night you dreamed of your husband?" is almost a threat, to which the Marschallin reacts with a joking rebuff. But when she says that in her dream he came home, Octavian shudders. He has only seen the Field Marshal fleetingly and has great respect for this commanding figure. The very power which emanates from his personality has been perhaps the piquant spice in Octavian's victory over his wife. For in his lack of experience he imagines that he has conquered, where actually he has only been chosen. . . . Suddenly the figure of the Field Marshal appears before his imagination and he would like nothing better than to hide himself and escape from those severe eyes.

Quickly he bends towards the Marschallin and whispers: "The Field Marshal?" She recounts her dream, telling of how he had arrived with much turbulence and his usual train of followers. For it was always like that: much noise, much rushing about, and then his sudden appearance. . . .

And now with the memory of her dream is mixed a strange

commotion from the courtyard which comes to her disquietingly.
The Marschallin is alarmed. . . . For heaven's sake, can it be her
husband? He hadn't intended to return so soon. And yet . . .
She remembers many times when his plans were suddenly
changed and he appeared like a devastating hurricane. Octavian
doesn't exactly reassure her in saying: "Yes, to be sure, I do
hear something—but must it be your husband? Think where
he is—in Raitzenland, way the other side of Esseg!" Marie
Thérèse knows nothing of geography. She is only half educated
like all the ladies of that period. It was enough to learn the
elegant customs, it was enough to be a "lady"—why burden
one's mind with useless knowledge? So with a touching innocence she turns to the young man: "Is that really so far away?"
And to his reassuring gesture she replies: "Then it must be
something else, then it is all right." But her eyes have not
entirely lost their expression of anxiety, and she looks repeatedly
towards the door, through which the strange sounds seem to
come. Octavian, noticing her anxiety, says immediately: "You
look there so anxiously, Thérèse?" Her answer: "You know,
Quinquin, even if it is very far away, the Field Marshal can
move very quickly," is a mixture of fear and a certain pride in
her husband's cleverness. Marie Thérèse is a soldier's wife.
Knightliness, imperturbability, eagerness for adventure course
through her blood. The Field Marshal has disappointed her as
a husband and as a lover, but never as a bold soldier, a strong
and fearless knight of the sword. For these qualities she admires
him and is proud of him. This pride rings through her words:
"The Field Marshal can move very quickly." And the memory
comes back to her of a day on which he almost surprised her in
a similar situation . . . almost—for she is still his wife. Had he
really surprised her there would have been no possibility of any
forgiveness. Even to-day she still feels the fear, even to-day still
enjoys recalling the cleverness with which she extricated herself
from that perilous situation.

She would like to tell Octavian about this—just as she would
tell a trusted friend. But at the last moment she remains silent.
Oh no, she couldn't tell this impetuous, jealous boy about that!
What a faux pas that would be. To tell him, who believes that
he is the only one. Laughing she buries her face in her hands
and avoids his violent question as to what happened once, by
saying: "Oh be good, you don't have to know everything."

Octavian has watched her, with increasing concern. How can it be possible? She has secrets? But I am really the only one—am I not? The only one whom she has chosen, who has won her, to whom she belongs? I must know, I must find out what it is that she was on the point of saying. "Bichette! What happened?"

When she refuses to tell him he throws himself upon the sofa in despair: "So she plays with me, O what a miserable being I am." From the heights of bliss he plunges abruptly into an abyss of jealousy.

Marie Thérèse, however, pays no attention to his rather comical despair: she listens intently to the sounds coming through the dressing-room door in the middle background. The hubbub has increased, someone is impetuously trying to force his way in. There is only one who would dare that, only one who would take it as his right: the Field Marshal. In sudden fear she is certain that it is he, and she interrupts Octavian, saying hastily: "Now don't be foolish, now it is serious. It is the Field Marshal."

Octavian, jumping up, listens for a moment as if paralysed. . . . Yes, it must be the Field Marshal, for if it were a stranger he would enter by the other door. No, only one would dare to enter through that door which is guarded against all intruders by faithful lackeys.

Octavian snatches up his sword which he has lain upon a chair and runs towards the door at the left, but is held back by the Marschallin. It isn't possible to escape that way: "My purveyors and a half-dozen lackeys are waiting there." No, the middle door seems the best, if one dares to try it. For the Field Marshal seems to have just reached the door of the dressing-room and is detained by the lackeys, who announce that the Princess is resting and cannot be disturbed—not even by her husband. . . .

Octavian wants also to escape by this door—but it is too late there too! The Field Marshal is already in the dressing-room and is trying to enter the room. There is only one thing to do: to hide. But Octavian doesn't fancy hiding, he wants to fight, he wants to enjoy this adventure to the full with a wild challenge to the injured husband. So he says boldly and defiantly: "I shall not let him pass, I stand by you." But the Marschallin with impatience pushes him into concealment behind the *portière*. It would really be unfortunate if she should come to grief through the thoughtless impetuosity of this boy! No, she will fight this through alone—she is now absolutely and

completely the master of the situation. And with flashing eyes
(as Hofmannsthal directs) she stands at the door, her arms folded
across her breast: "I should like to see someone dare to enter
this door while I stand here. I am no Neapolitan general, where
I stand, I stand . . ." Challenging, almost laughing, the wife of
a soldier, the bold master of a dangerous adventure—that is the
real Marie Thérèse. . . . She hears with delight that the lackeys
are refusing to admit the intruder in spite of violent demands.
The lackeys have a very good idea of what is going on in the
Princess's bedroom. They see through this piquant situation,
and as they all love and adore her, they want to help her.

Marie Thérèse says benevolently, with a smile: "They are
good fellows, my lackeys, don't want to let him in, say I am
sleeping, very good fellows." With a few steps she moves towards
the foreground, considering quickly what it is best for her to do.
Without any question it is best to open the door and meet the
Field Marshal in complete innocence, then just wait to see what
he will say. . . . Perhaps he knows about Octavian. Perhaps
someone has told him. Perhaps this will be the end. Well, then
it is the end! Marie Thérèse is fearless. She has snatched at
happiness when it has come her way and she will take the
necessary consequences. She goes energetically to the door at the
rear, ready to meet her husband.

Then, at the last moment, she suddenly hears outside an unfamiliar voice. It is not the Field Marshal, it is a stranger, a
visit. . . . She is saved, delighted. "Quinquin, it is a visit," is a
happy whirling into a lighthearted Viennese waltz. And she
continues in waltz tempo, laughing gaily in her relief: "Who
is that? Lord God, if it isn't Ochs, it is my cousin, the Ochs of
Lerchenau—what does he want?" She remembers a day when she
was sitting in a carriage with her youthful lover and a messenger
brought a letter to her. Certainly, that was the letter from Ochs!
"And I haven't the faintest idea of what was in it." She had
been so occupied with her charming Quinquin—how could she
have found time to read a letter, especially one from this unsympathetic cousin. But what will happen now? He comes
to-day regarding the letter—and she hasn't the slightest notion
of what he has written. Octavian is entirely to blame. She
reproaches him laughingly.

Half listening to the coarse complaints of Ochs, who un-
deterred by all refusals is determined to force his way into the

Marschallin's room, she looks about for Octavian. Where can he be? Why is he still hiding now that the danger is over?

In the meantime Octavian has put on the dress of a chambermaid which he has found in the alcove. He is really not much more than a boy and he seems to be much amused by the whole situation. But this isn't only a matter of wanting to dress up—it is a very good idea. As the chambermaid he can slip between the lackeys unnoticed and escape the attention of the people who are waiting for admittance. In any case he will attract less attention than if he leaves the Marschallin's bedroom as the dashing young Count Octavian.

There are many servants in the house—no one will question him as to who he is or what he is looking for. Of course, he should have left earlier—at the break of dawn. Then he would only have been seen by the soldiers who guard the Marschallin's suite, and they would have been understanding and looked the other way. Of course, that would have been more intelligent! But who can be intelligent or reasonable where Marie Thérèse is concerned? He is so helplessly in love—he just couldn't tear himself away. Now this fine idea occurs to him of disguising himself and everything will be very simple.

But he can't refrain from playing the chambermaid for the Marschallin's benefit. He trips out from behind the *portière* very elegantly and greets the Marschallin in the Viennese dialect of the common people (which is quite untranslatable) saying: "Command, Gracious Highness, I haven't been long in your Grace's service." Marie Thérèse is enchanted. Laughing she stretches out her hand to him. He immediately rushes to grasp it and, no longer the chambermaid but completely Octavian, covers it with passionate kisses. She can't help giving him a quick kiss as a reward for this flash of brilliance. She says laughingly: "Slip boldly through the lackeys. He is a clever rascal! And come again, my treasure, but come clothed as a man, and through the front door, if you don't mind."

Octavian wants to go, but at this moment the door is suddenly thrown open and Baron Ochs fills the doorway as he says with great arrogance to the servants: "Of course, her Grace will receive me."

Baron Ochs! Oh how can I write of him without letting my thoughts stray back to Vienna and Salzburg, or without paying tribute to the memory of Richard Mayr! There are others who play and sing the rôle of Baron Ochs excellently. Perhaps if I had not known Mayr, I would find them ideal. Mayr was first of all Viennese to the roots of his being. He was Viennese in an easy-going way, but he was at the same time an aristocrat. He was coarse, he was a peasant, he was a boorish aristocrat, his impersonation always gave one the feeling of a man of "class". When he broke into the Marchallin's room it was not only with the unrestrained coarseness of an ignorant peasant, there was also an exaggerated consciousness of his high nobility, the bearing of one who does not allow that he be turned away by servants. One felt all this in Richard Mayr at the very moment of his entrance. How often I have sung with him—first as Octavian, then through many years as the Marschallin. He was always a new delight, and again and again I was inspired by the many subtle details of his impersonation—by his enchanting whims, by the irresistible charm of his whimsical personality which could make even Baron Ochs ingratiating, illuminating him through his rough and hearty humor which was priceless. He made of him a delightful rascal, a drink-loving half-demoralized spendthrift whom one really couldn't be annoyed with because he was so amusing. There can never again be an Ochs like him! This personality only existed once and will never be found again. To be sure, no one is irreplaceable and many Ochs have followed him, creditably, even excellently, and with great success. But the absolutely personal note which Mayr brought to this rôle—this we will never again experience. I never sing the Marschallin without a feeling of longing for this revered friend who was taken so much too soon from the life he so loved. I am grateful that his voice at least has been made immortal through a recording of *Der Rosenkavalier*.

Baron Ochs has been successful in forcing his way in, but his impetuous entrance just at the moment of Octavian's departure results in their colliding in the doorway. The Marschallin watches this unexpected and unfortunate turn of events with concern. She stands in the foreground at the right of the stage. The portrayer of the Marschallin must be careful to leave the center of the stage at the moment of Octavian's departure: she is not now the central figure and must not obstruct the view of Ochs and Octavian in the doorway. Ochs must without any question have the center of the stage. His entrance is impressive, pompous, striking. The Marschallin has the intention of going to her toilet-table in the background, but her attention is distracted by this meeting of Ochs and Octavian which she watches. Then, somewhat preoccupied, she continues to the table where she looks into the mirror and powders her face, looking around from time to time to watch Ochs.

Baron Ochs who seemed in such a desperate hurry to reach the Marschallin now apparently has all the time in the world. At the moment the young and pretty chambermaid interests him more than the dignified Marschallin. So, with no concern for etiquette, he devotes his whole attention to the supposed maid.

Octavian plays his part excellently. He wriggles about coyly and when the Baron asks him: "I haven't really hurt you?" he shakes his head vigorously.

The Marschallin resolutely and slowly turns around. She wants to put an end to Octavian's dangerous game.

The servants who are much disturbed by the Baron's incredible nonchalance in the presence of the Princess bend over him and with politeness gently remind him of "Her gracious Highness". Ochs immediately turns and greets the Marschallin with his best form. She replies, smiling politely: "Your Highness is looking very well." This is a smooth *façon de parler* which the Baron takes too literally. He turns quickly to the lackeys and says triumphantly: "Don't you see that her Grace is delighted to see me?"

The Marschallin is taken aback by the crudeness of his behavior. A visitor doesn't address one's servants in such a tone. She is not accustomed to having any one speak over her head to someone else, disregarding her presence. So it is with a frown that she leads the Baron forward, while she looks distractedly over her shoulder at Octavian. Octavian is enjoying this ridiculous situation wholeheartedly. Playing the chambermaid amuses him hugely. He busies himself in the background in his efforts to avoid as much as possible the surprised and curious glances of the servants. He pretends that he is arranging the bed and throws the pillows about very conspicuously. He knows that he shouldn't attract Baron Ochs's attention, but it intrigues him to spin out this delightful comedy a little longer. So he pays no attention to the glances of the Marschallin but goes on behaving rather conspicuously. He is little more than a boy—this is a game, it is fun and he just can't help making the most of it.

The Baron now makes conversation with the Marschallin, who only gives him half her attention. He is thoroughly unsympathetic to her and his arrival is particularly disturbing. It is only with the greatest effort that she manages to be at all polite to him. But when he says that he has very often visited the Princess Brioche in the early morning hours she becomes suddenly attentive—there is always some scandal about this Princess. Marie Thérèse is much interested and amused when Ochs tells her that she has received him while in her bath and only concealed by a small screen.

The Marschallin motions to the servants who are waiting in the background to bring up a sofa. The servants then leave the room. Ochs's eyes follow them and he recalls the difficulty he had in trying to force his way in. He would like to be sure that the servants who dared to refuse the Baron Ochs will be punished. For after all he had announced his visit. The letter —which the Marschallin had forgotten to read—had mentioned the day of his arrival, but nevertheless he has had to wait until the servants receive the order to admit him. Marie Thérèse immediately asks his pardon—"I beg your pardon, they did as they were ordered. I had a migraine this morning." In tender remembrance her eyes rest for a moment upon Octavian, who, delighted, throws her a kiss. He is still standing in the alcove, hesitate to leave, for he thinks that Ochs will soon depart and he will again be alone with his beloved.

At this moment Ochs turns towards Octavian—of course not in time to see the kiss which he has thrown the Marschallin. The little one pleases him extraordinarily. Disregarding the fact that the Marschallin has complained of a headache and is eager to be rid of him he seats himself upon the sofa which Marie Thérèse, giving up all hope of his departure, has offered him. Noticing that without interruption his eyes seek the supposed chambermaid she says quickly and with embarrassment: "I am afraid my chambermaid, a young thing from the country, disturbs your Grace. . . ." She would be only too happy if he would say "yes", and give her an excuse for dismissing the daring boy and so putting an end to this game. Octavian's shortsightedness irritates her: he apparently doesn't realize that the best thing he could do would be to get out of the Baron's sight as quickly as possible.

Sooner or later the Baron is bound to meet the young Count
Octavian and it would be very embarrassing if he should recall
the features of the chambermaid. Ochs would perhaps be tactless
enough to express his astonishment. And the Field Marshal has
the eyes of an eagle. He would probably put two and two together, and the result would be tragedy . . . So the Marschallin
isn't exactly amused by Octavian's thoughtlessness, although
within her heart she must secretly laugh at the boy for carrying
this comedy through with such grace.

Ochs feels that he must apologize for taking so much interest
in this pretty young girl. He is actually a bridegroom. The
Marschallin looks at him with astonishment: "A bridegroom?"
Now it is Ochs's turn to be astonished. The letter—it was all
in the letter. The Marschallin has to laugh. The letter! Yes,
of course. Now she must play a comedy and find out what really
was in the letter.

To whom is the Baron engaged? She has heard nothing about
it—she has no idea who may be the chosen one—"the fortunate
one" as she says scornfully. Scarcely noticing what she is saying,
Ochs continues to watch Octavian with increasing interest, until
finally in response to her very emphatic question "Do tell me who
is to be the bride?" he gives her name: "Fräulein von Faninal,"
annoyed that the Marschallin should ask her name when he had
already mentioned it with the greatest clearness in his letter. He
knows that this marriage is really beneath him in the eyes of the
aristocracy. The father Faninal is *nouveau riche* and one doesn't
marry that kind of a person. He thinks that the Marschallin is
deliberately forgetting the name by way of expressing her dis-
approval. To make matters worse the Marschallin says: "Of
course! Where is my head? Were they born here?" The poor
lady is only doing her best to find out what was in the letter, and
doesn't realize that Ochs interprets her questioning very differently. He is annoyed, so he says with emphasis: "Yes, indeed
they belong here. Her Majesty has raised them to the nobility."

Marie Thérèse hasn't the faintest interest in the affairs of the
Baron. She seems to listen with attention but actually she
watches Octavian, who having become bored has left the background and now stands provokingly in full view of the Baron.
How thoughtless! How careless! With a frown she tries to
make it clear to him that he should disappear as quickly as
possible. But Octavian is having much too good a time. No

power on earth can make him budge from here! He is more than ever in love with the Marschallin, he enjoys seeing her so formal and so much the "great lady" as she speaks with the Baron, he enjoys throwing her secret kisses and seeing her look of annoyed reproach melt from time to time into one of tender warmth for him—for him alone. . . .

Baron Ochs has noticed the Marschallin's disturbed expression, but he has misinterpreted it. He thinks she is annoyed because he is marrying a commoner, or which is almost worse, one raised only recently to the nobility. He tries to make her understand this unsuitable marriage. His much too conventional cousin must realize that the father is incredibly rich, that the girl is pretty as an angel and has just come out of the cloister—half Vienna belongs to her father, and his health isn't very good.

The Marschallin has listened. She isn't at all amused. Suddenly she sees the picture of the young girl, who through her father's ambition is being forced into a marriage which can only result in unhappiness for her—for she knows her fine cousin. It annoys her that this vulgar girl-hunter, who is not at all ashamed of waylaying the pretty chambermaid in her presence, should marry a lovely girl—and still more that it is he who has the idea that he is marrying beneath him.

But after all why should she be concerned about it? She has no right to be mixed up in this. There are many people like Baron Ochs, many like the rich Faninal—one just can't do anything about it.

So she takes refuge in a half-joking figure of speech: "My dear cousin, I know what you mean." Winking slyly Baron Ochs begins to speak of the children which will be born of this marriage. Of course, they will not have pure and noble blood, but he is such a great man that he will know how to make a place for his wife and children at court. And even if the children can never wear the golden key of the Marshal (only those of the most noble blood may do that) they still will be contented with the iron key of twelve houses—twelve houses!—which belong to their father.

The Marschallin is very much amused by such naïve frankness. Laughing she says with wit and charm: "Oh certainly, surely the children of my cousin will be no Don Quixotes."

Things are going much too slowly to suit Octavian. He has finally decided to obey the command of the Marschallin and leave the room. Taking the tray with the remainder of the breakfast he is on the point of leaving, but he just can't go inconspicuously behind the Baron's back, he has to attract his attention again by passing before him as he leaves.

Baron Ochs immediately reacts as the bold youth had intended that he should. Calling the chambermaid (Octavian) back, he forces the Marschallin to offer him breakfast, which she does half laughing and half annoyed. Ochs now divides his attention between the Marschallin, with whom he speaks formally and conversationally, and the supposedly charming young girl, of whom he has decided to make a conquest. While he tells Marie Thérèse the story of his approaching marriage, he whispers to Octavian promises and requests, which he, in silent play, answers coquettishly and unabashed.

The Marschallin really has to laugh and begins to find this incredible comedy quite delightful. She acts as if she doesn't notice the daring farce which is going on before her eyes, but asks her cousin politely who will be the bearer of the rose—a custom of this period which lent an especial glamor to the marriage ceremony. (Before the bridegroom comes to his fiancée he sends a young cavalier of noble birth, who must deliver to her a silver rose as a token of his love.) The Baron knows no one in his immediate acquaintance who seems noble enough to be the cavalier of the rose. So he comes to the Marschallin with the hope that she may suggest someone. All this was in the letter which the Marschallin had never read. He is astonished that she doesn't seem to know anything of the request which he expressed in this letter—but she immediately pulls herself together and quite in the picture quickly considers whom she might suggest as the cavalier of the rose. "Cousin Preising? How would cousin Lambert do?" She will think it over, and when they next dine together she will give him the name of someone. "When may we dine together? Shall we say to-morrow?"

Octavian makes pleading and irate signals to her. "No, not to-morrow, have you forgotten, Marie Thérèse? I want to be with you to-morrow and the day after to-morrow and every day." Marie Thérèse pays no attention to him. The only thing which concerns her is getting rid of the Baron. Her question "Can I serve my cousin in any other way" is an unmistakable command that now at last he should really go.

But the Baron doesn't understand such delicate innuendoes.

He still would like to have a recommendation to the notary: it is for him an especially important matter—the marriage contract is to be completed, certainly a gala moment for the Baron, in which all the pretty young girl's large fortune will pass into his "highly noble" hands. The Marschallin smiles at his tactless haste—this gives her a pretext to send Octavian away. The youth will take the hint and go without attracting attention. She knows that the notary, as usual in the morning, is waiting in the ante-room. But she wants an excuse to get Octavian away, and so tells him to go to the ante-room to see if the notary is there. But Marie Thérèse hasn't reckoned with Ochs. He is very eager to keep "the little one" here. . . . The Marschallin laughs—and to his objection that such a sweet child shouldn't be permitted to mix with those rascally lackeys, she only replies scornfully and ironically: "Your Grace is too concerned." At this moment the ante-room door is opened and Struhan, the house steward, enters with dignity. The Marschallin engages him in conversation and the Baron uses this time for trying to arrange an appointment with Octavian. He draws him, half resisting, closer to him and asks him if he has ever dined *tête-à-tête* with a cavalier. Octavian shakes his head violently. To Ochs's urgent "Will you?" he answers in common Viennese dialect: "Oh, I don't know if I am allowed to."

The steward stands with his back to Ochs and Octavian, bending politely over the Marschallin. She talks with him, turning over letters and petitions but never loses sight of them. On the contrary she follows Ochs' efforts and Octavian's bold game with concealed amusement.

I should like to say a word of caution regarding this scene: Octavian is very easily overplayed here. The singer should never forget that Octavian is from a "great house", that grace and nobility of bearing are born in him, so that it just wouldn't be possible for him actually to simulate the coarseness which he would like to. Usually the Octavian forgets this and plays to the audience for laughs, instead of remaining within the limits of the refined comedy which *Rosenkavalier* is and should always be. For instance, throwing his legs high into the air when he is pulled by Ochs towards the seat is in my opinion very bad taste. In the first place the Baron would never permit himself to behave so vulgarly in the presence of the Marschallin or the house steward. The advances which he dares behind the Marschallin's back must be strictly within the bounds of possibility. Octavian should know how to draw away from him with a quick and clever turn, without exaggeratedly and boorishly throwing his legs into the air in a way which is so out of the frame of the play that it is really disturbing.

With suppressed amusement the Marschallin sees what is going on between Ochs and Octavian, and giving the steward a sign of dismissal sits back in her chair with great grace, saying very decidedly and with scornful politeness: "My cousin, I see, takes his pleasures where he finds them."

Ochs is glad that she takes his crude behavior so mildly. For a moment he was embarrassed and feared that without mincing words she would tell him what she thought of his conduct. But no: isn't she a charming woman? She only laughs—she is a woman of the world, she understands, she pardons. It seems to him that he is paying her a great compliment when he says, as he gratefully kisses her hand, that she has no nonsense, no etiquette nor Spanish affectation.

But she reminds him half jokingly that after all he is a bridegroom. Now that is a real challenge for Ochs. He must tell her of his ideas about love—he must picture more clearly for her the only true and real joys of love. So he launches forth on lavishly illustrated stories, to which the Marschallin and Octavian (behind the Baron's chair) listen slightly shocked but much amused.

The Marschallin asks him rather ironically if he pursues this so-called love as a profession. He answers proudly: "I certainly do! I know none which would suit me better . . ." This very long narrative of Ochs is generally cut. In Vienna we had a much longer version than is customary outside of Austria and Germany. I remember that for a time we even had the whole story uncut, but that is much too long, especially if there is no Richard Mayr to sing Ochs.

Ochs winds up his colorful recital of the joys of love with a description of how one must conquer an uncouth peasant girl and to illustrate this noble accomplishment he seizes Octavian and tries to kiss him. This scene ends with a very quick and dashing trio, in the course of which Octavian manages to break away and flies across the stage to the Marschallin, panting with relief.

They are all in very high spirits. It amuses the Marschallin that Octavian through his play-acting has been almost kissed by the coarse Baron, and when Ochs asks her if she won't let him have this charming maid as a servant for his future wife she can no longer restrain her mirth. She is especially delighted, when praising the maid's good manners he asserts that there must be a drop of good blood in her. The Marschallin and Octavian exchange merry glances: "A drop of good blood! Your Grace has a sharp eye . . . !" It may certainly be said that the blood of the Count Rofrano is good. Unwittingly Ochs has said something very true. He has an understanding for "aristocratic slips". He has an illegitimate son, Leopold, whom he always has with him as his valet. It is he who will bring the silver rose to the Marschallin—she must notice him—that is his son.

Suddenly the Marschallin conceives a plan. It has dawned on her in a flash when Ochs spoke of the "good blood" and his illegitimate son: she will show him a picture of Octavian—she hopes he will see the resemblance between him and the chambermaid, and she will tell him that it is quite possible that this maid is the daughter of the Count Rofrano. In this way she will do away with any possible danger in his meeting Octavian. He won't find the resemblance at all surprising or suspicious, but will remember: Aha, the Marschallin did tell me of an illegitimate affair from which her chambermaid was born. . . . Yes, she will even hasten this meeting, so that he will have no chance to forget this fictitious story. So she selects Octavian as the cavalier of the rose, which otherwise she might not have done.

Octavian doesn't see through this finely spun intrigue of the Marschallin. He is quite horrified at her showing the Baron his picture and hesitates to take it from its hiding-place as she orders him to. But "she must know what she is doing"—and he must obey her command.

She lovingly takes in her hand the medallion with the picture of Octavian. It is beautiful, and reveals her charming lover in all his seductive youth and grace and boyish manliness. She quite forgets herself as she looks at it. Then in a light conversational tone she asks: "Would your Grace care to take this young man as the bearer of the rose?" The musical phrase flows in light waltz-time—the sweetest of memories dance through the mind of Marie Thérèse. There must be all the warmth and feeling of one in love in the words: "My young cousin, Count Octavian"—

they must have the sound of a caress from which she parts reluctantly. But then with quick decision she hands the picture to the Baron. He immediately notices the astonishing resemblance. The Marschallin takes a deep breath. The plan seems to be working out. He sees the resemblance, he will believe her and will not look for the solution to a puzzle in view of this explanation. She is very pleased and says with exaggerated importance that she herself has often thought about it: the old Count Rofrano, the brother of the Marquis—Oh, not the father of Octavian. Oh, no, the second brother—does he know him? He seems to be the one—her noble cousin will understand! . . . So, knowing that the little maid is of high descent, she has always considered her as something "rather special"— and rising the Marschallin playfully draws Octavian to her side and adds: "always near me". . . .

But now there has been enough of this, and she wants to put an end to this ridiculous situation. Her idea of leading the Baron into confusion has been completely successful. With great authority which brooks no refusal she sends Octavian away: "Now go, Mariandl, hurry and let the people in." She pays no attention to the Baron's weak protest. Octavian opens the door to the ante-room and in coarse dialect calls in a disguised voice: "You can come in." . . . He then leaves through the middle door, shoving the Baron, who has hastened after him, right into the old servant who is entering with the washbowl.

For a moment the Marschallin follows this encounter with amusement, but she then turns to the sleeping-alcove to which her maid follows her.

In this period the morning bath was rather a dubious procedure. The little bowl of water, a hand-towel, much eau-de-Cologne—were all that one needed. . . . To-day it seems strange that in a time of such over-refined culture real cleanliness was actually very much neglected. But perhaps one shouldn't question the hygiene of this period, and so disturb the picture of the radiant Marschallin. . . .

In any case the "ceremony of making up" was a much more elaborate affair than that of bathing. And every morning this and the festive ceremony of the *coiffeur* (which was an art in itself) constituted a public occasion: the levee was the hour in which petitioners, salesmen, scientists, artists, came in droves to the Marschallin, pressing up to her and surrounding her seeking a look, or a word, or a gift. . . .

A merry crowd now begins to form on the stage. A pet dealer comes with little dogs, a monkey, a parrot. This often results in very amusing situations and I always look forward to the moment when the pet dealer appears—generally with a different dog for each performance. In Vienna the animals caused so much difficulty that for a long time we had only one very old and phlegmatic dog, who wasn't in the least disturbed by all the noise and confusion around him but sat placidly on the dealer's arm, blinking disinterestedly at the audience. The monkey had to be abandoned because his adventurous escapades were much too distracting and no one listened to the very difficult aria which the tenor, accompanied by a flutist, sings for the Marschallin. Who would ever listen to singing when a monkey is leaping about the stage chattering excitedly? This really seems to me too much and too dangerous rivalry! . . . Had I been the tenor I would have forbidden the presence of the monkey as unfair competition.

Once Elisabeth Schumann (the enchanting Sophie) sent to me on the stage her Pekinese "Happy", adorned with a glowing red bow. When I called him he wagged his tail violently and tried to climb up on the toilet table—much to the delight of Elisabeth who was watching from the wings. Another time I had quite an adventure with my own Pomeranian puppy whom I had only owned for three days. He came directly to me from a kennel and had a deathly fear of every one. My maid Marie, whom I had brought with me from Vienna was standing in the wings with my sweet little puppy on her arm. It just happened that no dog had been sent this evening for the pet vendor's scene and the director at a loss as to what he should do was delighted to see in my Mausi a way out of his embarrassment and took him away from Marie. As she spoke very little English she couldn't understand what he was saying, and couldn't explain that the puppy was so terrified that he would probably have a heart attack or do something dreadful on the stage. In any case no one paid any attention to her despairing efforts to express her horror at being robbed of the dog. And suddenly on the stage I had the shock of seeing my Mausi on the vendor's arm, so completely paralysed by fear that he was absolutely rigid and couldn't budge. In his terror he didn't even recognize me and

sat there like a wax puppy. But after all that is better than the
bad manners of some dogs who hurl themselves delightedly at
the Marschallin and with frantic tail-wagging try to climb up
on her lap. I always enjoy this scene tremendously, for in my
almost pathological devotion to animals I can never have enough
of them around me, no matter what the situation.

But I am wandering too far astray. The Marschallin returns
from the alcove and is received with reverential bows. She does
not give a real greeting in acknowledgment, but passes through
the gathering smiling benevolently, and proceeds to her toilet
table as the assemblage bows before her. This mixture of complete superiority and charming benevolence must characterize
the Marschallin. It is the old Viennese aristocratic way of "being
democratic", which she personifies. The real Viennese aristocrat
can never seem really arrogant, however much he may be in his
heart. He has so much charm and inborn nonchalance that even
his awareness of his superior position seems lovable.

The Marschallin seats herself before her toilet table and,
chiefly concerned with her make-up, only passively goes through
the form of greeting those who come to her in a colorful
procession.

To-day she is not satisfied with her hairdresser. Annoyed and
irritated she repeatedly tells him that she is dissatisfied with his
arrangement. Looking into the mirror she sees that she is
looking tired. . . . Tired from the night in which she had felt
younger than for a long time, tired from caresses and tempestuous passion. But it seems that to-day she must pay for
this. To-day from the pitilessly truthful mirror, there looks back
at her the image of an ageing woman. But she will not admit
that to herself. She must put the blame upon the clumsy hairdresser. She still refuses to seek the reason in her years. . .
And when, interrupted by the violent outburst of the Baron who
is quarrelling with the notary in the background, she thinks of
putting an end to the reception, she once again looks intently
into the hand-mirror and half turning towards the unhappy
friseur, says: "My dear Hyppolyte—to-day you have made an
old woman of me." To sing this phrase with the right expression is of the utmost importance. It would be wrong to say these
words too forcefully, wrong to make this reproach too emphatic.
Through these words must vibrate her whole helpless resignation

disguised as wounded pride. She says them with restraint, quietly, softly, but with decision. With a gesture of suppressed anger she throws the mirror on the toilet table. She *plays* the injured one who is served without sufficient care, the lady who is annoyed by inexcusable neglect. . . .

But within her heart she has realized that it is through no fault of a *friseur* that she who was so radiant has changed into a tired and ageing woman. She knows this—she has the evidence before her, and her irritation is an escape, nothing more.

The *friseur* plunges feverishly into trying to improve upon what he has already done well. But the Marschallin with nervous impatience dismisses all those present with a sharp and ill-humored command which is most unusual for her. She only says: "All are dismissed", whereas usually she has a friendly word for every one.

While the people are slowly leaving, and the pair of Italians approach the Baron scenting business, Marie Thérèse tries to improve her appearance with pearls and rings which she first picks up and then discards. She looks sadly and searchingly into the mirror, paying no attention to her surroundings.

Generally at this point a learned man with a tremendous book under his arm comes up to the Marschallin and she looks at the book with a polite and condescending interest. I personally don't like this universal and customary idea of direction. It seems to me to smack a little of artificially "filling out the pause". In any case it seems a hindrance rather than a help. In my opinion the Marschallin should now be left completely alone. The whole scene is a wonderful preparation for her magnificent monologue, and the less she is disturbed through unnecessary interruptions the better I find it.

It is only a bad actress who cannot through her facial expression alone make clear the feelings which she is experiencing. To be sure, opera houses are vast in size and the audience far away, and so one may think that the play of facial expression will be lost, and merely sitting motionless will give the impression of being lifeless. I have a very different conception. I believe firmly that vibrations emanate from the actor which can reach to the last row, regardless of the size of the house. Perhaps it is the power of personal magnetism which is capable of holding an audience spellbound—I don't know enough of such things to be sure what it is. But the mystery of personality goes much deeper than its momentary effect upon a receptive audience. Just as there are human beings who through their gaze can control wild animals, softening and dispelling their savagery, so the artist can hold an audience through his power of expression dispelling its natural restlessness and holding its attention. When in singing I feel any restlessness in the audience—that confusion of rustling movements, coughing and shuffling feet— I never seek the cause in the audience but in myself. It is I who have failed to fulfill my mission. There is no such thing as a mediocre audience—it is only the artist who is mediocre if she cannot hold her audience. So even on a great opera stage one must be able to hold the listeners as if under a spell—and they must feel this spell, even if they cannot actually see the facial expression of the artist standing quietly and motionlessly before them. The artist will always unconsciously assume a bearing which corresponds to her thought. The body is such a delicate instrument of thought and expression—how could any one misunderstand what seems so self-evident!

A face which has an extraordinary power of expression is that of Katherine Cornell. I saw her in Chekhov's *The Three Sisters*, and was fascinated to see how without a single overt movement she lived and was the focus of the action through her magnificently expressive face. This face, which for me is much more than beautiful was the mirror of her thoughts, a song without words to listen to which was inspiration and delight. . . .

So at this moment the Marschallin should sit quietly, almost without any movement at all—only her face should mirror what is passing through her mind. As she sits before her mirror her melancholy gaze falls slowly to her hands which are holding the beautiful pearls. But these hands, though cared for and protected from anything which might lessen their beauty, are also treacherous: more than anything else hands betray the age of a woman, while she may through a thousand remedies be able to keep her face still looking young.

Of course when one is not alone on the stage one must follow the orders of the stage director. That is to be taken for granted. Order must prevail—there must be one head which oversees everything and grasps the total effect. Usually I hate to broach too many of my own ideas—a director, strangely enough, often seems deeply hurt if a singer has ideas of her own. And the

more my reputation as an opera singer developed the more I
tried to fit into the frame and to avoid being the much-feared
prima donna which one is so easily considered if one introduces
objections. I have always found a way to retain my own conceptions and individuality within the prescribed frame. It is
even a kind of artistic challenge for me if I am compelled to make
a virtue of necessity. I never came to a stage rehearsal with
a fixed idea as to how I would play a part. I let myself be too
much guided by the inspiration of the moment to do that. I
have always found that the most important thing is a deep
understanding of the part itself, so that its outward expression,
the gestures which one makes, where one stands upon the stage,
is of no consequence. In this respect I always followed the
suggestions of the stage director—unless something went too
much against the grain.

We had as stage director in Vienna von Wymetal (the father
of Wilhelm von Wymetal, who is known in America), who was
an exceptionally fine *régisseur*. For his never-failing attention
I have much to be grateful. He watched us at every performance, censuring severely any bad habit or awkward movement.
He was especially delighted by Maria Jeritza's incredible flair
for theatrical effect. He once said to me: "She is like wax in
my hands—I have only to make a suggestion and everything is
there which I had just thought out in that second." During this
time Jeritza was subject to his strict control, and her passion for
acrobatic escapades was dampened through von Wymetal's good
taste. At that time her Tosca was magnificent, and the idea of
singing the prayer while lying on the floor didn't appear at all
out of place, as it seemed genuinely and deeply felt. If her hair
fell down it was not the sought for effect which it later became.
When she was no longer subject to von Wymetal's influence I
found it really disturbing that her hair always fell at exactly the
same moment, for one saw the practised grasp with which she
tore out the pins and her tragic grief no longer seemed quite
credible. Von Wymetal watched her with pitiless severity and
eliminated everything which might seem like a striving for effect.

Lothar Wallerstein, who is very knowing and brilliant, has
a slight tendency to exaggerate. When he first came to Vienna
I often had battles with him, for while he brought with him a
modern spirit it was one which had not yet been purified in the
fire of long experience. However, out of bitter disagreements

there developed a sincere and mutual respect, and I liked very much to work with him then, although I don't believe that he liked until much later my not doing everything which he wanted. When I didn't do as he said he would always turn a little pale, and I felt him pulling himself together in order not to lose his patience. But we always reached a mutual compromise and understanding and I very much enjoyed working with him. He is a stage director from whom one can learn a great deal, if one knows how to retain one's own freedom—or better, how to fight for it.

Among the many directors with whom I have worked, I liked Herbert Graf very much. He has ideas and he has enthusiasm which is most essential in this very difficult, perhaps most difficult and most thankless of all professions. For what Wallerstein once said to me is really true: "If singers act well, every one says: what inspiration! What a personality! The way that singer acted was wonderful, there one could see that he is a genius." But when the singer is awkward they say: "Of course, that is the fault of the director. . . . How could he let the man run around like that . . ."

It is quite true that the stage director is the hardest worker of all during rehearsals, yet he receives the least gratitude from the audience. However, one shouldn't exaggerate this fact. Someone once said to me: "If the director arranges everything—every position, every movement which the singer makes—then all the singer does is only imitation. Then the only original one is the director." That is, of course, pure nonsense. A truly artistic personality will always merge from the pattern which is perhaps woven by the director. . . . She will let herself be advised, even influenced, will consider and agree, but within the frame of what is prescribed she will always emerge as a real personality and go her own way.

The artist who is submerged by the ideas of another is no real *personality*.

Even a Toscanini, a Walter will give one freedom, if this freedom is artistic. It would be inartistic to shackle what can only truly develop through freedom.

But I have digressed a long way from my Marschallin. Let us come back to her as she sits sadly before her mirror. Returning to reality, turning her head slightly, she sees the two Italians beside the Baron and puts an end to their conversation by rising. She does this at the moment in which the Italians sing: "We are here!" Often I have gotten the impression that the Marschallin rises because Ochs speaks to her. This must never be the case: on the contrary, Ochs turns to her because by rising she has shown that she wants to put an end to the conversation.

The Baron wants to present to her the illegitimate son of whom he has spoken. She smiles a little when he asks if he may present the counterpart of her pretty chambermaid, but it is the smile of one withdrawn and distracted. With a slight turn she casts a half amused glance at the ridiculous Leopold who approaches the Baron, carrying the large red box with the silver rose. With scarcely suppressed scorn she says: "I congratulate your Grace. . . ."

All she wants is to be left alone. She wants to be alone with her thoughts, wants to try to clarify the thoughts which had affected her so deeply as she sat before the mirror: that her day is turning to evening, that resignation is lurking amidst the shadows. . . . But once more she is almost forced to laugh when the Baron tries to get the chambermaid into the room again. Quietly and determinedly she prevents this by repeating her promise that he shall have the Count Rofrano as his rose-bearer —"He will so gladly do it for me," she says with much charm. Once more there passes fleetingly through her thoughts the picture of the young girl who will be compelled to marry this unsympathetic cousin, and the inner revulsion which it stirs within her makes her break off suddenly, saying: "And now, my cousin, I say good-bye."

She wants to go to church—there she will find absolution from the priest to whom she has many times before confessed her fleshly sins. As the Baron leaves with the two Italians who had lingered in the background, and the servants follow quickly behind them, the Marschallin goes with quick steps to the other side of the stage looking towards Ochs.

At last she is alone. At last she can let her mask fall, that mask of politeness which to-day has oppressed her as never before. How she despises this Baron! How despicable he seems, he who dares to stretch out his greedy hands for a young innocent girl—"and pictures to himself that it is he who is lowering himself. . . ."

Marie Thérèse trembles with anger. In great agitation she

again crosses the stage and at the other side pauses, and with her characteristic humor, scolds herself: "Why do I work myself up, it is the way of the world . . ."

Now comes the rather long prelude to the wonderful monologue, and the less the singer of the Marschallin "acts" here the better. The thoughts which move her are not tragic thoughts: "one must accept what life brings, one doesn't go to pieces so easily . . . and this girl won't go to pieces either, but through secret tears and attempts at resistance will resign herself and become a good wife and have charming children and be on the whole contented with her lot. But she will do what every one in this circle does, she will find her happiness in other arms, she will sin and atone for her sin and it will be forgiven. So why this anger? It is just 'the way of the world'. . ."

During this reverie the Marschallin, half smiling, should just stand in quiet contemplation. She has learned to smile the knowing smile of one who has been tested. From the revolts of her youth she has wrung a philosophical resignation—and this has been the best victory of her life. . . . Slowly and thoughtfully she goes to the toilet table and seats herself hesitantly, absorbed in her thoughts. She should in no way give the impression of being sad. The music is light and graceful. So her thoughts only glide over the troubled times that have passed, in which she was forced into an unhappy marriage. But that is all so far back, that has all become settled and clear like old wine, like a half forgotten song which perhaps makes one a little melancholy but which one can still hum with a smile.

Her own girlhood rises before her. She sees herself just out of the cloister, sees herself in a marriage into which she had been "ordered". And with a melancholy look in the mirror says: "Where is she now? Where is the snow of winters that have passed . . ." That was I—that half-child, who dreamed and hoped, that was I. . . . And soon—in the near future—I shall be old, really old. . . . The Marschallin must almost laugh at this thought. It seems so impossible: she—old, withered, cold. Last night, in Octavian's arms, she had been so young. Life's passionate pulse had throbbed within her as of old—and yet: soon no one will any longer whisper to her words of love. She will be an old woman, the old Marschallin. . . . Bending forward she imitates the people who will call to one another on the streets: "See, there goes the old Princess Resi. . . ." There is something ghostly in this thought—with a sudden gasp of fear she clutches her throat. How can it be? I am always the same. I feel the same pulsing of my heart, the same longings, the same yearning dreams to-day which I felt when I was a mere child—they only take different forms, different melodies. But I am always I—I will not become the ghost of myself. . . . Only God knows why that should be. Why must I experience this so consciously? Why may I not pass slowly and imperceptibly from one period to another? Why must all the warmth and beauty of life slip away while I look on with full consciousness—with the ghastly realization: now the time has come.

Perhaps what God has decreed for us poor mortals must remain a secret. We must accept it, we must live through it and endure it.

A wonderful and serene understanding smiles within her—she raises her head and says half aloud, as if in warning to herself: "And in the *how*—there lies all the difference . . ." To experience growing old with dignity, to endure the inevitable with a smile, that is her determination, her philosophy, her realization.

Octavian enters the room in his riding-uniform. Looking up, Marie Thérèse is almost astonished to see him, for the moment she had quite forgotten him—he had seemed so far away.

Involuntarily she now gathers about her the cloak which had half fallen from her shoulders, for day has come and with it the need to be more formal. As she has said to Octavian: "Everything has its proper time."

She greets him with a friendly glance. He has entered quickly, throwing his gloves and sword on the chair, and in two steps is beside her—eager to clasp her again in his arms. He is so young—for him it is always time for love. But he restrains himself as he sees Marie Thérèse's calm gaze. To-day she is no longer the radiant lover. She looks tired—and sad. He stands beside her filled with tenderness: "and you are sad . . ." To her gentle denial he tells why he is proud and happy: she is sad because she has been worried, worried about him! For in his youthful egotism he thinks that everything which the Marschallin says and does must concern him. So he believes that she had only trembled for him, her lover, when she thought that her husband had returned. His heart is overflowing with joy and gratitude, and he tries tempestuously to draw her to him. But with a tender gesture Marie Thérèse pushes him from her. The

dear fellow! How sweet he is! How touching is his faith that
he is the only one who plays any part in her life! So she says
to him whimsically: "A little sad perhaps . . ." In a flash the
danger of that moment rises before her: if the Field Marshal
had really come home! What then? There is nothing which
can justify fear. She is the dauntless wife of a soldier—she
might even have accepted tragedy and dramatic discovery as a
challenge, and held her position. *She* is *she*—from head to toe!
Whatever might happen, it wouldn't alter anything, she would
always be the same—looking into the face of danger, taking the
consequences for whatever she has sought, accepted, enjoyed.

Octavian only thinks that she is happy to have escaped this
danger. So he says with gay and scornful triumph: "And it
was not the Field Marshal!" But the Marschallin doesn't like
the way in which he mentions her husband again and again. She
will not permit this boy to make gay over the husband whom
she respects, and moreover she doesn't want to be reminded of
him. To be sure one *does* things but one doesn't *talk* about
them . . . Octavian has much to learn. So she rejects his fervent
embrace rather coolly. She would much prefer having him
leave. She feels tired and sad and wants to be alone. Play and
laughter, ardor and fire—in this moment all that is over. He
must understand that. But it seems that, like all men, he is
egotistical, inconsiderate. That one must always experience the
same thing. Always this being taken possession of, which she
hates. This boy here—whom *she* has taken as her lover—he also
thinks that she belongs to him, that through a couple of nights
of love she has become his possession. It disturbs and oppresses
her, the worshipper of freedom, that he should already want to
play the master. But her reproach that he shouldn't be like every
other man has a surprising effect: instead of replying passionately
as she had expected and feared he would, he says discouragedly:
"I don't know how men are," and turns towards her with great
tenderness: "I only know that I love you . . ." He thinks she
seems changed, she is no longer the same—what have these
people done to her, who came to her—why have they estranged
her from him? He is very unhappy. Marie Thérèse, touched,
charmed, reconciled, reaches out her hand to him: "She is here,
Herr Schatz" (Sir Precious). This enchanting "Herr Schatz"
says so much: it shows her superiority, her tender scorn for
Octavian, who wants to show that she belongs to him. No, he

is a mere toy in her hands, the young "Schatz". He plunges towards her outstretched hand, he feels that she has only reached out to him fleetingly—but he will not have it so: "Herr Schatz". . . . He wants to be more to her—everything, everything to her. He will clasp her, that through his embrace she may feel how she belongs to him. He wants again to hear the fervent stammering of the night, he wants no more of this light and scornful trifling, he is a man! Oh, has he not become a man in her arms? So he will prove how much he is a man. She is his, she belongs to him. . . . But with gentle determination Marie Thérèse disengages herself from his arms and goes slowly to her toilet table, where she stands leaning against it. She would like to tell Octavian what it is which disturbs her, she would like to try to gain his understanding—and she explains to him how deeply she is aware of the transitoriness of time which rushes on unceasingly. The days and years seem to flow away in an ever-increasing tempo. Everything seems to slip between one's fingers, everything passes away which one would like to hold fast, all reality seems to become just a dream.

But this youth, who stands upon the threshold of life, cannot see that tragedy may lurk behind happiness. He does not understand Marie Thérèse. Why should one so full of laughter and radiance speak so sadly? Why should she think of all that is transitory in the midst of the glowing present? Perhaps she is tired of him—already? She would not speak so joylessly if she loved him as he does her. . . . Weeping he throws himself upon a chair and chides her: "She only wants to show me that she isn't dependent on me." The Marschallin smiles sadly. How little this youth can understand of all she wants to say! She turns to him as if he were a child, saying comfortingly: "O be good, Quinquin." As she goes to him and strokes his head which is bowed in grief, she realizes the tragi-comedy of this situation: "Now I have to comfort this boy because sooner or later he will forget all about me." This is not a reproach. She says it tenderly and with a kindly irony. But Octavian won't stand for this tone of superiority—he jumps up impetuously. What is it that has so changed her? Who is it that speaks through her? This is not the Marie Thérèse whom he loves, whom he has held in his arms. . . . What words are these which she speaks, which make her seem so far from him?

The Marschallin does not heed his complaints. She goes

slowly back to the toilet table and, sinking on to the chair beside it, sings the beautiful "Time Monologue". She tries to make clear to Octavian that it is not the outer world around us which is changed by time—no, time is within ourselves. One lives within it, without realizing that time runs away, one just doesn't notice it. But suddenly there comes a day when one feels its nearness. That is the day which is the beginning of the end, the beginning of the descent—the slow fading away of life. Then one starts to consider time. Now one feels it in one's body—trickling away like the incessant, soundless flow of the hour-glass—in the face, in the mirror, everywhere time is melting away, dissolving. . . . With a deep sigh the Marschallin turns to Octavian and says, filled with love: "O Quinquin, often I hear it flowing away—irresistibly." Time flows between him and her—even if she would like to hold it fast. Lost in this thought she confesses to the boy what she has never confessed to any one before, and she speaks, almost forgetting his presence: "Often I get up—in the middle of the night and stop all the clocks . . ." Doesn't he understand? He, who like time will vanish as the sand, who to-day is still close to her but to-morrow may be far away—far away in his love, in his devotion. And far away and strange will be the sweet mouth which knows how to kiss so passionately. . . . Time like an evil enemy awaits her hour. That hour which must come, which is approaching: the hour which means separation. Marie Thérèse straightens herself—her eyes look into the distance with an expression of fear. She listens—she seems to hear the pulse of time. Time, which the mere stopping of clocks cannot deceive.

Gently she throws off this stark oppression and says with a wise smile: "Yet one must not fear it—it too is the creation of the Father who has created us all. . . ." There it is again: her philosophy of life, her ready resignation, her quiet self-surrender. . . . "It is the way of the world." There it is again: the deep understanding and the acceptance of all that God has given to this world: joy—and renunciation.

Octavian has listened at first with sympathetic interest, but then with these strange words which he cannot grasp he becomes restless. Oh, of course, he knows what she means! But why does she have to say such sad things while he is here—why doesn't she let him wipe away with his kisses all that smoulders so somberly within her? All her thoughts should only belong to him, just as he thinks that he only lives for her whom he loves. She should forget all about time—what is time, anyway—what do years mean to such a wonderful woman? Isn't she more beautiful than any young girl whom he has met? Isn't she more attractive than all of them? She shall not speak of what is transitory—of resignation. He looks at her lovingly—feeling that she is suffering more than she admits. With deep tenderness he goes to her and takes her hand in his. Out of his loving reproach arises his passionate question: "Now that I am here, just now—you feel so depressed?"

Marie Thérèse realizes that the time has now come in which she must make clear to him how it will end between her and him. He should know that she faces this fact calmly. No concern for her shall hold him—she couldn't bear any cruel and misplaced sympathy. Time, which destroys everything, shall take its course. . . . With deep seriousness she turns to him (while he was speaking, she has risen) and clasping his hands says: "Quinquin, to-day or to-morrow you will leave me for one who is younger and lovelier than I . . ." Richard Strauss directs: "somewhat hesitantly at 'lovelier' . . ." It is very touching and so absolutely feminine that it is the fact that the other may be "lovelier" which disturbs her much more than that she will be younger. Younger—oh, that, of course, is to be taken for granted! He will soon tire of the ageing woman and seek his happiness in other arms—that is the way of the world. But she has always been a celebrated beauty to whom every one has paid homage. That this beauty should also fade and pale beside the fresh glow of a youthful face, that is what unconsciously hurts her. So she moves slowly and hesitantly away from Octavian, crossing the stage to the left side. In despair Octavian reproaches her. She only wants to be rid of him—that is it. She can't shove him away as she would something burdensome, but she would drive him away with cutting words which wound him. That is it—he sees it clearly. She doesn't love him any more.

Over her shoulder Marie Thérèse replies in a tone of forced lightness: "The day comes of itself—to-day or to-morrow the day will come, Octavian." She turns her face towards the window. At this moment she is incapable of meeting Octavian's eyes with calmness. She loves this young man—loves him as the personification of the youth which she feels fading from her. He means for her passion and laughter, light-heartedness and all that is graceful in life. Looking away from him she listens to his outburst of passionate excitement: Oh, he doesn't want to think! What is to-day, what is to-morrow? He has no interest in this ghastly to-morrow, he doesn't want to know anything about it. He doesn't want to see that day. And she should stop tormenting him. Sobbing, he falls to his knees embracing her.

(Very often this scene is arranged so that while Octavian is speaking the Marschallin has slowly moved behind the sofa at the left of the stage. He now throws himself upon the sofa and she stands behind it, bending over him as she sings the following phrase. I don't find this a good arrangement and have always played it differently. I always take the center of the stage and stand very erect above Octavian as he kneels before me. What the Marschallin now says is the absolute climax of the first act and is of the utmost importance. To hide behind the sofa seems to me very mistaken. Even from the visual standpoint, which should never be neglected, the Marschallin must here have the *center of the stage*. Her figure should not be cut off by the sofa.)

With great significance she says to Octavian: "To-day or to-morrow or the day after . . ." So it will be: he will leave her. She knows it, and she wants him to know that she expects this and expects him to go his way. Oh, no, she has no idea of tormenting him! But it is the truth—and is it not much more a warning to herself than to him? He will lose nothing, with his youth and his impetuosity he will go forth into a life which will be rich in exciting experience. It is she who will be the loser. Knowing, expecting this, she must find a way to endure this loss. One can endure everything in life, it is just a question of taking it lightly enough. One should never cling to anything persistently, that is the main thing. To be light in taking and light in leaving. To receive all that life has to offer with the awareness that it is only lent not given one. Only those who look upon life and value its joys in this way may go unpunished through the years. For God who created everything also created time with all its constructive as well as destructive power. He wants us to understand it rightly—and accept it as it should be accepted. He gives us nothing more than the ability to understand. He leaves to us alone the settling of our problems, and we can only do this if we do not consider them as problems but take them for what they are—the way of the world.

Octavian is deeply hurt. Is she trying to make the parting

easy? That parting of which even the thought can only mean torture for him, that parting which must never, never come to pass. Doesn't he love her for ever? How can there be any thought of separation for those who love so deeply? But she, whom he loves, speaks to him like a priest of the church. She speaks of God and punishment and compassion. He doesn't want to hear any more of this. He wants to hear words of love, not philosophical wisdom. With much emotion he says to her: "Does that mean that I may never kiss you again until you have to gasp for breath?" That strikes to the heart of Marie Thérèse. Yes, the time will come when she will never again be kissed, when she will no longer drain youth from the lips of this enchanting boy. It will come soon. Not only time which passes through *him* will bring the end—perhaps even sooner the cruel time within her own veins will bring it. For she is weary of stormy ardor—she longs for solitude and reflection. So she turns away from his violent embrace, and when he doesn't immediately follow her says with an authority which brooks no contradiction: "You must leave me. . . ."

Octavian now gives up. He sees that all his pleading and tears, his storming and his tenderness, are in vain. She doesn't want him here any longer—he must go. For a moment he stands there silently, but when he hears her say "Now I will go to church" he goes with vigorous and agitated steps to the background, and disappears into the alcove where he has left his sword. He immediately returns with it in his hand, fastening it around him. He acts as if he were not listening to the Marschallin. He is offended and hurt. His bearing is defiant and obstinate.

The Marschallin pays no attention to him. She slowly returns to her toilet table and seats herself before it. She will devote the morning to the duties which she has neglected for the sake of her charming lover. The church—oh, yes, that is very important! Her good priest will expect her and will hear her confession as he has so often before. She will leave the church feeling like a different person—pardoned, strengthened, renewed. Then she will visit her old Uncle Greifenklau, whom she hasn't seen for a long time, and will have lunch with him. It will be rather boring, but it will be a kind of atonement for all the sweet delights which she has enjoyed. For the other Marie Thérèse, the one who will leave the church, must think of doing good deeds. The priest will insist upon it. She knows that. Now, after all, it will be a good deed to endure being so bored by her good old uncle. The hours will drag along very slowly. Fleetingly her eyes sweep to Octavian. How she has hurt him! How sad he looks—sad and defiant. Perhaps she could see him in the afternoon. Yes, she will send a messenger to him if she should drive in the Prater. If she should, perhaps he would like to come? And he will ride beside her carriage through the long Praterallee which will sparkle like a road between lighted Christmas trees with its flowering chestnut trees. She will lean against her silk cushions and look very beautiful in her new feather hat, and he will be very dashing and captivating upon his black horse —this handsome youth who has made her so happy and so sad. . . .

Octavian has listened with renewed hope as the Marschallin spoke of sending a messenger to him. He had hoped to hear that he might return, that he might be called again to her arms. But it is only a ride in the Prater which she promises. He agrees. Just to see her means happiness for him! He will ride beside her carriage and she will steal glances at him with that tender fire which he knows, which he has enjoyed to the full—and which he wants to enjoy again.

So he turns to her radiantly and gratefully, kisses her outstretched hand and seeks to press his lips to her arm in an ardent kiss. But with a gesture of light restraint she holds him back, and says in a friendly way as if to a child: "Now be good and do as I say. . . ."

That means clicking his heels together as is seemly for a cavalier, and leaving. More pleading, more tempests would now be of no avail. So he says between his teeth: "As you command, Bichette . . ." and with quick strides he is gone.

The Marschallin had not wanted any more pleading. She only wanted him to go. But now he has gone and her hand which had been raised to emphasize her command slowly falls. The hand feels an emptiness—and her eyes, which had just been raised half disapprovingly to Octavian, take in the large empty room in all its coldness, now that the lovely boy who made her so impatient is no longer there. Oh, what a senseless vacillating heart!

She might at least have said a kind and warm farewell instead of sending him away with scarcely concealed irritation. With a sudden start she rises: "I didn't even kiss him once . . ." She has let him go away without once kissing this young mouth—

why did she deprive herself of this sweet moment? Will there be so many others? Is she so rich, still so rich that she can afford to be wasteful of such delights? Excitedly she calls in the lackeys and with ill-concealed haste orders them to summon back the Count immediately.

But the lackeys return—without the Count. He had left too swiftly. He had ridden away like a devil and was away beyond hearing.

Turning her back to them Marie Thérèse leans against her toilet-table. With an effort she tries to regain her composure. She should not let the servants suspect her agitation. Having composed herself she turns to them and orders them to send to her her body servant, the little colored boy. As he enters she hands him the red box with the silver rose and is about to give him the order—but taking the box with a deep bow he trips hastily away. She calls him back impatiently but kindly: "You don't know where to take it . . ." In a quiet tone she gives him the order: "Take this to the Count Octavian—it is the silver rose—the Count knows the rest. . . ."

As the little colored servant leaves her, her eyes follow him— absentmindedly. Suddenly an evil premonition sweeps over her; it is as if, in sending away this silver rose, she is sending away her own happiness. It seems as if she must call the boy back, but as she starts to, the door closes behind him—and she controls herself. She thinks: what can be the matter with me? I am nervous—this has been too much for me. I am not young enough for so much storming. How silly that I was so frightened. Nothing will happen. I am only upset. I will rest.

With dragging and weary steps she goes to her dressing-table and sinks down before it in an attitude of exhaustion. Involuntarily her eyes seek the mirror—from it there peers at her the countenance of an ageing woman, on whose features is written: It is over. . . . Hastily she picks up the little hand-mirror and observes carefully the lines about her eyes. As if with a gesture of wiping out the image her hand glides over the surface of the cruelly truthful mirror which she has let slip down through the folds of her gown. She would like to break into sobs, would like to give way to a quiet despair—tears would do her good. But no: "One must take things lightly, holding and taking with a light heart and light hands—holding and letting go. . . ." A soft smile of resignation plays about her lips. She bows her

head not as one who is defeated but as one who is resigned—
smilingly resigned. "For in the *how*—there lies all the difference."

The curtain falls very slowly, and the last picture is of the
Marschallin sitting in complete loneliness, in full daylight—
tired, lost in reverie, relaxed in complete self-surrender.

The Marschallin does not appear at all in the second act. The
long period of rest is rather unwelcome, as it is much more tiring
than uninterrupted singing. The inner tension is lost and the
mood dispelled, with the result that reappearing on the stage
after such a long intermission involves all the strain of starting
a new performance. My dressing-room in Vienna always seemed
transformed into a reception room—it was almost like the levee
of the Marschallin: visitors came and went. Not outside
visitors, of course, but colleagues who were also taking part in
the opera but were free at the moment. When the stage
manager came to call the singers for their entrances he always
came to my room first, as he was quite sure of finding the tardy
ones there rather than in their own rooms. Bella Paalen, the
Annina, looking very Italian with her black hair and classic
Roman features; Alfred Muzzarelli—"Muzzi" to every one—
who played the notary, very much enjoyed filling out his long
wait laughing and chatting with me. He was possessed with
becoming a perfectionist and always seemed to have just discovered a wonderful new singing teacher, which gave him new
hope. His deep dark bass voice persistently refused to develop
the delicate head tones which he longed to acquire. This cost
him many a headache and much disappointment. But again
and again he would come saying that at last he had really found
the right teacher and the correct approach to the coveted head
tone.

When the war ended and letters again began to reach me from
Vienna I received one from "Muzzi". It was so typical of him,
I didn't know whether to laugh or cry: like every one in the war
zone he had lived through terrible experiences; he had been in
the opera house when it was bombed and had escaped as it was
burning. Its destruction affected him deeply, as it did every
good Viennese. (I have received many letters telling how people
in no way connected with the opera house stood sobbing as they
watched it burn. It was for them a shrine of musical culture.)
How much greater a tragedy it was for the singers who looked

upon this opera house as their home, just as it once seemed home to me! "Muzzi" wrote very touchingly of the destruction of this magnificent building, and of the personal loss it meant for him. But then the real "Muzzi" showed himself: he wrote that he had at last achieved his head tone—it was *his* now, and no one could any longer teach him anything about technique. To my great joy I realized that there was one person who had not changed a particle. Even though the world had been almost destroyed and Europe seemed dying he had found happiness through achieving his head tone, and could devote a large part of his first letter to this accomplishment in spite of having undergone such devastating experiences.

This seems to me really enchanting! It reveals so clearly the unreality of the world in which we artists live. The actual life around us seems almost unimportant—we have our individual problems which, from afar, may seem rather childish. "Muzzi" is an exceptionally intelligent person; he is amusing and interesting, and fascinated by subjects which are in no way related to his profession. But his profession is much more to him than a means of livelihood, and even though he has never succeeded in making a great career he loves it with his whole soul. Although he may scold and complain he considers the satisfaction of knowing that he sings better than ever before his greatest boon, even though it comes too late to make of him a great singer. One must love singing in this way to be a true artist. Though he has never reached the top and knows that he never will, he is immersed in the theatre to the limits of his being. So it must be!

Unfortunately lack of space makes it impossible to devote myself to *Rosenkavalier* as I should like to. I must restrict myself to the rôle of the Marschallin, instead of considering the other rôles in detail. But for the sake of those who are unfamiliar with the opera I will indicate the content of the scenes in which the Marschallin does not appear, so that they may follow the thread of the story.

In the second act Sophie, the fiancée of Baron Ochs, awaits the Cavalier of the Rose. She is tremendously excited and tries to humble herself as she has learned to do in the convent which she has just left.

I can never forget the incomparable Sophie of Elisabeth Schumann. No other Sophie has had her aura of untouched purity, nor her combination of graceful charm and childish timidity which, with Ochs, could change into a daring defensive pertness characteristic of suburban Vienna.

Sophie listens with delight to the description of Octavian—her "Duenna" Marianne Leitmetzerin is looking through the window and reporting how he looks with the greatest of detail: "He is dressed entirely in cloth of silver, he looks like an angel. . . ." How could Sophie be expected to pray now! She awaits him with a beating heart, the messenger of her bridegroom whom she has not yet seen but who will certainly—oh, certainly!—be much more handsome than his messenger.

The entrance of Octavian is accompanied musically with a splendor which only Richard Strauss seems capable of creating. The really heavenly duet between Sophie and Octavian has all the shimmer of youth and beauty, which these two young people embody.

The inevitable takes place: Octavian falls head over heels in love with the young girl.

After the subtlety of the Marschallin he turns instinctively to the untouched youth of this girl before him, who seems little more than a child. What she says is shallow nonsense. But he has enjoyed so much intellectual conversation—he listens touched and delighted to Sophie's childish chatter. It is pleasant for once, not to be "the boy". He feels like a man; he knows that this girl looks up to him, and that flatters and enchants him. . . .

When Ochs enters Sophie is deeply shocked: so *that* is her bridegroom, this old, ugly, vulgar man who makes her shudder. His behavior is so arrogant and demanding that Octavian is more than once on the point of drawing his sword, but controls himself since he is a guest of the house. Ochs immediately sees the resemblance between Octavian and the supposed chambermaid and is tactless enough to comment upon it. How right the Marschallin had been to weave her intrigue so finely! Now the Baron has no suspicion. He is in a very jovial mood: Sophie has pleased him very much—he has put her through her paces as if she were a horse he is buying—and he is "satisfied". The future father-in-law is very obsequious, and with the rest of the household laughs at the Baron's coarse jokes. With the exception of Octavian and Sophie every one is delighted by the "aristocratic" bridegroom—and poor little Sophie gets no attention or understanding from her father when in desperation she seeks deliverance from the amorous advances of her obtrusive fiancé. Octavian is beside himself. He foams with rage and struggles heroically against his desire to put an end to this unworthy farce with his sword. Still he restrains himself and tries to behave as is seemly for a guest of the house. But his blood boils with anger at the boldness of Ochs, and with love and sympathy for the charming child whom he must protect from the terrible fate of becoming the wife of such a man.

The Baron finally leaves the room to devote himself to important—for him, the most important—business, the drawing-up of the marriage contract—and Octavian and Sophie are left alone. Octavian promises her his protection; he declares his love and asks Sophie if she wouldn't rather marry him than the Baron. Their ecstatic duet is interrupted by the pair of Italians: they have been engaged by the Baron to watch his bride, to serve him in every possible way. They promptly fulfill their contract by surprising and capturing Sophie and Octavian, and summon the Baron.

A heated quarrel now develops between Ochs and Octavian. Octavian demands that he give up his intention of marriage, since his fiancée does not love him. Ochs finds the whole affair very humorous. He scoffs at Octavian and wouldn't dream of giving up this girl with all her fortune. On the contrary he wants to force her to follow him in signing the marriage contract. Finally Octavian draws his sword and in a brief duel wounds the Baron in the arm. At the Baron's undignified cry for help the whole household comes rushing in. Sophie's father, Faninal, is beside himself over the behavior of Octavian. He forbids him his house and threatens to send his daughter back to the cloister if she does not marry the Baron. In the general tumult Octavian disappears but is detained by the two Italians, who have quickly realized that they have more to expect from Octavian's generosity than from the rather shabby Baron. They offer him their services without any concern for their obligation to the Baron. Octavian listens to them hesitantly. Then an idea occurs to him and he orders them to follow him.

The Baron, left alone, complains to his servants about his adventure with this "damned boy", but he has to laugh a little over his daring, remembering his own youth. Sophie makes him laugh too—yes, her temperamental defiance has pleased him. He loves girls like that—he loves to have them defiant, because it gives him such pleasure to tame them. In high spirits from the wine which the doctor has forbidden him, he looks with satisfaction into his rosy future.

The Italian Annina now appears in the doorway with a letter in her hand. Octavian has learned from the Marschallin of the pleasure to be found in the game of intrigue. So he has devised the following plan: as the said Mariandl he writes a letter to the Baron suggesting a rendezvous. He knows the Baron well enough by now to know that he will be delighted with the idea and will surely select a place for the rendezvous which will fit in with his own intentions. There he will try to arrange a scandal, so that the Baron will get into difficulties with the police on the ground of immorality. Then Sophie's father will see at last that it is better not to let his daughter become the wife of such a rascal.

The Baron immediately falls into the trap. The act closes with the waltz of the Baron who, exhilarated by wine, thinks that he holds everything in the palms of his hands: Sophie and all her money—and as an additional delight the charming Mariandl, the pretty chambermaid. . . .

And as the curtain falls I still see Richard Mayr's mischievous face, and can still hear his laughing, slightly tipsy: "With me— no night is too long for you. . . ."

The third act is played in a questionable tavern to which the Baron has invited the supposed maid. A whole play, a real comedy, has been worked out by Octavian, and the act begins with the general rehearsal of this comedy. Valsacchi, the Italian, has efficiently carried out every order. People are concealed everywhere, who at the designated signal will peer out of windows, chests and from under the table to confuse the Baron, and by bringing him to the point of calling for help make him expose himself. The Italian Annina is to arrive dressed as a grieving widow, accompanied by a whole row of children who are all to say that the Baron is their father and that he has deserted their poor mother. . . . All this is contrived to force the confusion to a climax.

Octavian enters the room, already disguised as the maid. He lets the comedy be played as it should proceed, and is quite satisfied with the shrewd Valsacchi who is rewarded with a purse of gold.

Then Octavian leaves in order to return with the Baron. Leaning shyly on his arm he again plays the chambermaid with amazing realism.

In a very funny scene he seems to become drunk and rather disappoints the Baron, who had promised himself another effect from alcohol than hiccups and deep depression.

Whenever the Baron becomes too pressing, those who have been concealed, suddenly appear from all sides. The Baron, seeing dishevelled heads eyeing him from every corner, becomes confused and thinks he must be having a nightmare. He drinks more wine and tries in vain to forget the strange and uncanny faces all around him. But gradually it becomes too much for him. Octavian's plan is working out beautifully. The Baron, surrounded by faces which he thinks he must imagine, tears open the window and cries for help. Pursued by the widow with half a dozen of "his children", he runs about the room breathless and quite beside himself, violently ringing the bell which should summon help. The whole so-called hotel now gathers around the Baron with shouting and gesticulations, with the result that he loses every interest in the rendezvous and has but one desire: to get away from here without being noticed. In the meantime, in accordance with Octavian's order, Valsacchi has sent for Sophie's father, Faninal. If he should catch the Baron here in this infamous hostelry with a girl it is to be hoped that he would have enough of this aristocratic son-in-law.

But in response to his cry for help the police suddenly appear. It had not been planned that they should come before the arrival of Faninal. For if the police commissioner should settle everything before the father arrives the scene certainly wouldn't be as effective as in the completely uninterrupted tableau which Octavian has so cleverly set.

The Baron thinks that he will now be rescued. He is a well-known figure among the aristocracy—the commissioner, influenced by his name, will immediately put out all those who are disturbing his peace, and he will be able to conclude the interrupted evening with the charming Mariandl as he had desired.

But he is mistaken. The commissioner says that any one can say he is the Baron von Lerchenau. He must bring witnesses. Ochs believes that nothing could be easier than that. He winks at the Italian, Valsacchi, who is in his employ, and the landlord of the hotel knows just as well who he is. But both say they can't be sure—"the gentleman may be a baron, he also might not be—I know nothing", says Valsacchi obeying Octavian's orders.

Leopold, the Baron's favourite lackey and illegitimate son, seeing with concern the dangerous situation of his master and father, wants to help him—and the glorious idea occurs to him of going to the Marschallin. She seems to be a friend of the Baron. So he disappears hastily. This little scene, which is so important for an understanding of the whole situation, is generally overlooked by the audience. If so, one must be puzzled as to why the Marschallin should come to this infamous hotel, how she could suddenly appear there to unravel all the knots like a good fairy.

Octavian has waited impatiently for the commissioner to notice him. He begins to wail loudly, and in apparent confusion runs into the broad curtain which has concealed a very indecent bed. Drawing the curtain aside, he makes clear to the commissioner the purpose for which the good Baron has wandered there.

The Baron, now forced into a corner, excuses himself with the commissioner by saying that the girl there is his fiancée, the Fräulein Faninal. It is quite immaterial to him that in doing so he puts Sophie in a very bad light and seriously endangers her reputation. The main thing for him is that he gets himself out of this embarrassing predicament.

Just at this moment Herr von Faninal appears upon the scene —certainly not to the pleasure of the Baron! Again Octavian draws the attention of everyone—including Faninal—to himself. Faninal is informed by the commissioner that this girl is his daughter, according to the testimony of the Baron. Faninal is beside himself that the Baron should have dared to cast such aspersions upon his daughter. Sophie, who has waited below in the carriage, is ordered to appear. When she arrives Herr von Faninal becomes ill, and, overcome by all the excitement, falls in a faint and is carried into another room, followed by Sophie (who has not seen Octavian) and all the servants. Remaining alone with the commissioner, the Baron feels his old confidence returning and says with a broad grin: "I pay, I go, I'll take her home now . . ." The commissioner, however, is not so easily appeased. He would have continued the hearing, but Octavian whispers something in his ear which amuses him hugely. Octavian in two words has confessed that it is all only a game and that he is really a man—the Count Rofrano. Behind a curtain the young Count, accompanied by a policeman, undresses, throwing the "maid's" clothing over the screen—much to the amusement of the police officer and the discomfort of the Baron.

Into this situation the landlord plunges, breathless with excitement: "Her Gracious Highness, the Princess Field Marshal. . . ."

Leopold, the Baron's servant, had gone to the Marschallin. In his very stupid and confused way he had told her that his master and father has gotten himself into a very unpleasant situation. The Marschallin was perhaps not entirely clear about it from his description, but she has gathered that the Baron has been caught in a rendezvous with the "maid—Mariandl" and that the police are now making life difficult for him.

It arouses the suspicions of the Marschallin, that Octavian in the disguise of Mariandl had met the Baron: what can be behind this? What is he up to? There must be some purpose in it. With quick decision she has followed the request of Leopold, and directed by him has driven to this questionable tavern, which otherwise she would never have set foot in. Of course she has agreed to come here not through a desire to help the Baron out of any unpleasantness but because she wants to find out what Octavian is up to.

She enters the tavern quickly. The entrance of the Marschallin is musically one of the most beautiful climaxes of the opera. From out the confusion of the previous tumult the broadly flowing theme which characterizes the Marschallin breaks over the scene in a flood of beauty. Tumult and hullabaloo give way to noble music, and the Marschallin is immediately the focus of attention. She looks around her with indignant eyes. It disturbs her that any one should suggest her coming to such a place, even though she herself has agreed to it. Now, for the first time in her life, she sees a tavern of ill-repute. She stands in the center of the room with an expression of great disdain. Of course, the Baron is stupid enough to assume that the Marschallin has come only in order to help him. He assures her that he is overwhelmed by this indication of her friendship. Octavian, again dressed as a man, observes the Marschallin through the curtains with astonishment and nervousness. It is most unpleasant for him that she should have appeared here. She herself has not yet caught sight of him, but stands motionlessly with her back half turned to the Baron. The police commissioner steps forward and stands at attention. Without heeding the interruptions of the Baron, who is trying to assure the officer that everything is now in order, the Marschallin turns with friendly courtesy towards the commissioner. A faint recollection stirs within her: somewhere she has seen this man before. Yes, of course, he was one of the Field Marshal's orderlies. He had aroused her attention because he is a very dashing young man, and she finds pleasure in handsome young men. . . . So she regards him through her lorgnette with a charming kindliness, and her smile is absolutely "Marie Thérèse" when the officer confirms the fact that he had been one of her husband's orderlies. In the meantime the Baron has motioned Octavian away. He is afraid that the supposed Mariandl will in the end reveal herself to Marie Thérèse. But noticing his efforts she turns around. At this moment Octavian in man's attire steps out from behind the curtains. Their eyes meet. . . . When she sees Octavian's helpless confusion the Marschallin is almost convinced he has devised this comedy for the sake of some girl. Who she is or what it is all about she does not entirely grasp. But with one blow it is clear to her that she has lost him to another. "To-day or to-morrow, or the day after . . ." The day has come.

The Marschallin is from head to toe a very great lady. She meets Octavian's confused glance with a look of questioning. Embarrassed, he stammers: "There was a different arrangement. Marie Thérèse, I am surprised to see you . . ." To be sure it had been arranged that they should meet in the Prater, and that he should ride beside her carriage. The last thing which he could have anticipated is to see her here in this ill-famed tavern, to which he has been brought through a farce, a farce which he has wanted to play for the sake of another.

At this moment Sophie enters from the door at the right. She does not see the Marschallin, who is concealed behind the broad expanse of the Baron. The young girl has now regained all her sense of security, and nothing could be more welcome to her than the terrible disgrace which the Baron has brought upon himself. But as yet she does not realize that she has Octavian to thank for all this. She still has no suspicion that it has been he who has put through this daring comedy with such brilliant success. But she does know that her father is enraged by the Baron's behavior and that the much-dreaded marriage is now out of the question. It gives Sophie a certain joy to have the opportunity to tell the abhorred Baron what she thinks of him. She boldly steps before him to deliver her father's very welcome message. Her words "I have a message for you from my father" are spoken with daring and arrogance.

The arrival of Sophie has been especially embarrassing for the Baron. He would like to keep the Marschallin from discovering all the details of his sad downfall. So he wants as fast as possible to get Sophie back into the room from which she has come. Anxious to conceal her from the Marschallin he tries to drive her away with forceful words.

The Marschallin immediately turns around and so far as the intervening figure of the Baron permits regards Sophie through her lorgnette. In dreadful embarrassment Octavian tries to explain what the Marschallin in a single flash has all too clearly understood. But she interrupts his stammering attempt by saying in a friendly tone: "Find you a little embarrassed, Rofrano. Can well imagine who she is . . . Find her charming . . ."

Everything which the Marschallin has wanted to accomplish, all her intentions of taking Octavian's abandonment of her for another lightly and kindly, are now fulfilled.

Concealing the tumult within her, she finds even in the first moment the light tone with which she brings to an end an affair which has meant much to her. That she should suddenly call him "Rofrano"—him, the beloved "Quinquin"—immediately puts a distance between them as she intends it to. From now on she will be to him the Princess Field Marshal. She can't quite conceal a certain irony which she feels in observing this young girl for whom Octavian has left her. Sophie is charming, certainly. But the Marschallin can't see anything exceptional in this half-child. The only outstanding thing about her is her great youth and an innocence of soul such as the Marschallin hasn't possessed for many a year. The words "find her charming" are spoken kindly, but have a rather condescending inflection.

Sophie has not yet seen the Marschallin. In her pert Viennese way she gives the Baron a piece of her mind, and the Marschallin listens to her, rather amused by her daring and her whole attitude, which smacks a little of surburban Vienna. It also gives her a certain pleasure to know that the Baron whom she so despises is now in the clutches of a dilemma from which there is no possibility of escape. His marriage with the pretty and wealthy girl seems to have gone completely on the rocks, and that delights Marie Thérèse. Whatever might have hurt her in this crazy affair she locks within her heart with all her characteristic energy. She is now the mistress of a game which has played into her hands without any intention or desire on her part. But she is accustomed to mastering any situation and so she masters this moment too. With slow steps she crosses the stage to the Baron, and just as Sophie closes the door in his face without listening to his furious protest the Marschallin lightly taps his shoulder with her fan and says: "Now don't try to mend matters, just go . . ." The Baron, quite speechless, turns around. He can't understand why the Marschallin should seem to take the part of this commoner. He had thought that she had come to help him. With much humor the Marschallin says: "Keep your dignity and take yourself away." Eyeing him scornfully from head to toe she assures him that there is only one thing which can save his questionable position as an aristocrat— to put a good face on a bad deed. Leaving him standing there, speechless, she turns to the commissioner. She doesn't want any scandal to come out of this affair. She doesn't want to see Octavian involved in a farce which is unworthy of him or be herself in any way connected with this affair. So she puts an end to the scene by assuring the commissioner that the whole thing has been no more than a comedy and is certainly not worthy of the attention of the police. The commissioner obediently leaves and the Marschallin turns with a friendly gesture towards Sophie, who bows deeply before her.

Contrary to what she had expected the Baron doesn't at all consider complying. Quite the opposite. He explains clearly that he hasn't the slightest intention of giving up Sophie.

So far as the Marschallin is concerned the whole situation has been very badly mismanaged. Her plan for keeping her affair with Octavian from the Baron seems to have failed completely. Octavian has arranged everything beautifully for Sophie but not for the Marschallin, for the Baron will certainly tell this story for all it is worth throughout his whole circle. He will say that the maid of the Marschallin had invited him to a rendezvous, and that this had been interrupted through the intervention of the police. The gossip will reach the ears of her friends—yes, the ears of her husband—and then, *where is Mariandl?* So all her fine plans are about to be wrecked. She must now make a counterplay and reveal her secret, for the Baron would never tell *this* story which would make him for ever ridiculous . . . He will protect himself from ever letting his friends find out that in the end it was he who was duped by his charming Mariandl turning out to be the Count Rofrano. So the Marschallin must risk lifting the veil from her secret. She is a woman of quick decision, and in the moment when she sees that the Baron is not satisfied she turns with an impatient gesture towards Octavian, who is waiting half hidden at the back of the stage. *"Mon cousin,* inform him," she says with sharp emphasis. With a very manly stride Octavian steps before the Baron, ordering him to to leave the room. With a start the Baron jumps back, and in response to his astonished question as to the meaning of this the Marschallin turns to him with a haughty sweep and says: "His Grace the Count Rofrano . . . Who else?"

The Baron puts a good face on a bad situation. With bitter amusement he observes Octavian, who looks him up and down with scornful arrogance. "So it's as I thought, have enough of that face . . . My eyes didn't deceive me, it is a man," he calls to him.

The Marschallin regains her inner security. Stepping closer she explains in a light conversational tone that this has all been a Viennese masquerade, and with a glance which puts the Baron at a distance she says very condescendingly: "It's fortunate for you it wasn't my Mariandl whom you tried to lead astray." Withdrawing into herself, turning slightly towards Octavian but without looking directly at him, she says lightly: "Just now I have a grudge against men—in general . . ."

In the meantime the Baron has recovered his composure. The meaning of all this begins to dawn upon him. He now sees that he holds a weapon which he can use against the Marschallin. This is all very interesting: so Mariandl was Octavian! Very piquant to find the young Count in the Marschallin's bedroom! He voices his astonishment with complete shamelessness.

The Marschallin is very much taken aback. In spite of her detestation of the Baron she has overestimated him. She wouldn't have dreamed that he could be so impudent and tactless as to point out to her that he has understood what it would be the duty of any cavalier not to understand. She holds back Octavian who, with evident indignation, is on the point of drawing his sword. She needs no protector! She knows very well how to handle people of this sort. So with apparent graciousness, although she is inwardly boiling with rage, she turns to the Baron and with a look filled with disgust says lightly and as if in a tone of friendly conversation: "You are, I think, a cavalier? Then you will refrain from thinking . . . That is what I expect of you." The word "expect" is very sharp —a threat, an absolute command—and the Baron feels the sharpness of this command. He pulls himself together, and tries with a lightness he is far from feeling to extricate himself from this very delicate situation. In some way or other he even feels flattered that the Marschallin should have expected so much subtlety from him. She is a wonderful woman! She sees that he is a cavalier. She won't openly forbid him to talk, him—the Baron von Lerchenau. She gives him a delicious wink, and he, the cavalier, understands and will obey. . . .

For a moment the Marschallin tensely awaits his answer. Then, seeing that this brutal man has been tamed, she slowly crosses the stage to the right side. It annoys her that now, instead of withdrawing, he expresses at length and fully his joy at being her confidant in such a piquant secret.

But the Baron isn't finished yet. With the shrewdness of a peasant he would like to make capital of his knowledge, and feels that a little extortion is quite appropriate. He has quickly figured out that by keeping his silence he will be doing the Marschallin a great favor. Now it is her turn to do him a favor, and he is sure that if she would put in a good word for him with Sophie's father his marriage with this rich young girl might yet be saved. For this reason he now says very clearly: "But now I need your help." And striding vigorously towards the door, behind which he knows Faninal to be, he seems on the point of calling him into the room, convinced that with two charming words the Marschallin can again change the situation into the very rosy one of the desirable son-in-law.

The Marschallin now completely loses her patience. The polite mask which she has assumed until now falls before the enormity of his behavior. It seems there is just one way to silence this vulgarity: to throw him out! Pointing towards the door she addresses him with great agitation: "You may retire without further words." Like a tempest she sweeps impetuously across the stage, driving him into a corner.

In a flare of temper she makes it clear to him that everything is over. The whole affair of the wedding and everything connected with it is finished and done with!

The Baron gives up. He.bows in resignation before her more forceful personality. Mechanically he repeats her last words: "Everything connected with it is finished and done with."

Sophie, standing in the background has followed all this without being able to make any sense of it. Octavian is here! Why? How has he suddenly appeared in this room? What has he to do with the Baron? With the Marschallin? She can't understand any of this. She only grasps the fact that something is not as it should be. She has a vague feeling that there is some connection between the Marschallin and Octavian which she cannot fathom. Her heart is oppressed by a vague fear. Has she lost Octavian? To whom? To the Marschallin? Is that possible? What does the Marschallin mean when she says: "Everything connected with it is over and done with from this hour"? Does she imply more than just the end of this undesirable engagement? Or does she mean that all that has budded and bloomed so beautifully with Octavian will be taken from her for ever? Softly and sadly she repeats with trembling lips: "Is all over."

After she has spoken these words, the Marschallin realizes the double meaning in what she has said. Yes, it is over. Octavian is lost for her. . . . She slowly turns her head towards the young count, and with a sad look of farewell says softly as if to herself: "It is all over . . ."

Octavian stands in the center of the stage, silent and pale. He knows well that it is he who is to blame. He would like to fall upon his knees before the Marschallin and beg her forgiveness, and yet he knows that he is driven by an irresistible compulsion and that what he had once thought would last " for ever"—his passionate love for the mature woman—now seems to fade. . . . His whole heart is Sophie's. Marie Thérèse was right—he really leaves her for another.

All the people whom Octavian had engaged to play a part in this trick upon the Baron now enter the room. They come with accounts and demands, for Octavian permitted himself the fun of making Baron Ochs bear the cost of this unfruitful adventure.

The Marschallin crosses to the right side of the stage. Octavian, who sees that she wants to avoid all the people, quickly brings up a chair which he offers her. But the Marschallin does not want to be near him. . . . She moves past him and remains standing at the window.

This is a somber moment in her life. She has done what had to be done. She has saved the whole situation without favoring herself in the slightest way. With a deep loneliness she stands beside the window, knowing that Octavian, whose eyes question her pleadingly, is in his heart a world away from her. She now must face the most difficult task of all: she herself must join together these two young beings. It is not easy for her to do this so quickly, before she has really had time to regain control of herself. She has been plunged too abruptly from the rosy heaven of her own love affair into this abyss of loneliness, which for the moment seems unending.

It doesn't matter at all whether Marie Thérèse loves the young Octavian so deeply that she will be unable to forget him. It doesn't matter at all whether this has been for her a so-called "great love", or whether he has only been a passing adventure which will soon be forgotten. I personally don't believe that Marie Thérèse can resign for ever. She is much too much the child of her time, much too full of temperament and radiance. She has much too much *joie de vivre,* worldliness and lust for adventure to resign herself so soon to growing old. But this doesn't lessen the tragedy of her feeling at this moment. If one loves, one always believes that it is for ever—even if it is only a lovely illusion. And the end of any love is always a kind of dying. So in this hour there dies within Marie Thérèse something which is very beautiful, and she buries it in her soul with the feeling: now I am alone. . . .

One must be able to imagine the struggle which is taking place within the Marschallin. Her impersonator should not just stand quietly at the window. One must feel that this is an hour of decision for her. Having slowly regained her composure she finally turns back towards the stage. She does not look at Octavian but seems to observe the boisterous group of servants with a distant haughtiness. When the two Italians, who leap about the Baron in a scornful dance and ridicule him, leave the stage with the others, only the Marschallin, Octavian and Sophie are left.

Sophie is terribly excited. She sees that Octavian only has eyes for the Marschallin. She can't understand why he doesn't come to her, why he stands beside the Marschallin's chair as if he is chained to it. He seems to have forgotten her. This woman, who with her splendor and her regal personality makes Sophie feel small and insignificant, seems to hold Octavian's heart like a toy in her hands. Sophie feels all this without really understanding it.

Octavian is frightfully embarrassed. He would like to excuse himself but doesn't know what to say. So he begins to stammer rather awkwardly, which makes the Marschallin very impatient. She would like to be through with this whole affair; would like Octavian to go to Sophie, to whom he now belongs, as quickly as possible. For this reason she turns to him and says with sharp emphasis: "Go quickly and do as your heart tells you."

Oh, how gladly Octavian would do that! But it tortures him to realize how deeply he has wounded the Marschallin. So he stands caught between the two women, not knowing what is right for him to do. Only when the Marschallin says sharply: "You are a fine picture of a man! Go to her," does he turn away from her and towards Sophie. But Sophie does not look at him. She stands with a defiant attitude, and only returns sharp replies to his pleading. He has made a fine mess of everything! She is not to be treated as a child any longer! She is a sensible Viennese girl with whom one doesn't act in such a way! She had thought that he loved her—and now what has happened? Now she feels ashamed before the Marschallin but doesn't know why she should be ashamed . She sees the somber eyes of the Princess levelled upon her. Eyes which make her tremble, and Octavian stands there without making any effort to help her.

The Marschallin has watched the conversation between Octavian and Sophie with inner excitement. When Octavian says the same words to Sophie which he has so often whispered in her ear during their hours of love: "I swear it on my soul . . .", it affects her deeply. She rises and says under her breath: "To-day or to-morrow or the next day . . ." And while Octavian assures Sophie of his love, the Marschallin again makes clear to herself that she is now experiencing what every woman must experience once in her life: resignation. . . .

At the end of the short trio she turns gently towards Octavian. Sophie, misunderstanding this, thinks that she has called him.

An interval of embarrassment!

The Marschallin stands in silent anticipation. She doesn't want to make it too easy for Octavian. He should show that he is a man and is capable of handling this situation like a man. But Octavian stands between them, helpless and confused. With an anxious gesture he keeps Sophie from leaving, and vainly tries to find the right words to make his feelings clear to the Marschallin. The Marschallin smiles sadly as he restrains Sophie when she in her embarrassment seeks to leave the room. It has gone so far that he is afraid to be alone with her! Does he really know her so little, does he believe that it would be possible for her to reproach him? With a sigh she turns away from him, and Octavian in great embarrassment stammers: "Did you say something?"

Marie Thérèse now sees that she herself must take the initiative. With slow and decided steps she passes Octavian without looking at him, turning now to Sophie, who curtsies shyly. With a friendly gaze she looks into Sophie's puzzled eyes and says with great benevolence: "Have you fallen in love with him so quickly?" To which Sophie can only stammer: "I don't know what your Grace means by that question." Marie Thérèse gently touches Sophie's face with her fan and says, smiling reflectively: "Your pale face gives the right answer." Sophie now tries to overcome her embarrassment by talking. In her childlike and pert way she tries to make clear to the Marschallin what a shock she had when her father fainted and the Baron behaved so badly, and how grateful she is to the Marschallin.

Marie Thérèse listens with a smile in which there is mixed a gentle irony. How is it possible that Octavian can have fallen so head over heels in love with this insignificant child? A woman can seldom understand why her lover turns to another, can seldom appreciate the worth of the other. So the Marschallin sees here only a very pretty girl who talks apparent nonsense and whose only redeeming feature seems to be her prettiness. She interrupts Sophie and says with great amiability, hiding her own feeling: "Just don't talk so much, you are pretty enough." "Pretty enough" . . . with that she says everything. It is a charming face, it can be only that which has enchanted Octavian.

Now she takes the whole situation into her own generous hands. She will go into the room where Sophie's father is waiting, and even if he has fainted she knows that what she has to say will be a good medicine for him. She will tell him that the young Count Octavian will make a far more acceptable son-in-law than the unsympathetic Baron von Lerchenau. She is quite sure that Herr von Faninal will believe her. She will invite him to drive in her carriage with her and Sophie and Octavian. She will invite them to her castle and—Sophie will now see, won't she, that her father will be very satisfied?

Octavian is deeply touched. He shyly approaches her and says with great tenderness: "Marie Thérèse, how good you are . . . Marie Thérèse, I don't know at all . . ." but he can go no farther. The Marschallin stands absolutely motionless. She doesn't want to hear any more. She wants no thanks, no explanations. She wants no protestations. She only wants to be left in peace. With clenched teeth she says to him tonelessly: "I also know nothing, nothing at all . . ."

In this moment Octavian does not know what to do. He goes closer to her, and his whispered "Marie Thérèse" conveys pleading and protestation and searching questioning. Yes, in this moment he is so overcome by the greatness of Marie Thérèse —by her goodness, her warmth of heart—that I have always felt that she holds his fate in her hands. I believe that if in this moment she should turn to him and say: "Be mine," Octavian would obey her. But the Marschallin is too great, too wise. She turns to him, and her eyes say—*farewell.* . . .

The heavenly trio which follows is the climax of this lovely opera. The three voices, which blend in indescribably pure harmony, flow together with the deepest of expression.

Sophie feels that the Marschallin is giving her her happiness. It is as if she is receiving Octavian from the hands of this woman as a gift for her whole life, and yet it is as if she has taken something away from Octavian which Sophie will never be able to possess.

Octavian feels that Fate has driven him into this new experience. He would like to ask the Marschallin if what he is doing is right, but he knows that she is the last person whom he could ask. Is he doing something wrong then? It is a compulsion! He must obey! It is a compulsion that he loves *no longer*, and a compulsion that he loves *again*. A compulsion that there should be but one face for him—Sophie's.

The Marschallin reminds herself that she has sworn to love him in the right way. To love him so that she would also be able to love the woman for whom he would leave her. All this might seem incredible to one who has not experienced it, and yet she knows that it is the truth. There was a time when she had felt one with Octavian—yet there he stands now and belongs to that girl who is a stranger, and he will be happy with her in the way men know how to be happy.

The Marschallin knows that she is no longer needed here. With a long look at the two young people who have eyes for nothing but each other she says: "In the name of the Lord," and leaves the room.

Neither Octavian nor Sophie has felt the Marschallin's presence, and they do not notice her departure. They fall into each other's arms and sing the love duet, whose simple melody is like a folk song. In a wonderful way Strauss lets this melody soar suddenly from out the waves of music as the expression of simplicity, of the feeling of being now at home of the simple average person, of the uncomplicated union of two beings attuned to one another.

The Marschallin, accompanied by Faninal, again enters the room. Faninal seems rather overwhelmed by the benevolence with which the Princess has honored him. He goes to his daughter, enfolds her in his arms, and then with great amiability shakes Octavian's hand. Then he turns to the Marschallin and says in a friendly and contemplative way: "That's the way they have—the young people."

Yes, that is it. Love and the future belong to the "young people"—and she, the Marschallin, stands here beside this old man whose daughter will be the wife of her charming young lover. With a resigned and smiling "Yes, yes," she acknowledges the rights of youth which are no longer hers.

Led by Faninal she leaves the stage. During this time she hasn't looked at all at Octavian—she has stood there completely "the Princess Field Marshal". But now, with a single gesture, as she is leaving she shows the whole generosity and warm kindliness of her nature. She once again stretches out her hand towards Octavian and he kisses it with impassioned gratitude. With this gesture she seems to say to him: "Don't be worried, I understand and—forgive . . ."

She goes out of the door with Faninal, leaving the two lovers alone.

After a short duet which repeats the theme of the folk song, they follow her, and the stage is for a moment empty.

But Hofmannsthal and Strauss did not want to end the opera on a sentimental note. This charming comedy *Der Rosenkavalier* must have a gay ending. The little negro, the Marschallin's body servant, dances into the room with lightly tripping steps. Sophie has lost her handkerchief, and he searches for it in every corner. When he finds it, he waves it triumphantly and runs out.

The curtain falls.

Chapter XIV

AND NOW THE LAST CHAPTER

THE ROSENKAVALIER has run like a lovely musical theme through my whole life in opera. Sophie was the first important rôle which was entrusted to me as a beginner. The conductor, Gustav Brecher, even considered letting me do the *première* in Hamburg. I think that was in 1911—the second year of my engagement there, but then he thought better of it and gave the part for the first performance to Elisabeth Schumann. She was dramatically much more talented than I, and in spite of her youth had already given evidence of her delightful gift for acting and her ripening artistry in several rôles, while I was still very much in the background and really nothing more than an ignorant and awkward beginner with a nice voice. Then too, Edith Walker who sang and acted Octavian quite enchantingly wanted Schumann as Sophie, for which I certainly couldn't blame her. But at the time I was bitterly disappointed and saw everything in a very false light. I felt persecuted and surrounded by intrigue—how I laughed later on over this ridiculous idea! Elisabeth's whole being is worlds apart from any intrigue; she has always been the best colleague one could imagine—a wonderful character through and through. And Edith Walker certainly had no ground for persecuting me with disfavor as the stupid little beginner imagined. She only wanted the performance to be as fine as possible, and so very wisely chose Elisabeth. But suddenly I found myself only the understudy, and sat through the stage rehearsals in the hall gnashing my teeth and comforting myself with the thought that I was the dramatic victim of a finely woven intrigue. Later, when Schumann was not available, I was allowed to sing Sophie and had a very nice success with it.

Then gradually I grew into the rôle of Octavian and sang this part for many years. It gave me much joy and I was told that I conveyed the quality of a young man very well. But my figure was by no means ideal for the embodiment of a youth. It is very strange how as a young girl I lacked any vanity in regard to my appearance; it never in the wide world entered my head to bother as to whether I was well enough built for this very revealing rôle. At this time the mirror was a very uninteresting object for me, and it was not until I went to Vienna that I began to realize that a woman must be as lovely as possible and that it is a part of the profession of a dramatic artist to approach the ideal from every aspect.

Director Schalk always wanted me to make up my mind to sing the Marschallin, but in some way I didn't feel sufficiently mature for this rôle. To portray a woman who is neither old nor young is infinitely more difficult than to act an old woman. I felt instinctively that I must first develop a penetrating understanding of this very subtle rôle. But then there came an opportunity which compelled me to sing the part. I received a contract to sing at Covent Garden in London, but it was dependent upon my singing the Marschallin. The conductor was to be Bruno Walter. Without any consideration I accepted. But I shall never forget the first rehearsal with Walter—the deadly fear which I endured. I confessed to him that I had never sung the rôle. If he didn't like the idea at least he didn't show it, and started to work with me. The rôle grew with each rehearsal until I really lived it and fitted into the frame of this wonderful performance without disturbing it, which is saying a great deal. Ochs was Richard Mayr, Octavian the enchanting Delia Reinhard—very convincing, slender, graceful and refined to her fingertips—the born "young gentleman of a noble family"; Sophie was the incomparable Elisabeth Schumann. Those were unforgettable performances and unforgettable times.

Since then I have remained faithful to the rôle of the Marschallin. Ever again, on the rare occasions when I sing it, I am filled with joy in feeling the words and music flowing from me as if I myself were creating them, so completely have I become one with this rôle. And each time when, leaving Octavian and Sophie alone together in the third act, I close the door behind me it is as if with a smiling farewell I were closing the door upon an experience of my own.

And isn't this really so? Isn't each time a farewell, now that I so rarely return to the opera? I am now only a guest. I no longer feel that I belong to the colorful world of the stage. Waiting in the wings for my late entrance in the third act I feel as a stranger to whom this fantastic world is something new.

Then I realize again with a kind of melancholy that this was once my whole life—the theatre and all that went with it. And the Vienna Opera rises before me in all its old splendor. I forget that it has been destroyed and can never be the same again. I see before me the familiar faces of my colleagues who for the most part are now retired. The good old Adelheid, our time-honored helper, whose pride it was to have everything prepared and as attractively arranged as possible when I came to my dressing-room: on the tables were covers which she had embroidered for me, at the windows extra curtains, everywhere cushions and toy animals of every description—I had a large collection of them. And in an inconspicuous corner of the dressing-table there was always a tiny bunch of flowers which Adelheid with embarrassment admitted placing there.

Then there was Mizzi, the hairdresser, with the wigs which she so carefully prepared.

The absorbing business of making up was spiced with the latest opera gossip—piquant scandals of which there was never any lack. From every dressing-room came the sound of singing —vocalizes or short fragments of rôles. In the midst of it all would sound the bell of the stage manager. Colleagues would stick their heads in at the door: "Good luck . . ." Each member of my family came or sent messages wishing me success. At the last minute Otto, my good husband, would appear, always elegant in his tuxedo, wishing me "Good luck". He always knew just where he must keep his fingers crossed for me—where I was nervous, where I was sure, when I enjoyed singing, when I was afraid. He was thoroughly musical and enjoyed my singing and the whole colorful life of the opera as if he belonged to it with every fibre of his being. My brother Fritz, looking worried: "Are you nervous?" A question which I always answered with a false lightness: "Heavens no—not at all," although I was actually trembling with stage fright. But it would have made me miserable to know that any one so close to me was nervous on my account, just as it distressed him to feel that I might be suffering with stage fright. So we reassured one another with complete nonchalance. My father, who lived through the first nine years of my growing career in Vienna, was filled with pride and touchingly biased. There existed but one singer for him—his daughter; all others were in his eyes only mediocre. He followed with jealous attention the criticisms of my "rivals", and was annoyed at each success if it did not contain the name of Lotte Lehmann. My mother, who liked best to hear me in touching rôles like Manon, Marguerite or Elsa, and would cry bitter tears if she had to see me die on the stage. It was quite impossible for her to listen to Desdemona, much as she loved the music, for seeing me strangled was more than she could bear. . . .

The last signal. A last quick glance at the family photographs on my dressing-table to bring me luck. And the Catholic city of Vienna had taught me to cross myself although I was actually a Protestant.

All the members of our marvellous orchestra, the Vienna Philharmonic, were my friends through many years. And our chorus! And the good workmen! I liked them especially, for they were gallant and honest men with a great understanding for our profession. I was always very proud when they praised me, for I knew that they didn't do that often. They go their own ways and generally don't bother about what is going on around them. But when they listen and nod approvingly—that is something to be proud of. When the war was over they sent me greetings. I was more touched by those greetings than by many others.

Once I was a part of this world; it was my home—the very breath of life for me. Now I almost belong to that other world which does not share the existence of that more fantastic one behind the curtain. Soon it will be so; soon I myself will close the door behind me and leave youth undisturbed before the footlights.

Yet I do not enter a world of reality: it is the infinitely beautiful world of Lieder which has opened before me, as with the passing of time the other has slowly closed behind me. I have left much that is beautiful, have renounced a wealth of living experience—but the rich, transfigured realm which I have entered is more than a substitute, it is a new world: the Lied. And more. With the slipping away of the colorful excitements of theatrical life, beauty has opened before me as never before. My eyes have awakened to the beauty of nature, to the wonders of artistic creation in fields new to me. Goethe says:

> "Greift nur hinein ins volle Menschenleben!
> Ein jeder lebt's,
> Nicht vielen ist's bekannt,
> Und wo ihr's packt, da ist's interessant."

Wherever you touch life it is fascinating. Once I devoted myself to the theatre. To-day I have become a part of the whole. Oh, so much richer! Rich in the understanding of things before unknown to me, rich in the knowledge that there is never an end to learning. That one door is closed only to open another. That life knows no end, and there can be no end to the experience which it may bring. . . .

So, like the Marschallin, I stand in the half-closed door, ready to shut it behind me. And with a smile I say with her: "In the name of the Lord."